IMAGES
of America

KENTWOOD

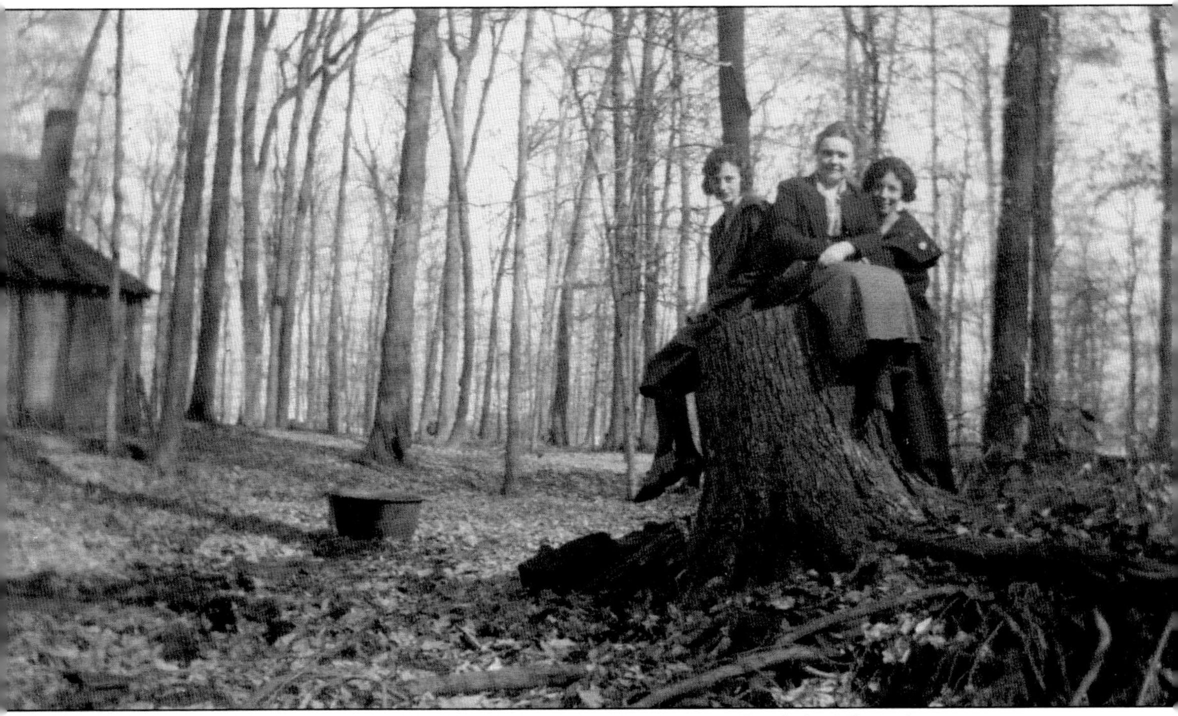

Paris Township residents Opel Welbourn, Cora Bowen, and Edith Allen share a seat on a tree stump outside of the Bowen family's sugar shanty. The Bowen farm had a number of sugar maple trees on its property. In the early spring, the family tapped the trees to collect sap, which they distilled to create maple syrup or sugar. Sugaring was usually a fun activity, since it let family and friends, separated by snowy winter weather for several months, get together.

On the cover: Burr Bowen sits proudly on his Fordson tractor. Even though tractors were available, many Paris Township farmers continued to work with their horse or oxen teams since they were more cost effective than a tractor. At the end of World War I, Henry Ford released the Fordson Model F tractor. The inexpensive tractor enabled Burr and others to do many tasks around their farm more quickly and easily.

IMAGES
of America

KENTWOOD

Katerie Prior

ARCADIA

ISBN 0-7385-4018-8

Published by Arcadia Publishing
Charleston SC, Chicago IL, Portsmouth NH, San Francisco CA

Printed in the United States of America

Library of Congress Catalog Card Number: 2005935048

For all general information contact Arcadia Publishing at:
Telephone 843-853-2070
Fax 843-853-0044
E-mail sales@arcadiapublishing.com
For customer service and orders:
Toll-Free 1-888-313-2665

Visit us on the internet at http://www.arcadiapublishing.com

This book is dedicated to my family
for their encouragement, patience, and inspiration.

Contents

ACKNOWLEDGMENTS

For years, the Kentwood Historical Preservation Commission has been collecting photographs, oral histories, maps, and other materials related to the history of Paris Township and the city of Kentwood. When I started writing this book, their collection of resources was both overwhelming and exciting. I would like to thank Esther Middlewood and the Kentwood Historical Preservation Commission for their enthusiasm in preserving the past and assistance in validating this history. Without their dedication, this book would not have been possible.

Special thanks are also extended to Karolee of the Grand Rapids Historical and Special Collections Center at the Grand Rapids Public Library; Ray Boisvenue, who loaned his extensive collection of private and donated slides of Paris Township and Kentwood; Judith Wiley of the Kentwood Women's Club; and the staff at Heritage Hall at Calvin College.

Most importantly, I would also like to thank the families and individuals who donated materials to the Kentwood Historical Preservation Commission. Their generosity with sharing images, stories, and experiences of the past have given future generations of Kentwood residents a valuable and timeless treasure.

–Katerie Prior

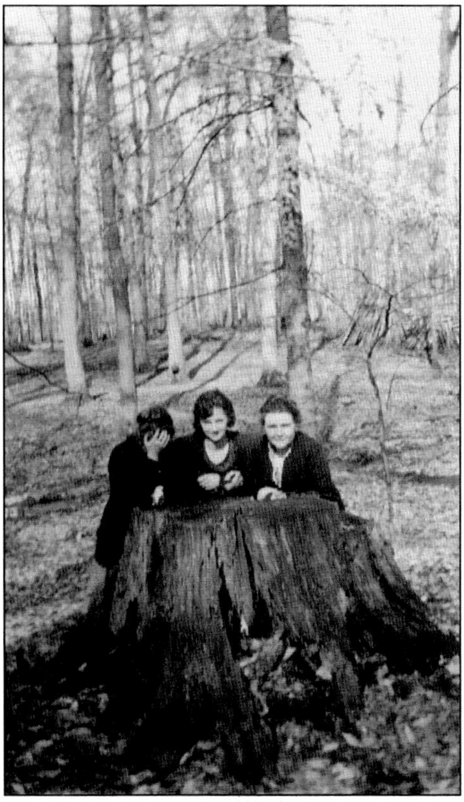

Edith Allen and Cora Bowen, along with friend Opel Welbourn, count the rings of a tree cut down near the Bowen's sugar shanty. The tree was 200 years old. During the latter half of its lifetime, Paris Township had evolved from a pioneer settlement to a thriving farm and rural area. Had the tree survived for another 50 years, it may have seen the community change dramatically again.

INTRODUCTION

For many people, life seems to run at a constant pace. People look around their neighborhoods and see the same houses they always have. On the way to work, they drive by the businesses that they have for years. In their children's schools, a fresh crop of kids sits in classrooms that have seen generations of students. Every Sunday, people worship in the same church where they were baptized.

While everyone knows the constancy of life is an illusion, people often forget. Small changes in a community seem like they have always been there. Nothing helps people remember quite like photographs. Flip through pictures from decades ago and the number of changes to an area may be startling. Virgin land becomes a bustling farm and then years later, a tree-lined, residential neighborhood. A business district grows around a main road, perishes in hard times, and is renovated into a trendy shopping area. New buildings go up. Old buildings come down. The children of a large family become adults who change the face of a community.

In many ways, Kentwood is a city where life has gone on as it always has. Children of its residents have passed through the schools, found jobs in the area, married in its churches, and raised families in its neighborhoods. But Kentwood and its predecessor, Paris Township, have always been in a state of gradual but constant evolution.

Like much of Michigan, the area that would be Kentwood was a vast wilderness that Native American trappers and fur traders called home. In 1785, the U.S. Congress passed a law that required all new territories to be surveyed. Once surveyed, the land was divided into townships six miles square. The section called T6N, R11W later became Kentwood.

In the 1820s, just north of this township, fur trader Louis Campau bought 72 acres of land around his trade store on the south bank of the Grand River. With plans to create a city he called Grand Rapids, he solicited farmers in upstate New York and all across New England to come to the area. Intrigued by tales of fertile prairie land and bountiful forests, settlers like Henry Whiting, Joel and Edward Guild, Daniel Coit, Porter Reed, Rachel Patterson, Orlean Spaulding, Abram Laraway, James Clark, Philonzo Bowen, and others bought land patents and then brought their families to the area to establish farms.

The first few years were hard for settlers. According to *History of the City of Grand Rapids, Michigan*, by Albert Baxter, many Paris Township families had little to eat other than potatoes and onions. Fortunately, the area's farms began to prosper after a few seasons. In 1839, the settlers gathered together in Hiram Allen's home to organize a government and give the area a name. Paris, the name suggested by Joel Guild, the township's first supervisor, was approved and christened the area for more than a century.

By the 1870s, Paris Township was a prosperous community. Large farms dominated a landscape dotted by villages. Several stores and businesses grew just west of the Bailey farm on East Paris Avenue. Bowens Corners, the intersection of Forty-fourth Street and Kalamazoo Avenue near the Bowen farm, was another village that became the site of Paris Township's first (and last) train station. Several small villages developed at Division Avenue, a plank road on the border of Paris Township. Eventually, schools and churches grew around these areas to support the educational and spiritual growth of the community.

By the early 20th century, Paris Township was an attractive area to many people. Hundreds moved into the community each year. Some bought sections of existing farms, while others, who worked in the burgeoning furniture industry in Grand Rapids, moved into Godwin Heights and Home Acres, the township's new neighborhoods. Many saw the area's potential, Grand Rapids city officials selected Paris Township as the home of the city fairgrounds, while Kent County officials selected the area for poor farm, and later the first airport.

The area's attractiveness eventually hurt the community. In 1915, a section of Paris Township was annexed into Grand Rapids, costing the area important tax revenue. This first annexation led to subsequent ones throughout the 1950s and 1960s. Township officials tried to stop the annexations by becoming a city. Each vote to incorporate failed until 1965, when business developers proposed building Woodland Mall on township land right on the border of Grand Rapids. Fearing the potential revenue from the mall would be lost in an annexation, residents of Paris Township voted to become a city, and in February 1967, Kentwood was officially born.

Since then, the community has continued to grow and change. Now the landscape is dominated by residential communities and flourishing businesses. While the Kentwood community looks to the future, they continue to preserve the past. Several farmhouses that once belonged to the Bowen, Bailey, and Patterson families still stand. One operating farm still produces the bounty of the land. They are the remaining reminder of a community's vibrant history, documented in part in this book.

Most of the images in this book were organized and preserved by the Kentwood Historical Preservation Commission. Each chapter looks at a particular aspect of life in the community as the area grew. Even though every effort has been made to include the images of people and organizations that were a part of early Paris Township and the beginnings of Kentwood, there are sections of the community's history that remain untold. The commission is always eager to hear from individuals who are willing to share their memories, photographs, and other artifacts of Paris Township and Kentwood. It's one way the history of a wonderful community can always live on.

One

The Pioneering Spirit

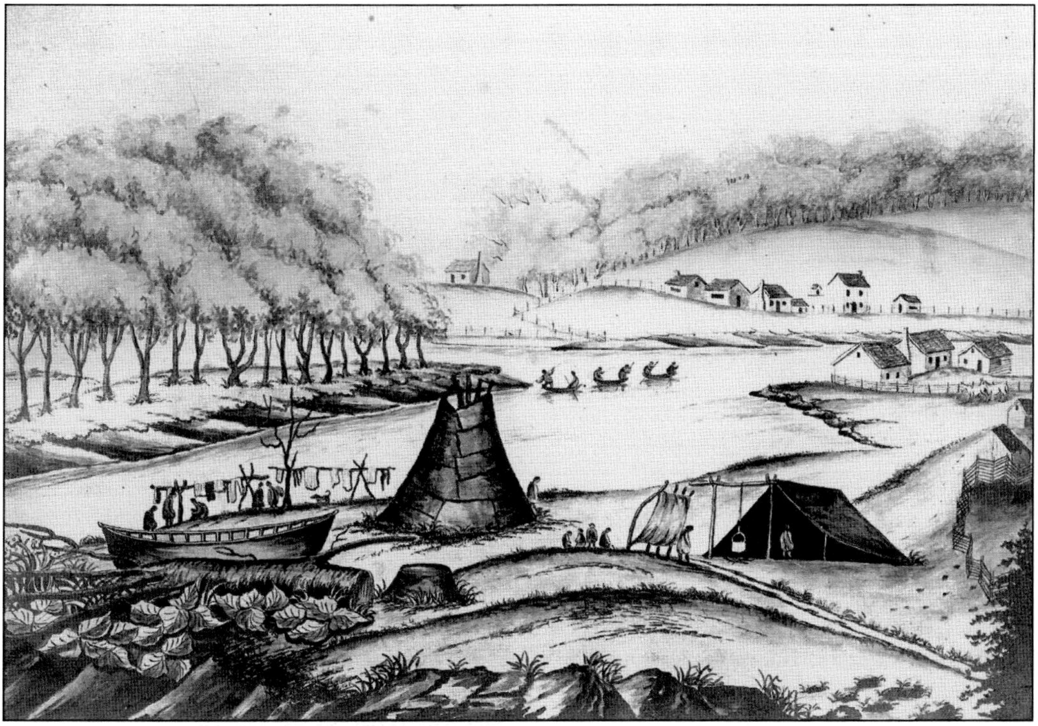

Missionary Isaac McCoy established a Baptist mission for Ottawa Indians on the banks of the Grand River. This sketch, drawn by Rev. John Booth in 1831, shows the McCoy settlement and on the opposite bank, Louis Campau's trading post. A fur trader, Campau was the first to solicit pioneers to come and settle the area. His land later became downtown Grand Rapids.

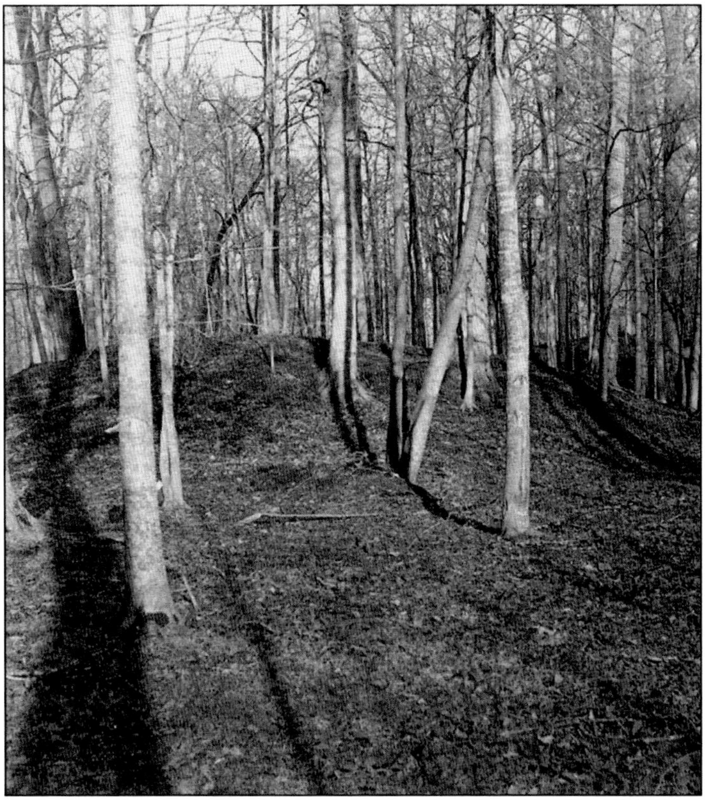

The Treaty of 1836 pushed many Native Americans north of the Grand River. Although a band of Ottawas reportedly lived near settler Philonzo Bowen's property for a few years before moving on, the only remnants of their existence in Paris Township (the first name for Kentwood) were burial mounds, such as these, and arrowheads and other artifacts farmers found when they plowed their fields.

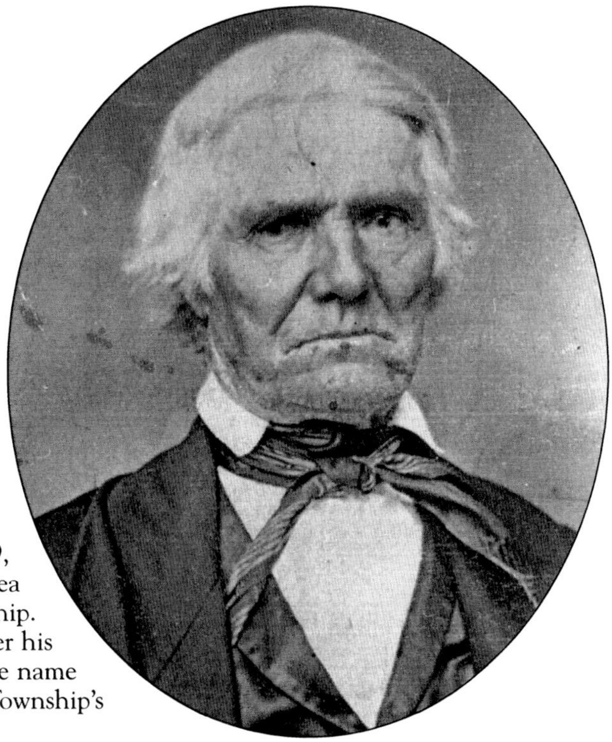

Joel Guild was one of many who followed Campau's invitation to come to Michigan. In 1833, Guild settled outside of Grand Rapids along with his brothers, Edward and Daniel. By 1839, so many people were living in the area that settlers met to organize a township. Guild suggested the name of Paris, after his former residence, Paris, New York. The name was ratified, and Guild became Paris Township's first supervisor.

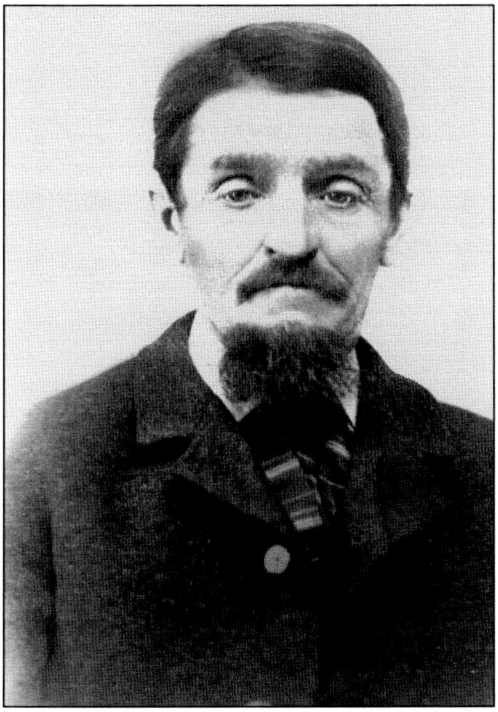
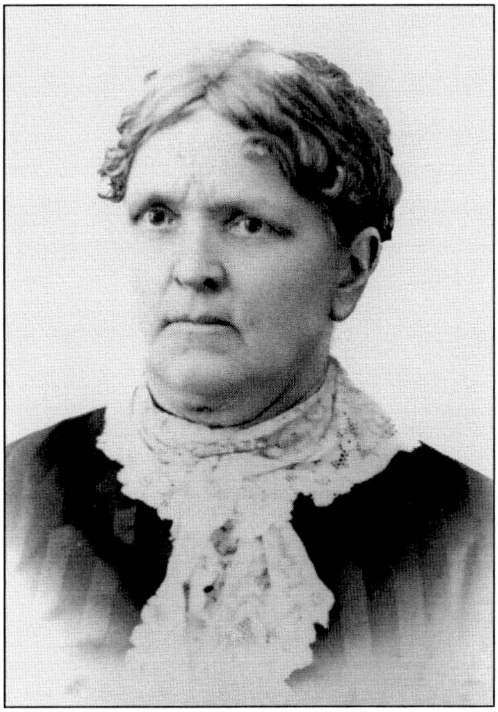

In 1836, Capt. John Davis brought his sons and grandson Isaac Dixon Davis (above left), to Paris Township. Although described as a man of slight physique, Isaac was well known for his ability to chop down trees. At the age of 18, he helped his family clear the land on their farm just south of Reeds Lake. He bought a farm in the heart of Paris Township after he married his first wife, Sophia Reed, in 1842. After Sophia's death in 1863, Isaac married Louisa M. Barr (above right).

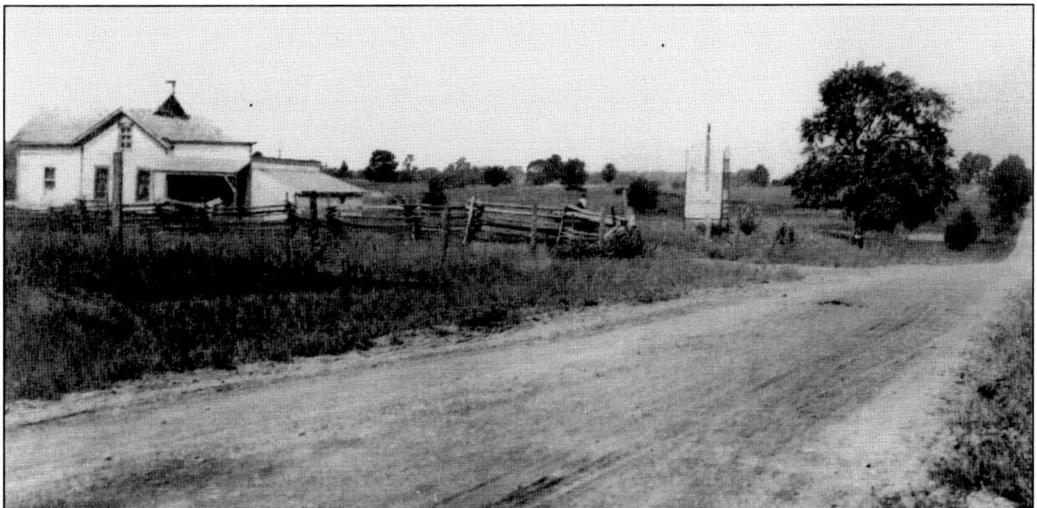

The Davis farm (pictured here in the 1920s) was located between Eastern Avenue and Kalamazoo Avenue and Forty-fourth Street and Fifty-second Street. Like many farmers in the area, the Davis family cultivated fruit trees, along with other crops. Isaac Davis also served as township clerk, township supervisor, and school district officer before his death in 1899.

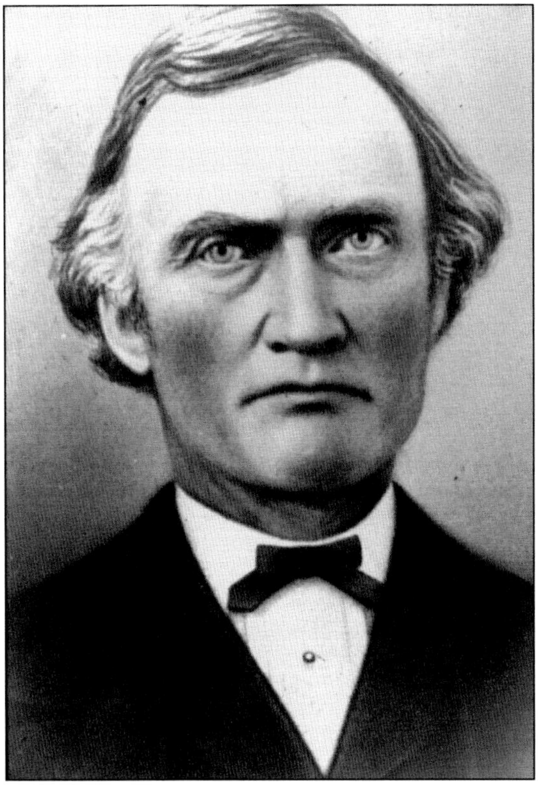

Philonzo Bowen was another New Yorker who moved to Paris Township. In 1836, Bowen acquired 320 acres of land in a deed signed by Pres. Andrew Jackson. He hired two men to travel to his property, clear the land, and build a small cabin for his new bride, Selestia Lucina Perkins. Together, the Bowens managed an extensive farm where they raised seven children.

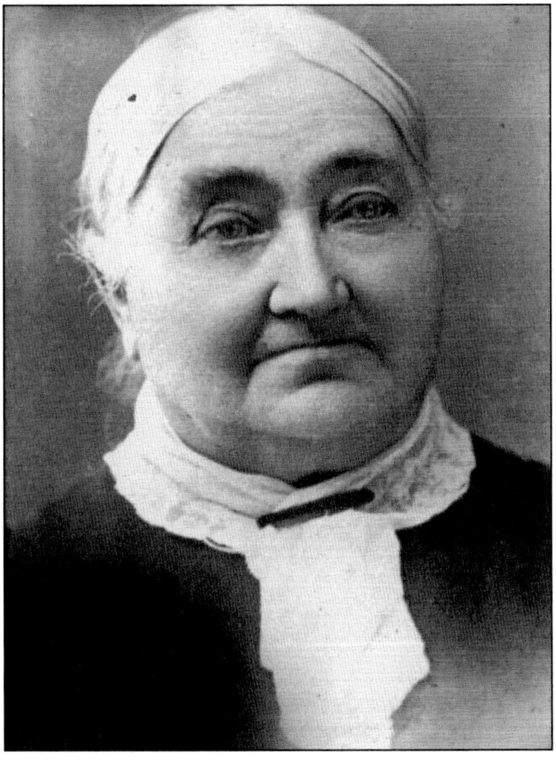

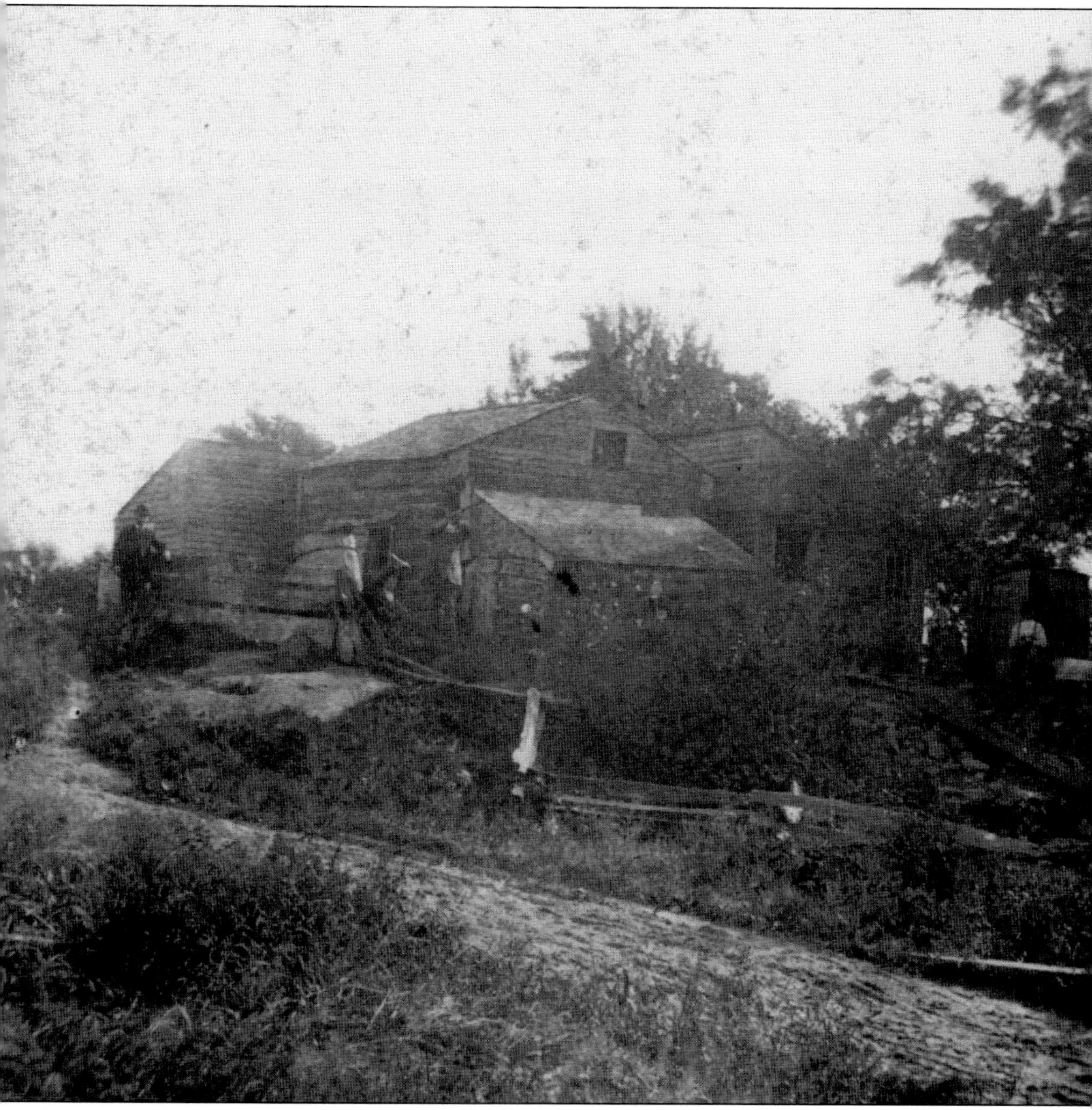

In 1839, Selestia traveled from Detroit to Paris Township by stagecoach to set up house in their new cabin, pictured above. Philonzo followed with a new team of oxen. Many Paris Township residents started their farms with cabins like these and later built larger houses. Toward the end of the 19th century, it was fashionable to keep cabins alongside new houses to show where the residents had come from.

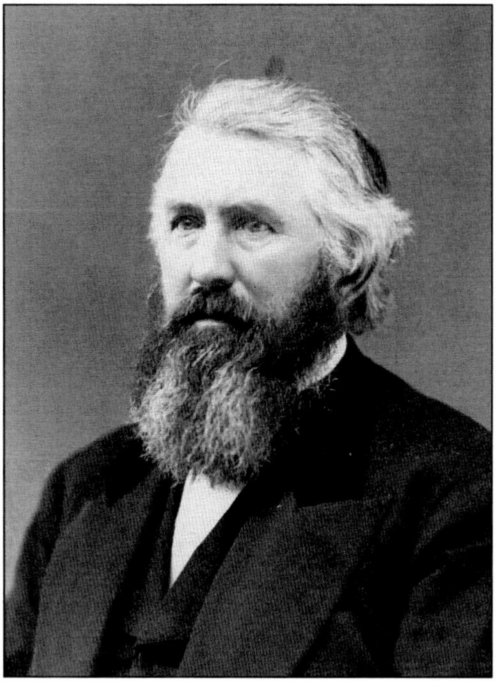

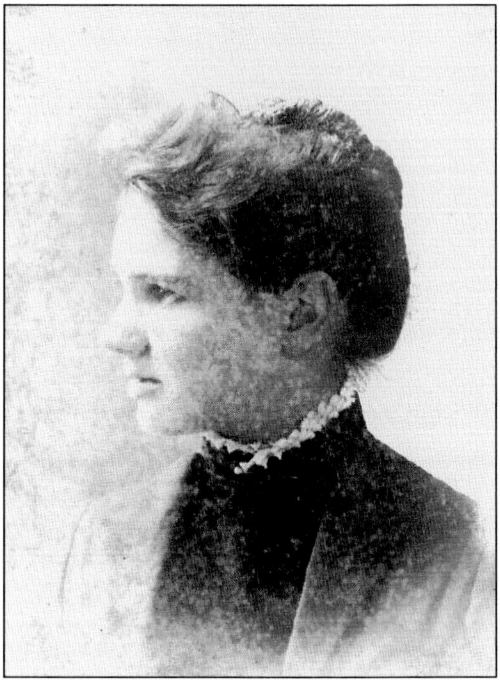

Sluman Bailey and his brother Freeborn visited Paris Township in 1845. Impressed with the area, Sluman bought 120 acres from a land agent in Detroit for $3 an acre. In 1846, Sluman, his wife Delia, and their newborn son became residents of Paris Township. In addition to farming, Sluman founded the Kent Agricultural Society and served Paris Township as school inspector, tax collector, and justice of the peace. He also served Kent County as sheriff.

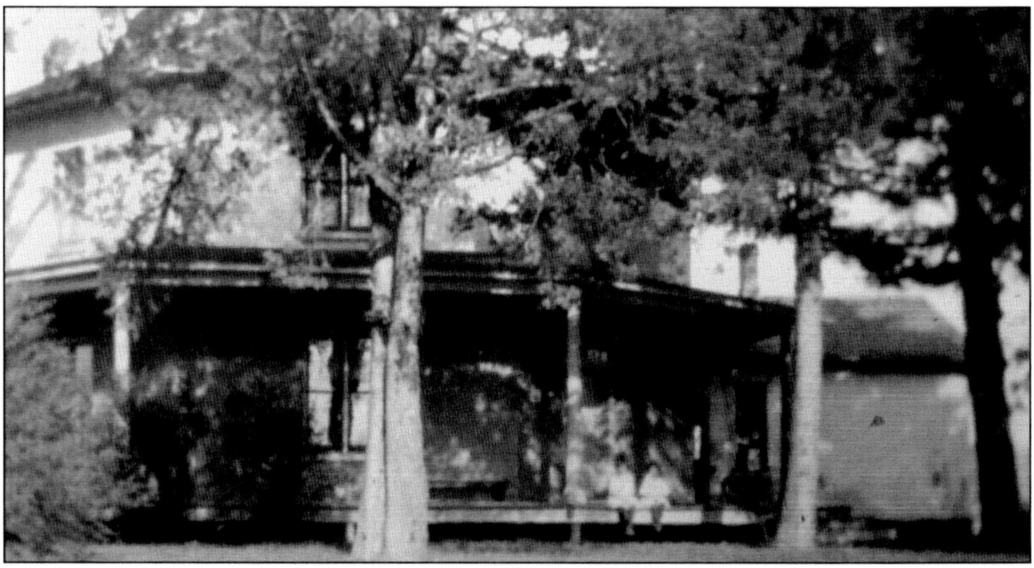

The Baileys' first home was a log cabin that Sluman constructed himself. By 1855, the family was prosperous, and a new house was needed. Intrigued by the benefits the octagon house was purported to have, listed in *The Octagon House: A Home for All*, Sluman followed a building pattern that author and builder Orson Fowler designed. Still standing today, the Bailey House is one of the few surviving octagon houses in the United States.

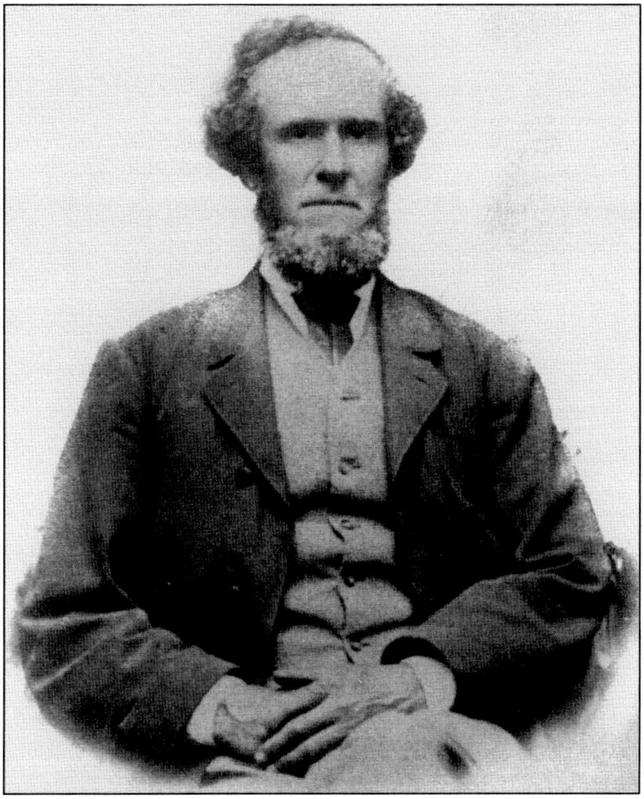

Like the Davis family, several generations of the Darling clan settled in Paris Township in the late 1830s. Silas and Rhoda Darling were the parents of Hiram (pictured at right). Hiram was well known and respected among Paris Township farmers. In 1840, they elected him to the office of township treasurer. After his first wife, Polly, died in childbirth in 1856, Hiram met and married Louisa Vosburgh (pictured below).

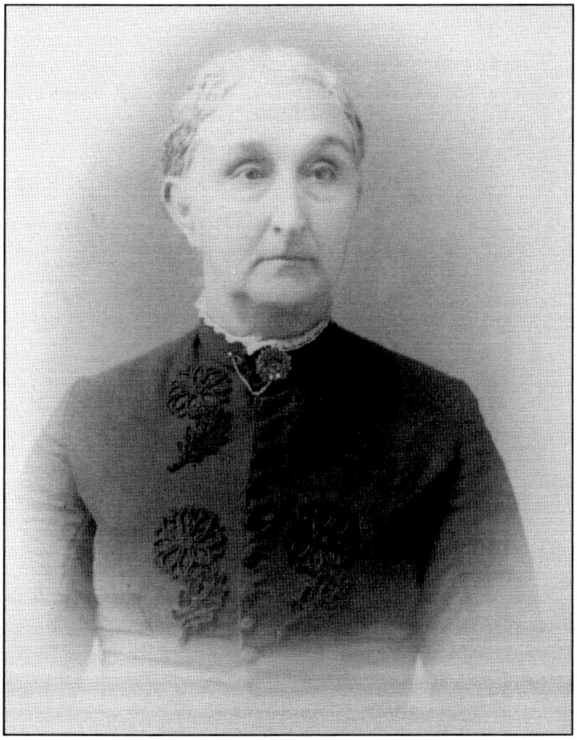

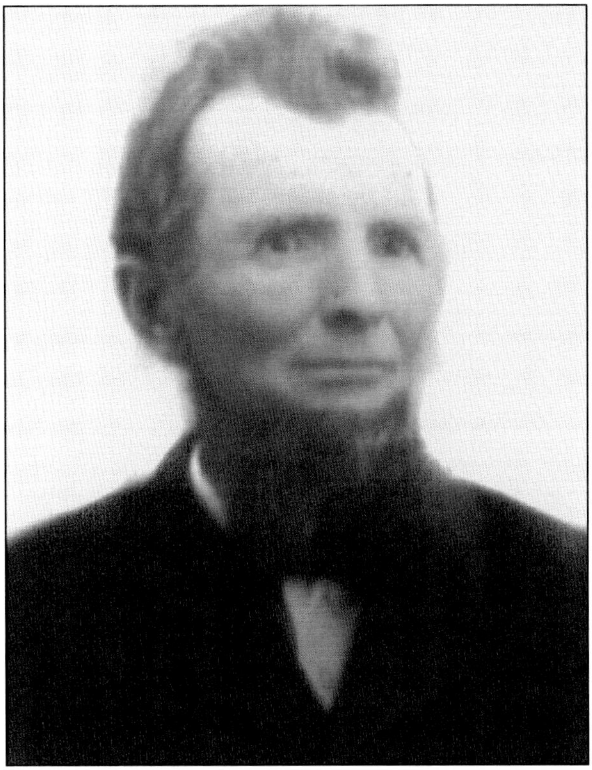

Aaron Aber, of Schuyler County, New York, moved to Michigan in 1853. After the Civil War, he purchased 160 acres in Paris Township. He and his wife, Catherine, made their farm an extremely comfortable and welcoming place for friends and visitors. An obituary called Aber's death in February 1899 "an irreparable loss, not only to the immediate family but to the entire community."

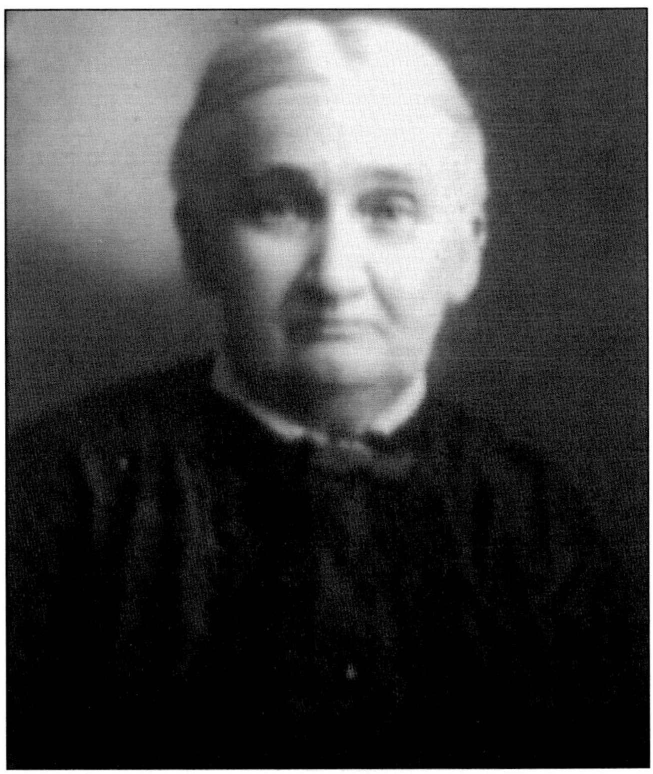

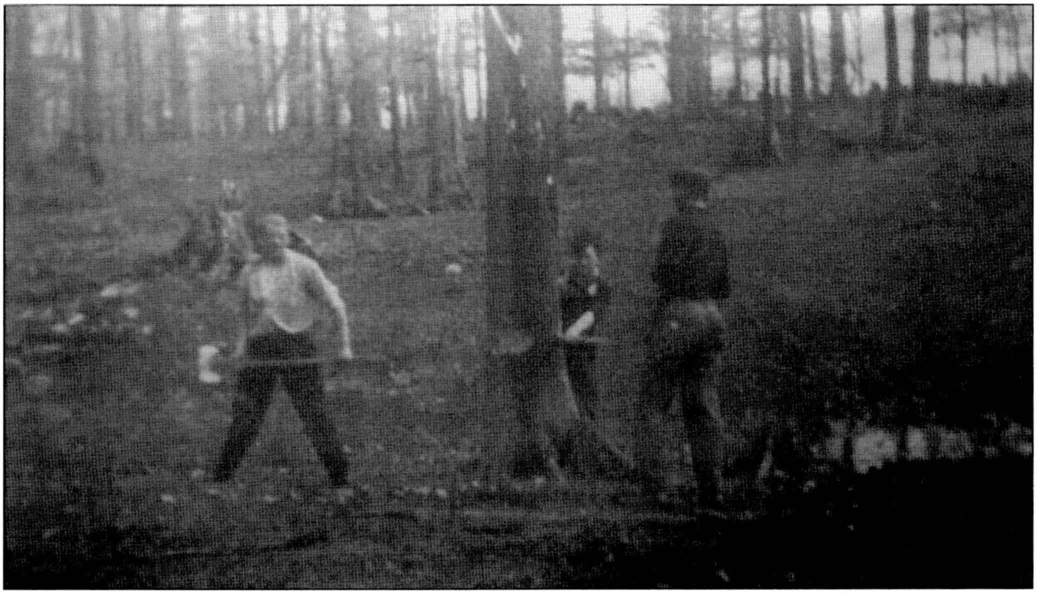

In the mid-1800s, hundreds of families bought land in Paris Township. Families, such as the Laraways, Clarks, Cutlers, Hardys, Pattersons, Spauldings, and others, cleared the land, established farms and other businesses, and became part of an ever-growing but close-knit community. Decades later, their children and grandchildren would continue to influence the development of Paris Township as it became Kentwood.

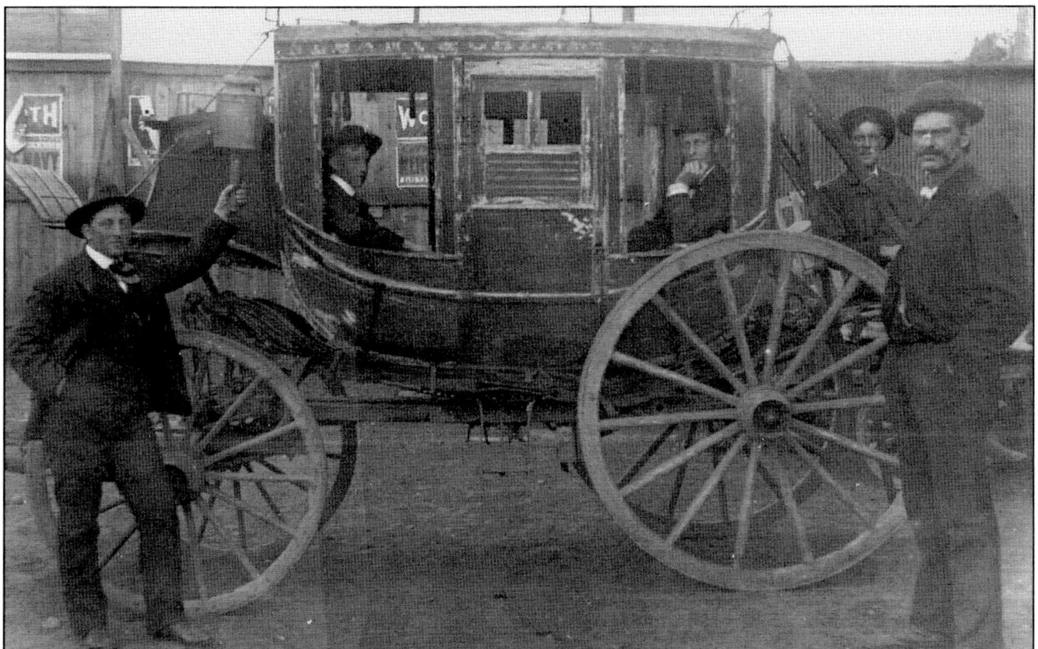

Many early settlers, like Selestia Bowen, arrived in Paris Township by stagecoach. Coaches, such as the Concorde, seated six to eight passengers. In addition to people, stagecoaches also brought letters and other news from the east to Paris Township. Before the 1850s, the only other methods of travel were horse, ox-cart, boat, or foot.

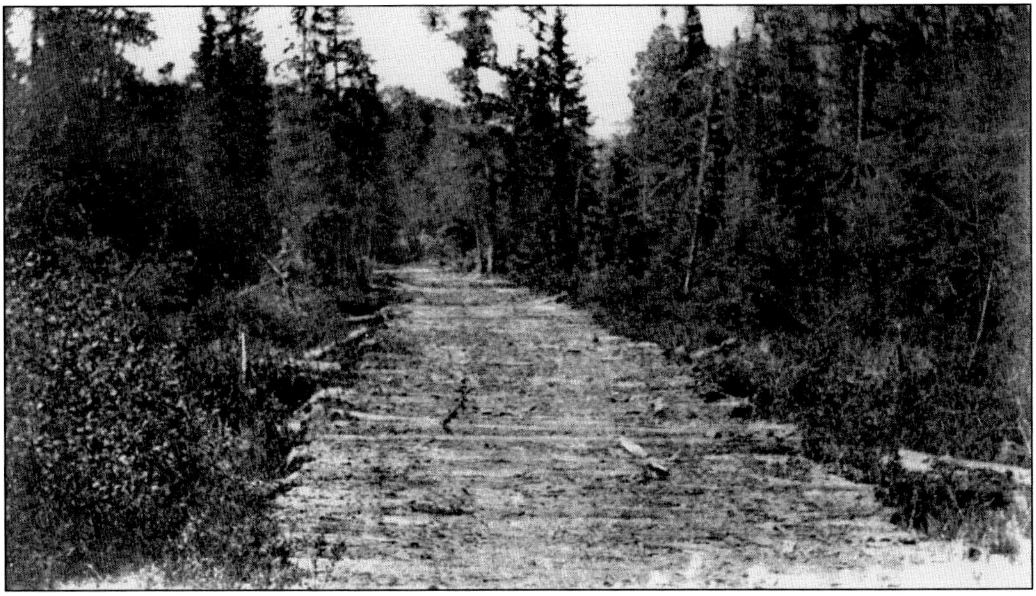

Before settlers arrived, Michigan trappers and traders used the river systems to carry goods (one of the reasons that Campau's trading post was on the river). At the time, most roads were muddy wheel ruts along old Native American trails. Seasonal rain and snow made travel along the roads difficult. As more settlers entered the area, plank roads like this one were laid down over the trails to make travel easier.

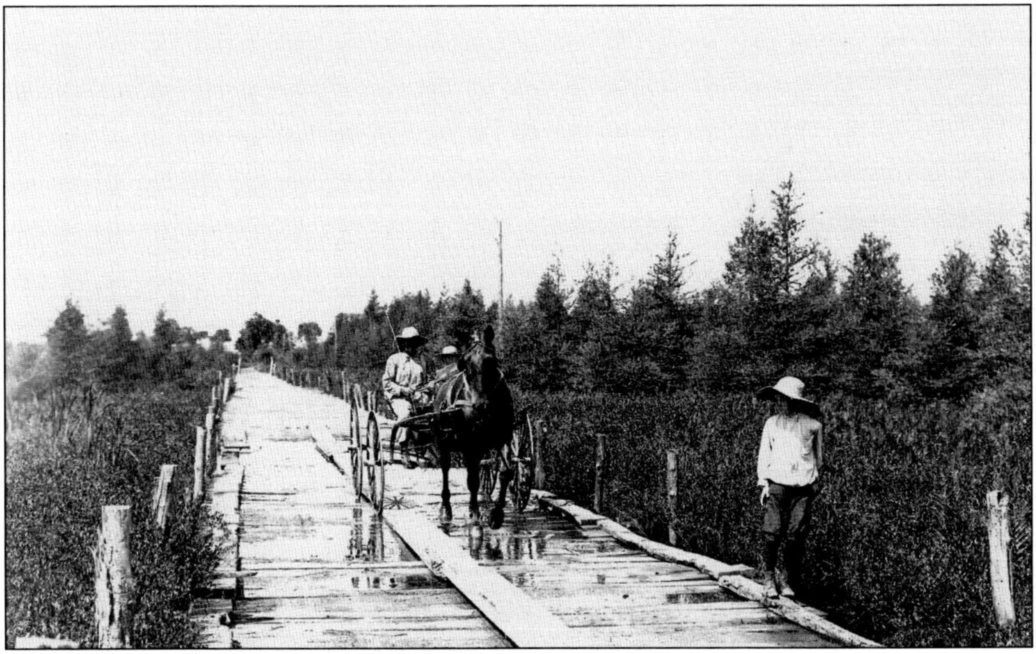

Plank roads, or puncheons, first appeared in Michigan in 1837. They were composed of pine or oak boards, up to 16 feet long, placed over stringer or sleeper boards covering the road. Division Avenue, which bordered Paris Township and ran from Grand Rapids to Kalamazoo, was one of many plank roads in Kent County. This road made it easier for settlers to come to Paris Township and helped farmers transport their goods to nearby markets.

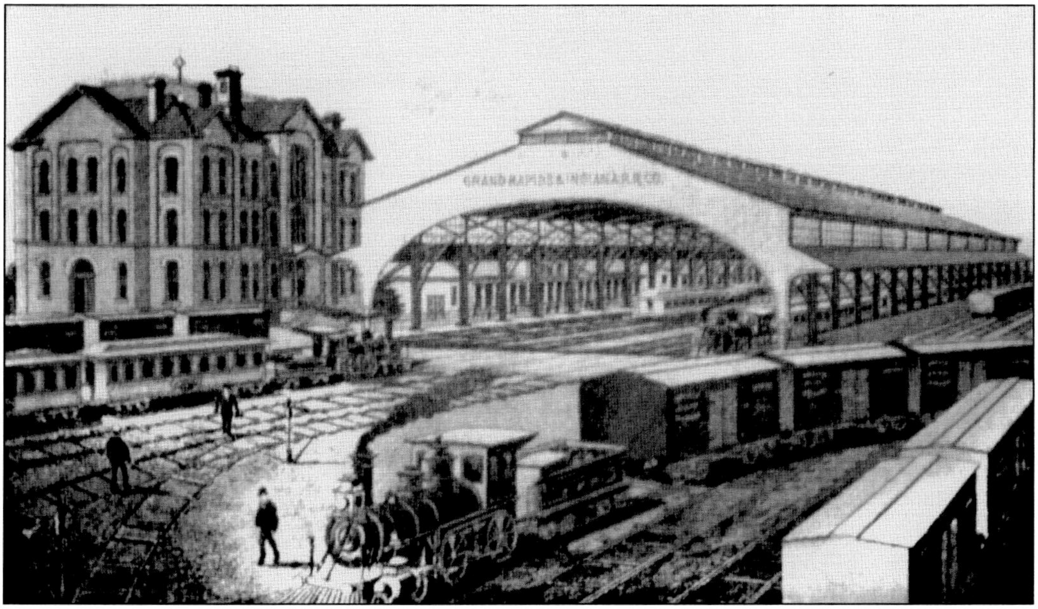

In the late 1850s, the state government began to build railroads across Michigan. Although the Detroit and Milwaukee Railroad ran from Grand Haven and Muskegon to Detroit, an extended line was added for Kent County in 1858 and came through Grand Rapids. Until Bowen Station was built in 1869, arriving by train in Grand Rapids and taking a coach into Paris Township was the easiest way to the area in the late 1800s.

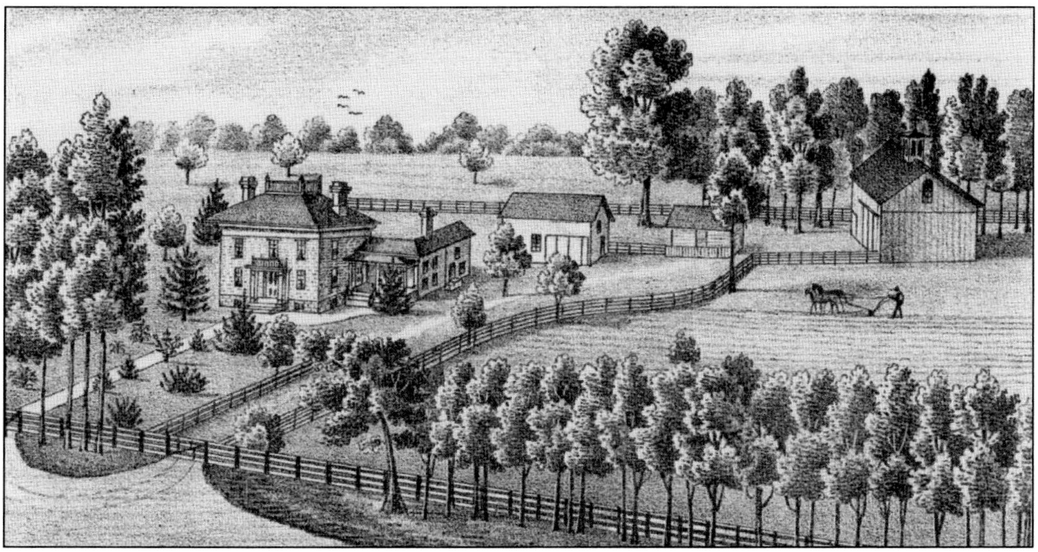

In 1876, the *Illustrated Historical Atlas of the Counties of Ottawa and Kent* was published. Several affluent Paris Township families paid to have their farms included in the book. Like many illustrations of the time, these drawings are heavily stylized and represent a more idealized picture of the farms than really was. The J. D. Alger farm, pictured above, had 80 acres in the northwest section of the township.

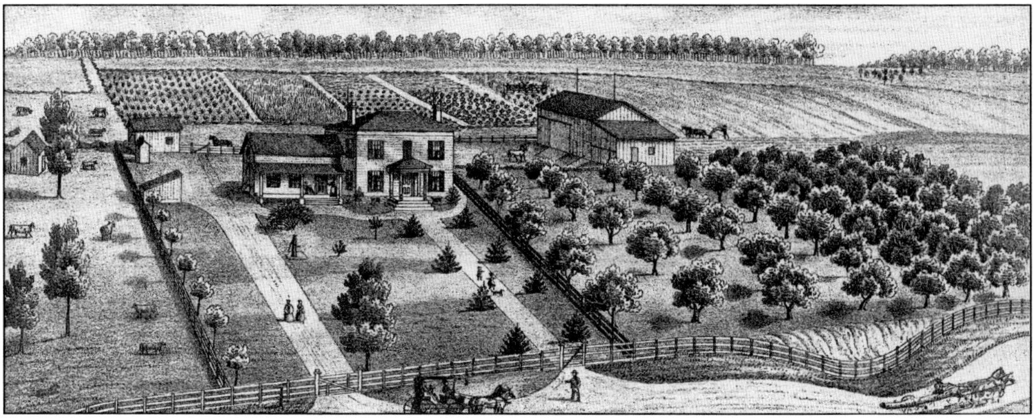

Freeborn Bailey purchased 90 acres of land near his brother Sluman's farm and in 1849 moved to Paris Township with his wife Ellen, an English immigrant. After losing their three children, all of whom died in infancy, the Baileys welcomed three foster children into their family and temporarily cared for many others. Freeborn's generosity earned him the nickname "Father Bailey."

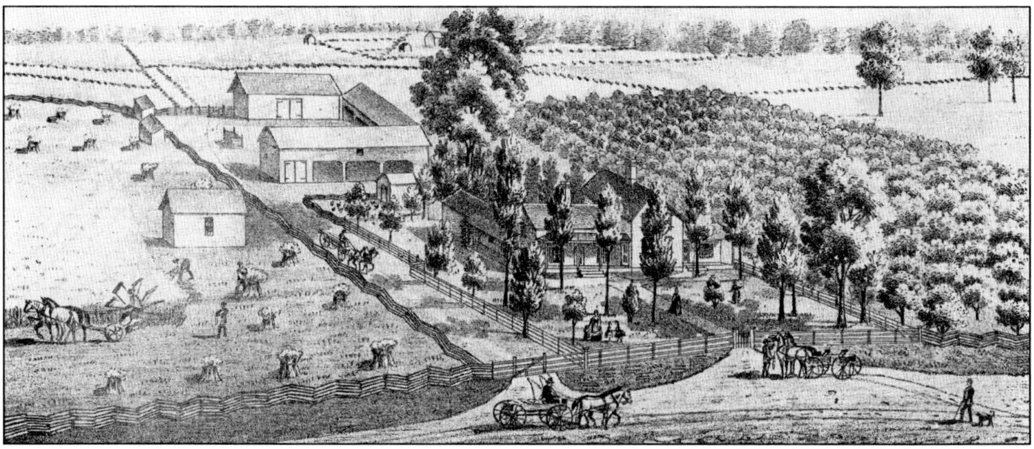

Carpenter Anthony Boden was a native of England who married Hanora McHahon of Ireland in Grand Rapids in 1837. In 1846, the Bodens bought this farm. Anthony continued to commute to Grand Rapids everyday to work. He left his son, Joseph, to manage the farm for him. Paris Township residents of the time considered Anthony a friendly man and his farm one of the finest in the county.

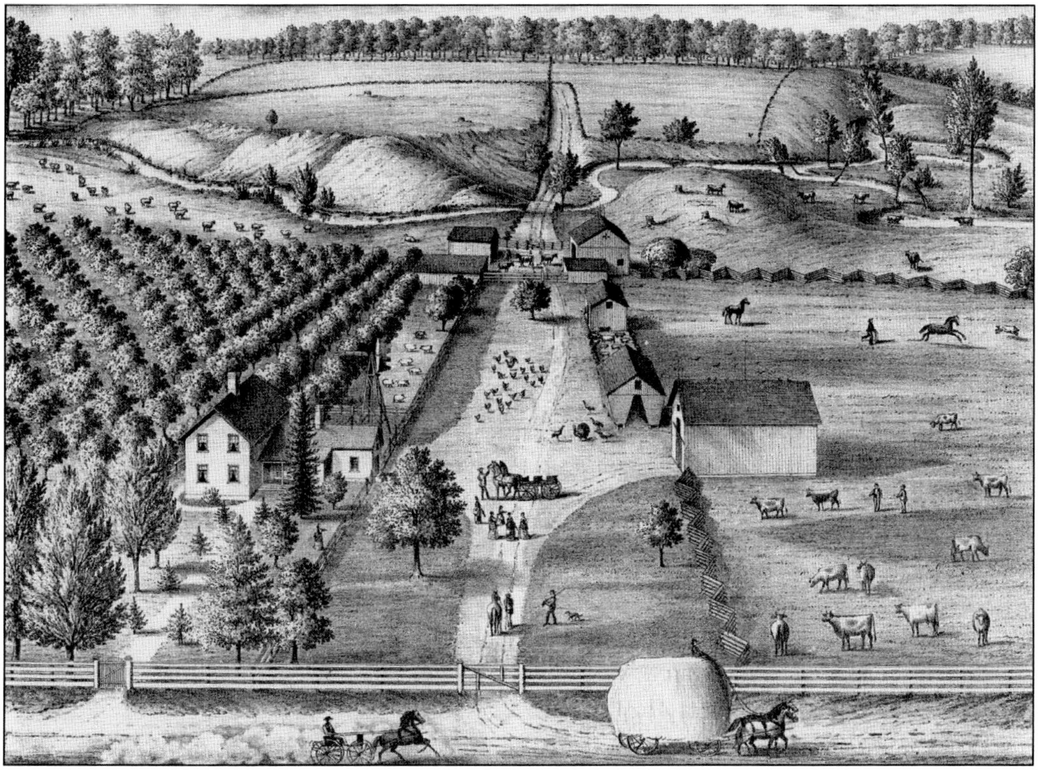

Stephen B. Davis (not related to the Isaac Davis family) owned an L-shaped section of land facing present-day Forty-fourth Street and East Paris Avenue. When he and his wife, Lovina, first moved to Paris Township from Canada in 1850, they bought 80 acres of land. With 10 children to help him, Stephen continued to invest in his farm until he owned 161 acres valued at $60 an acre.

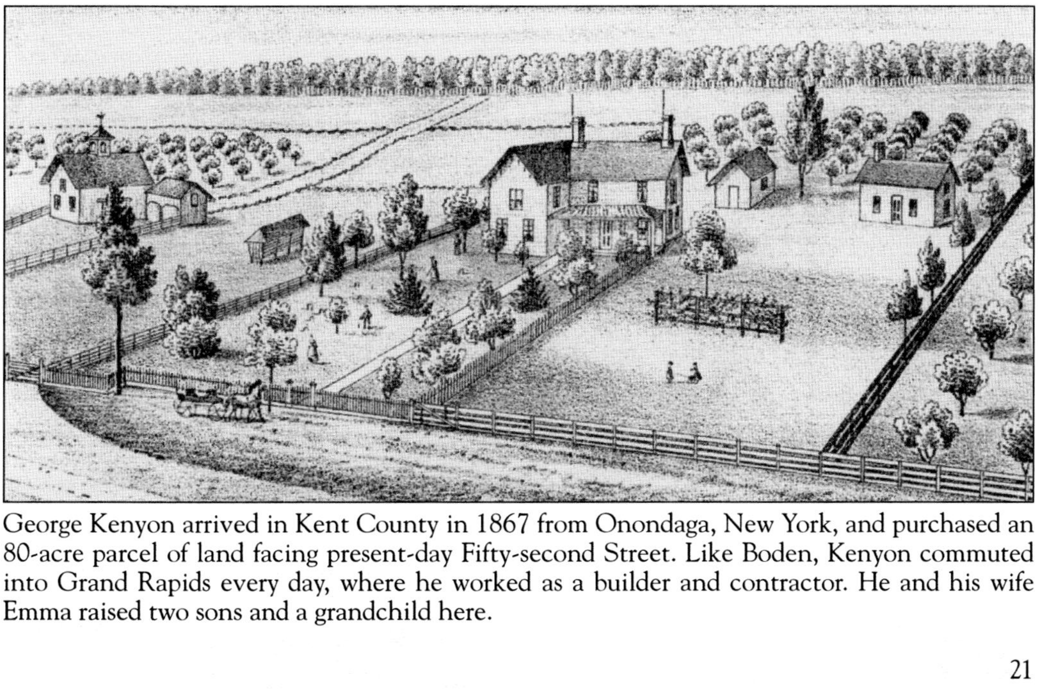

George Kenyon arrived in Kent County in 1867 from Onondaga, New York, and purchased an 80-acre parcel of land facing present-day Fifty-second Street. Like Boden, Kenyon commuted into Grand Rapids every day, where he worked as a builder and contractor. He and his wife Emma raised two sons and a grandchild here.

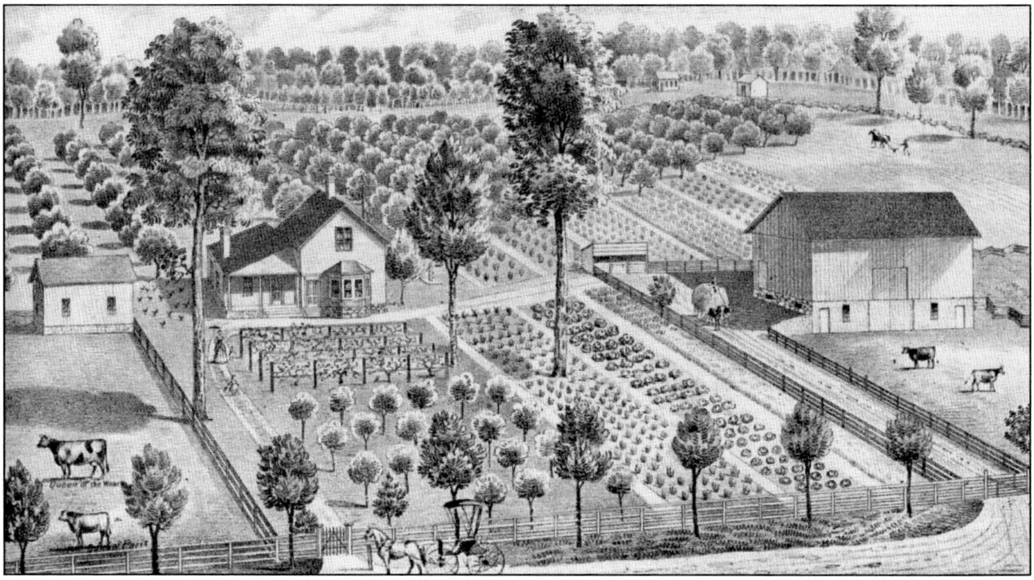

George Prescott moved from New York to Grand Rapids with his parents in 1844. After serving in the Civil War, Prescott returned to his hometown in 1866 and bought 80 acres of land along the border of Paris Township and Grand Rapids. He and his wife, Agnes, had three children. The Prescotts sold garden seeds, which were renowned by Paris Township farmers as being highly reliable.

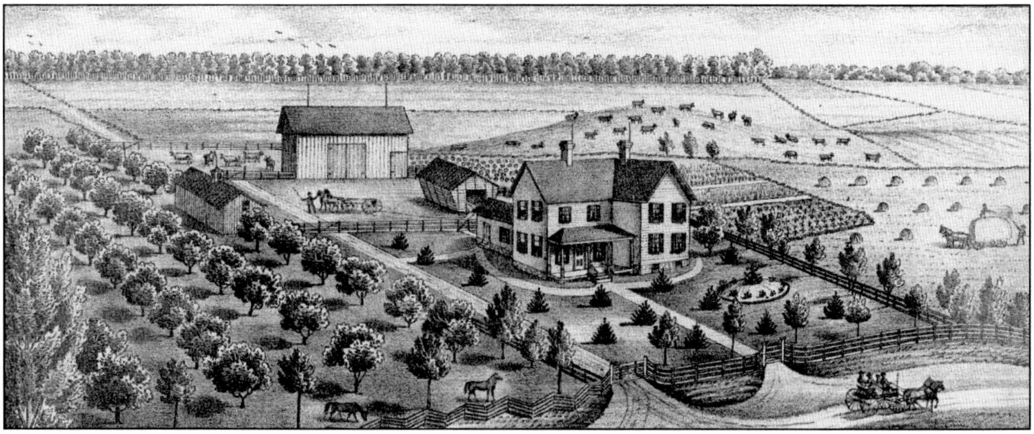

Leroy Thompson moved from Seneca County, New York, to Paris Township in 1851. He built a log cabin and worked for neighbors, chopping trees and splitting rails in the winter and helping with the harvest in the summer. He saved his money and eventually sent for his family, who joined him a few years later. In 1861, Thompson married Eliza Earle of Grand Rapids. Together, they managed an 80-acre farm along present-day Thirty-sixth Street.

Two

THE FARMING LIFE

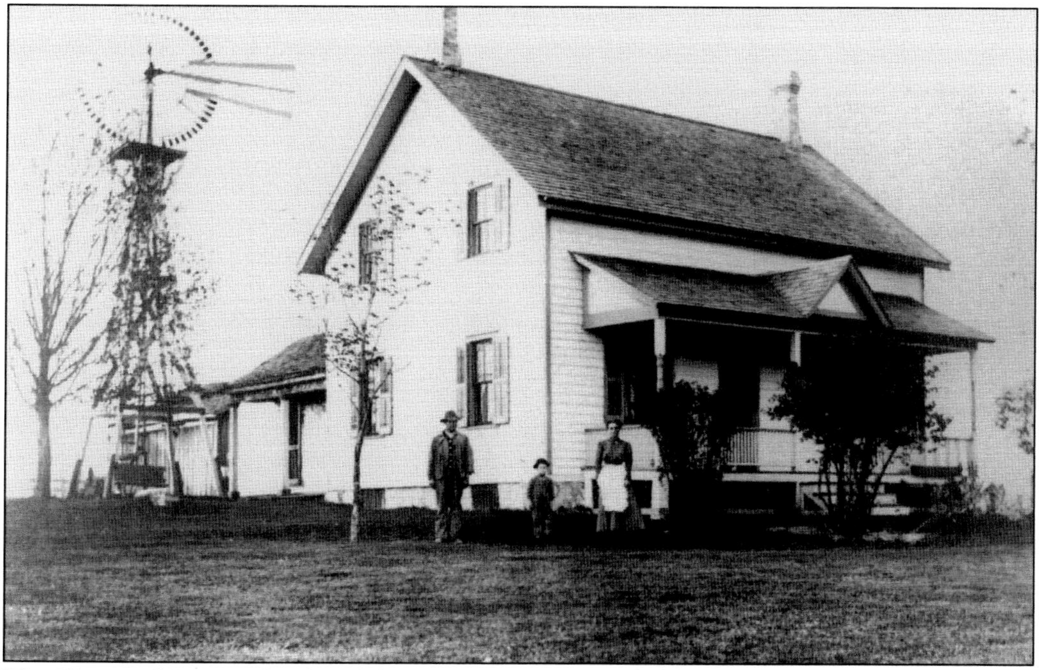

The *Illustrated Historical Atlas of the Counties of Ottawa and Kent* notes, "many excellent and finely kept farms are found" in Paris Township. An example of one was the Sternbeck farm, shown here with the Davis family. Fred Sternbeck was a German immigrant who settled in Paris Township in 1870. He married Hiram Darling's widow, Louisa, in 1874. The couple grew a variety of crops until the early 1900s.

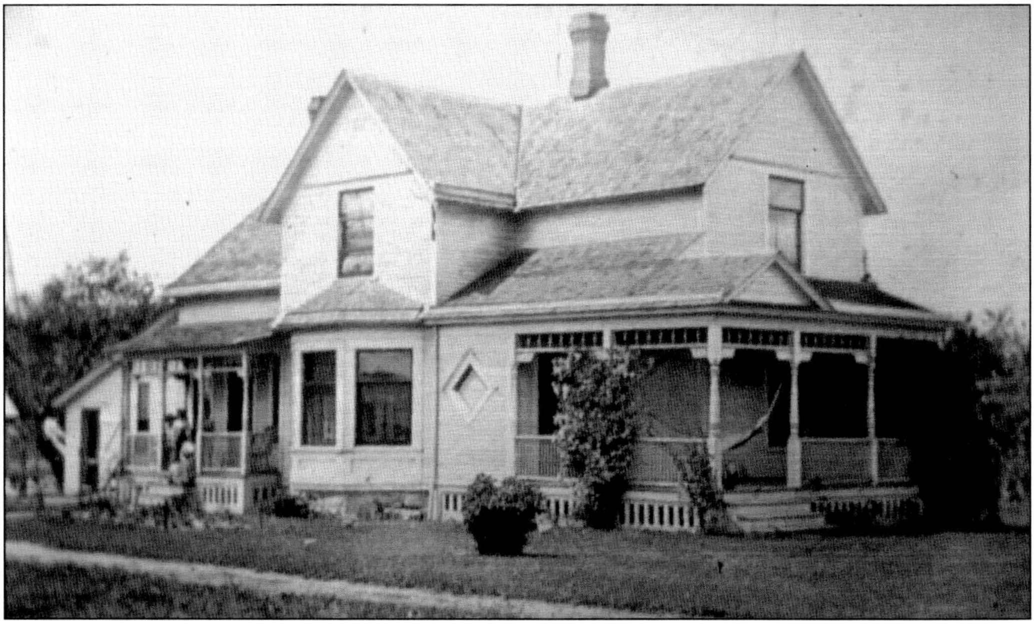

By the early 1900s, many second and even third generation Paris Township families ran successful farms. Their prosperity is evident in homes like this one, where Bert and Minnie Davis lived. The house, with its wide front porch and diamond window, was clearly influenced by Victorian architecture, which was popular at the time.

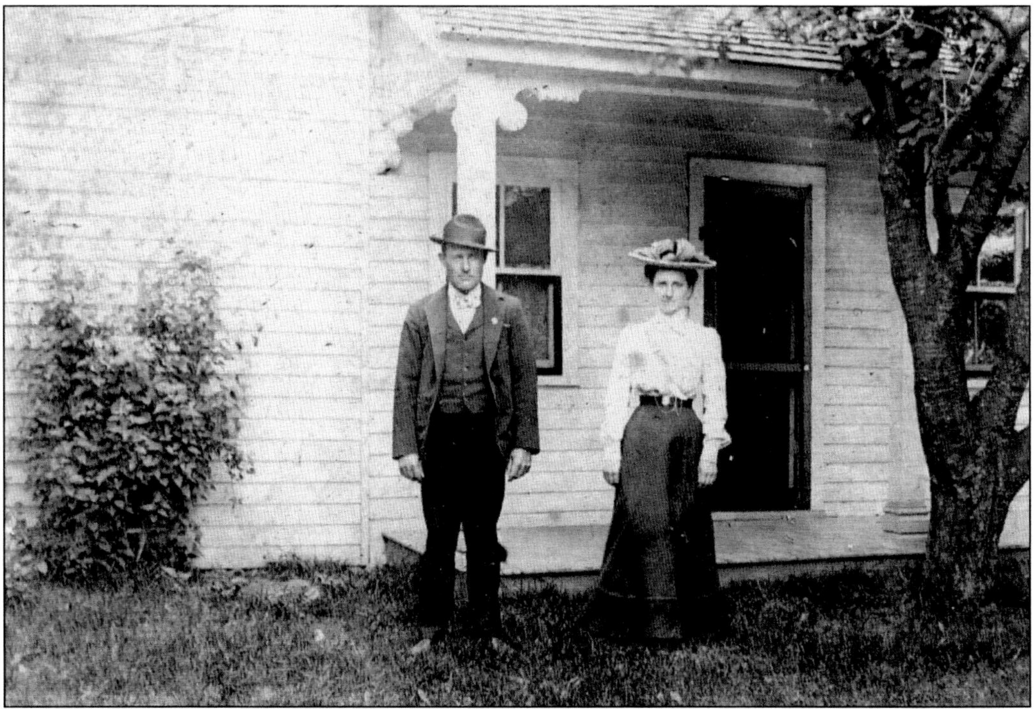

Bert and Minnie Davis stand on the side of their house dressed in their best for a photograph. At the time this picture was taken, Burt and Minnie were in their late 20s and had only been married for a few years. Together, they raised several children on their farm.

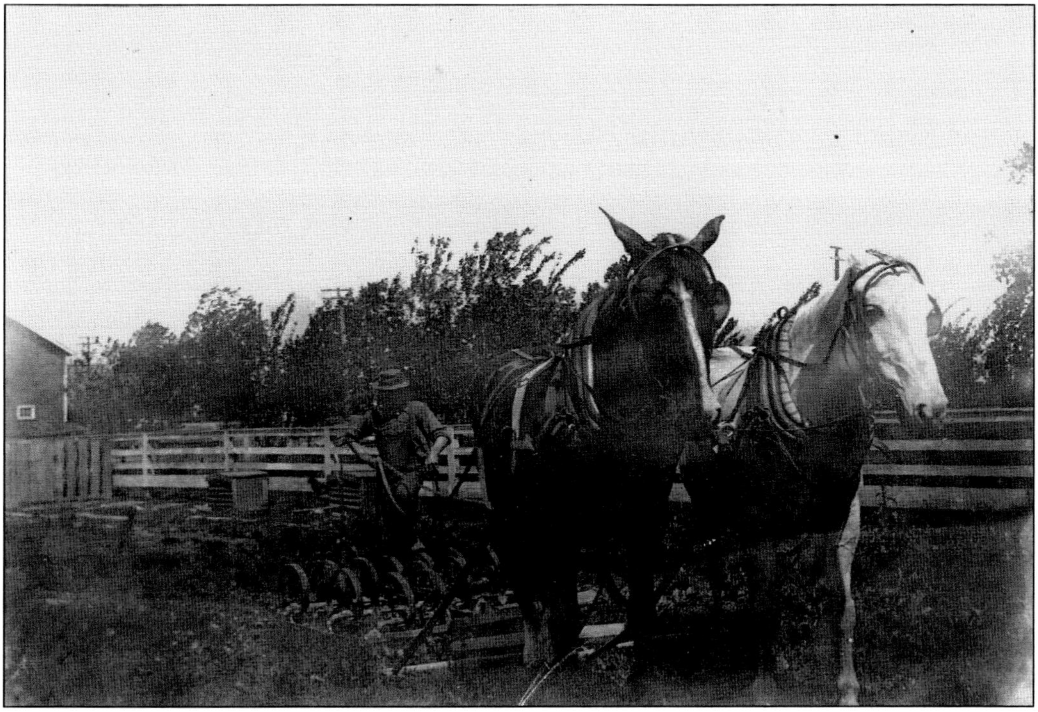

Draught animals, like these horses belonging to Bert Davis, were essential to Paris Township farmers for their ability to pull farm machinery and transport produce and other goods to markets around Grand Rapids. Even with the extra muscle these animals provided, farming was hard, time-consuming work. When plowing, for example, farmers needed to stop and let the horses rest every half hour.

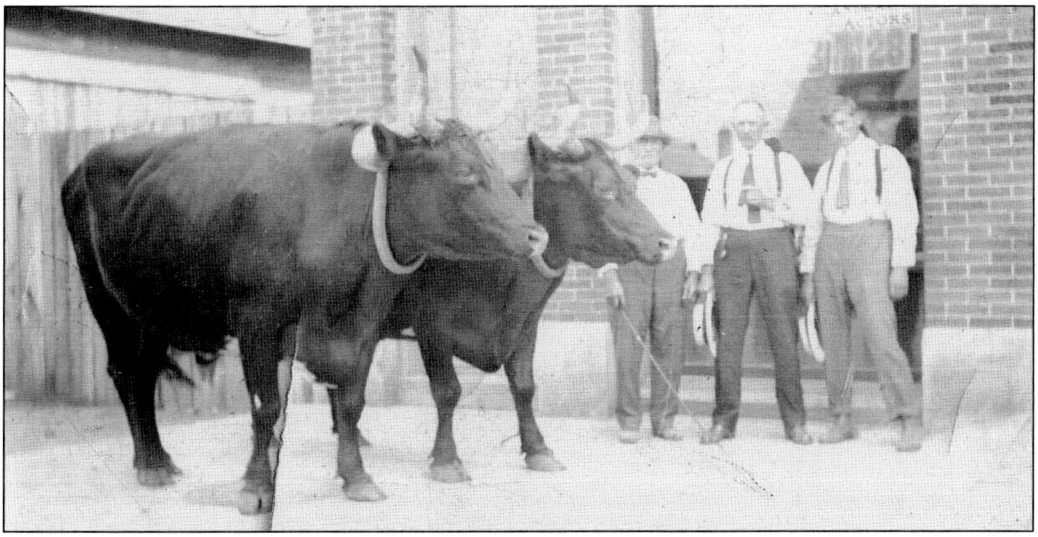

Some Paris Township farms also used oxen as draught animals. Oxen are bulls picked as calves for their intelligence (they could be taught to properly respond to commands like "get up" and "whoa"). Although they moved more slowly than horses, oxen could pull heavier loads for longer stretches of time. The Bowens were proud of their team, named Jack and Bill, and in this picture, showed them off for an event in Grand Rapids.

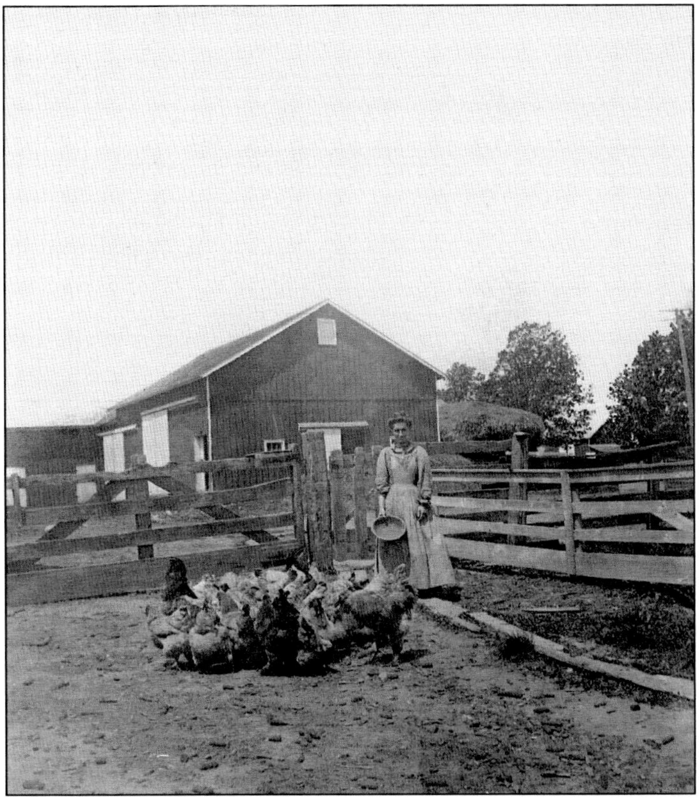

All of the animals on a typical Paris Township farm served a purpose. In this picture, Minnie Davis throws feed to her chickens. Before the invention of refrigeration, the Davis family, like many farmers, kept chickens for their ability to produce fresh eggs. Any chickens that did not produce were usually butchered and became dinner on Sunday or other special occasions.

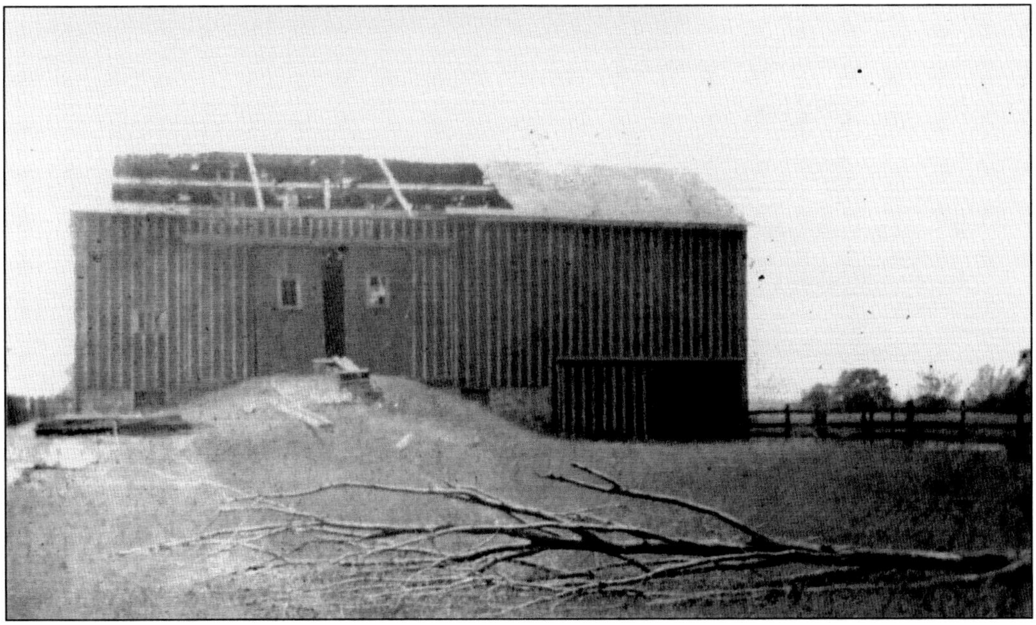

Barns were also an essential part of a farm. This bank barn was built on the Aber farm (located on present day Thirty-sixth Street). Bank barns were usually constructed on the side of a hill, so farmers could enter multiple barn levels from the ground. Instead of a hill, the Abers built a bank to the second level.

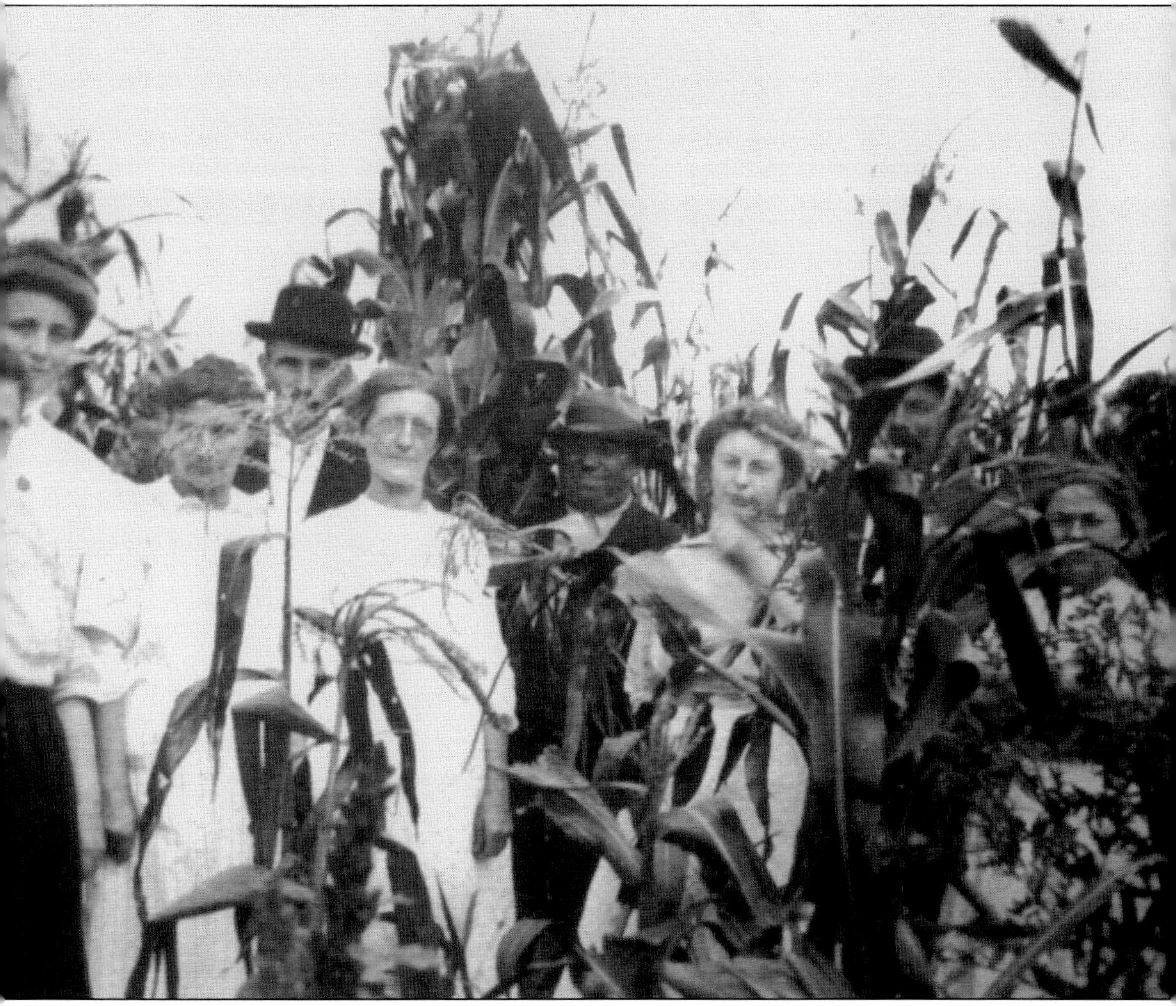

The settlers who first arrived in Paris Township purchased large sections of land. As their children became adults and more settlers arrived in the area, farmers sold parcels of their land. By the early 1900s, Paris Township had numerous small farms, which grew a wide variety of crops, including corn. Here, members of the Feenstra family and their friends display the bounty of their farm.

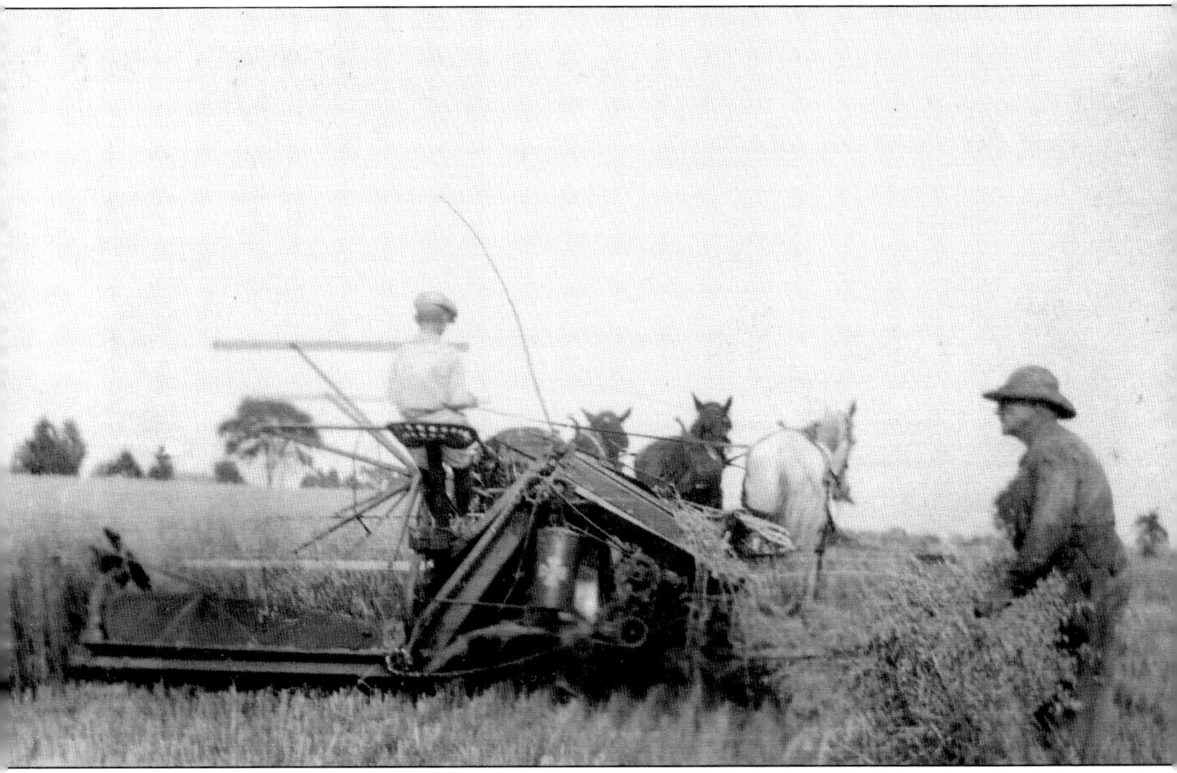

Wheat was one of the main crops grown by Paris Township farmers. Since the Bowen family raised cows as well as crops, they rotated their crops every year following the acronym COW, C for corn, O for oats, and W for wheat. In this photograph, Bostwick Bowen, son of Philonzo Bowen, holds a shock of freshly harvested wheat as his nephew, Jack Rogers, drives a team pulling a binder. The binder was another piece of essential farm machinery since it could cut wheat and then tie it into shocks or bundles.

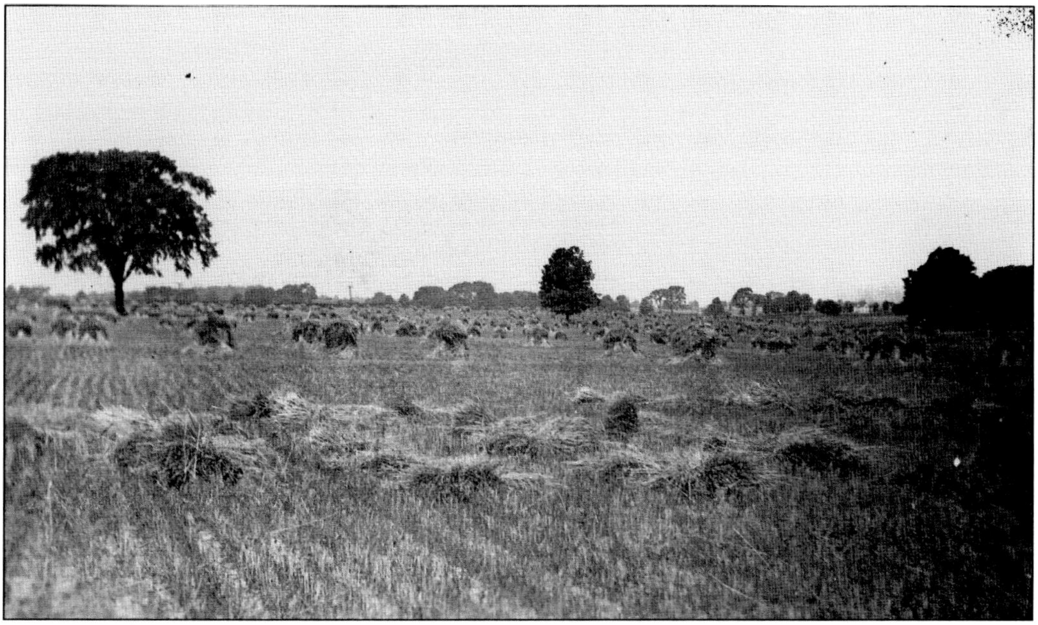

Once Bostwick and Jack were done harvesting, a photograph was taken of the harvested wheat field. The Bowen's new house, built by Bostwick in 1910 after the original was destroyed by fire, can be seen in the distance. Paris Township farmers usually left shocked wheat stacked upright in the field for several days in order to let it dry out.

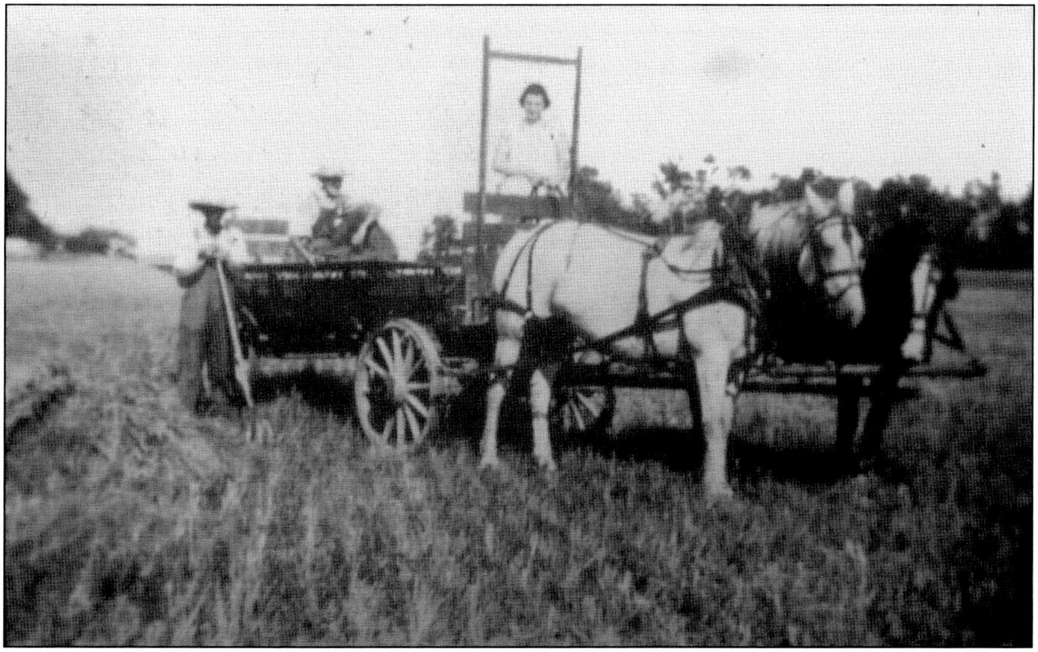

Once dry, the shocks were collected and loaded into a horse-drawn cart to be brought to the thresher. Depending on the size of the field, collecting shocks could be a large task. Time was also a factor since smaller farms hired threshing teams to come to their field on specific days. Naturally, everyone in a family (in this picture, from left to right, Stewart, Fred, and Ruby Darling) worked together to bring the shocks in on time.

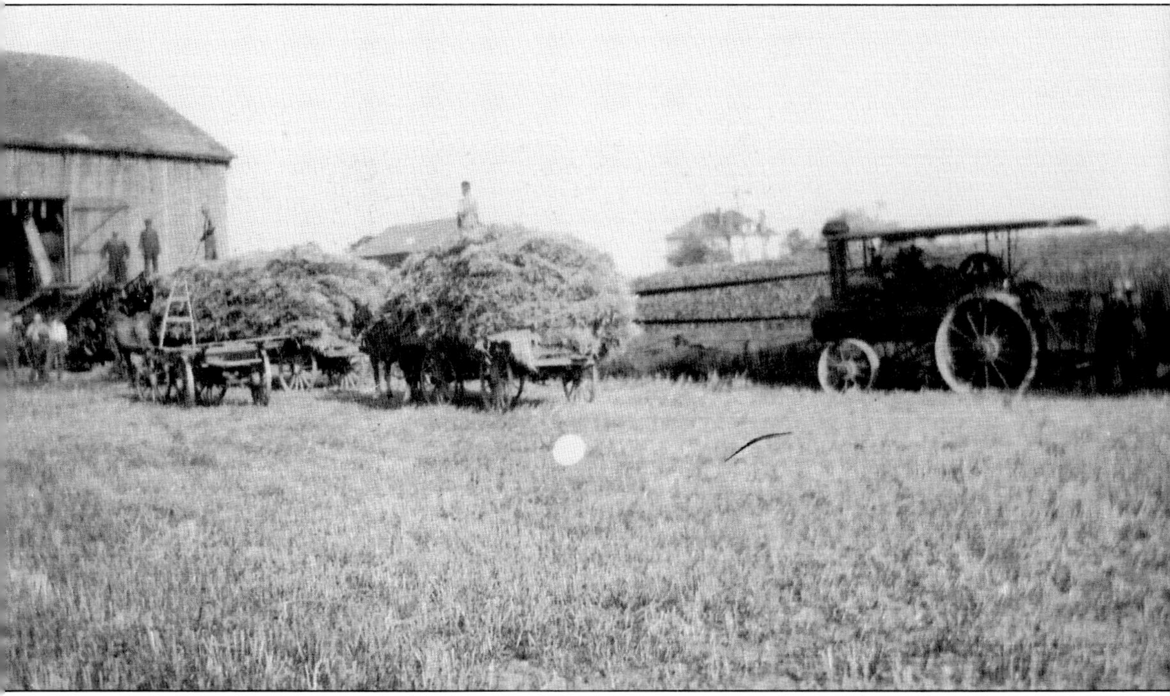

Collected shocks are being brought to the Bowen family barn. Next to the fence on the left sits the steam engine, which would run the threshing machine. Large farms, such as that of the Bowen family, often owned their own threshing machines. Even with the convenience of a machine to thresh their own wheat, threshing was a complex task and required many hands. The Bowens hired farm laborers and even housed them on their property.

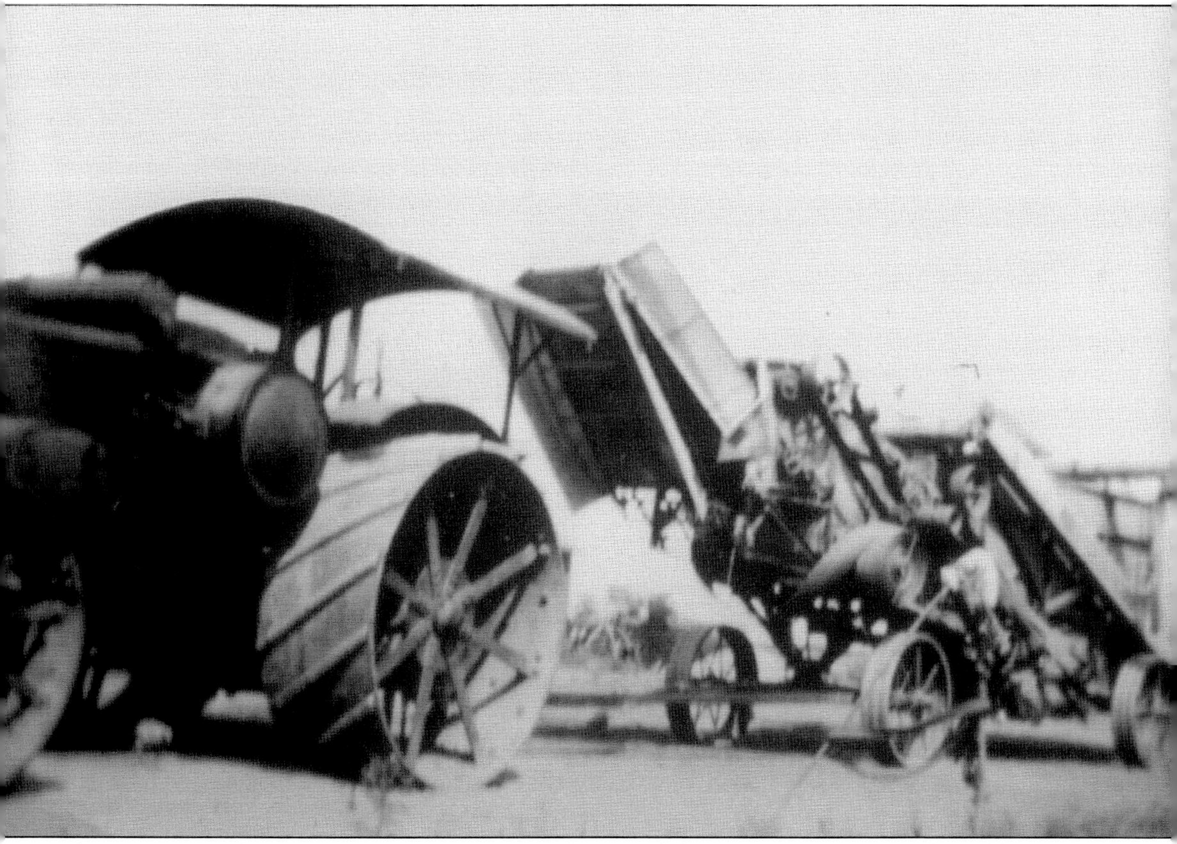

When Henry Ford released the inexpensive Fordson Model F tractor at the end of World War I, he created a price war in the market. Other tractor companies, such as the International Harvester Company, which created the Titan tractor, slashed their prices in order to compete. Naturally, many Paris Township farmers took advantage of the opportunity. In this photograph, a Titan tractor tows a threshing machine to a local farm.

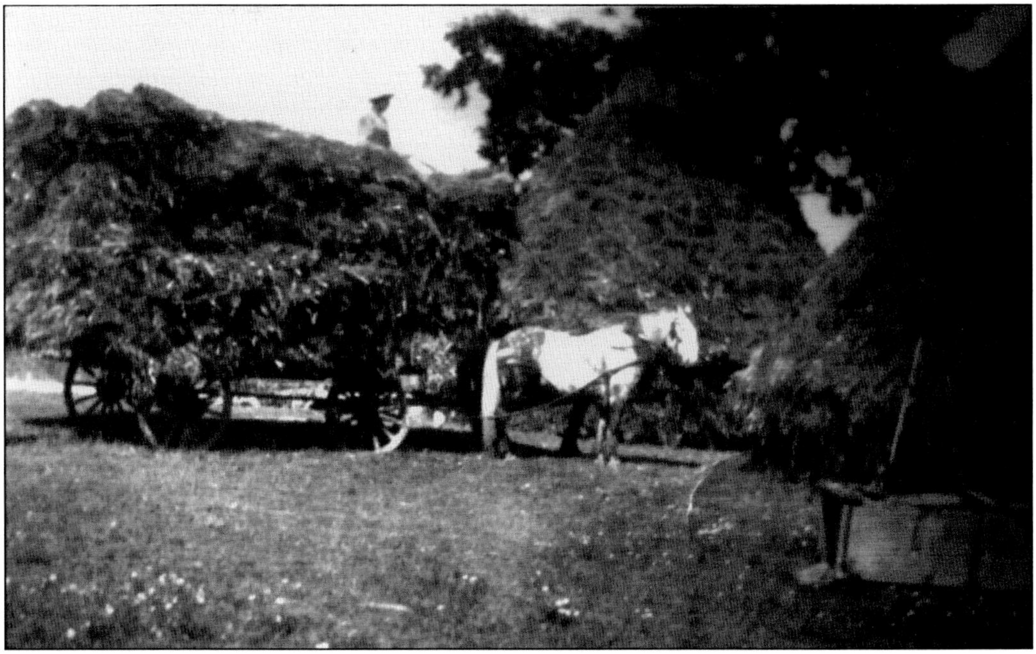

Once threshed, grain was separated from the stalks and the chaff. The grain was placed in a grain wagon or bagged. Paris Township farmers either used the grain themselves or sold it to area markets. The straw from the wheat was blown out of the thresher into stacks. Even the straw was valuable to farmers, who used it for animal litter.

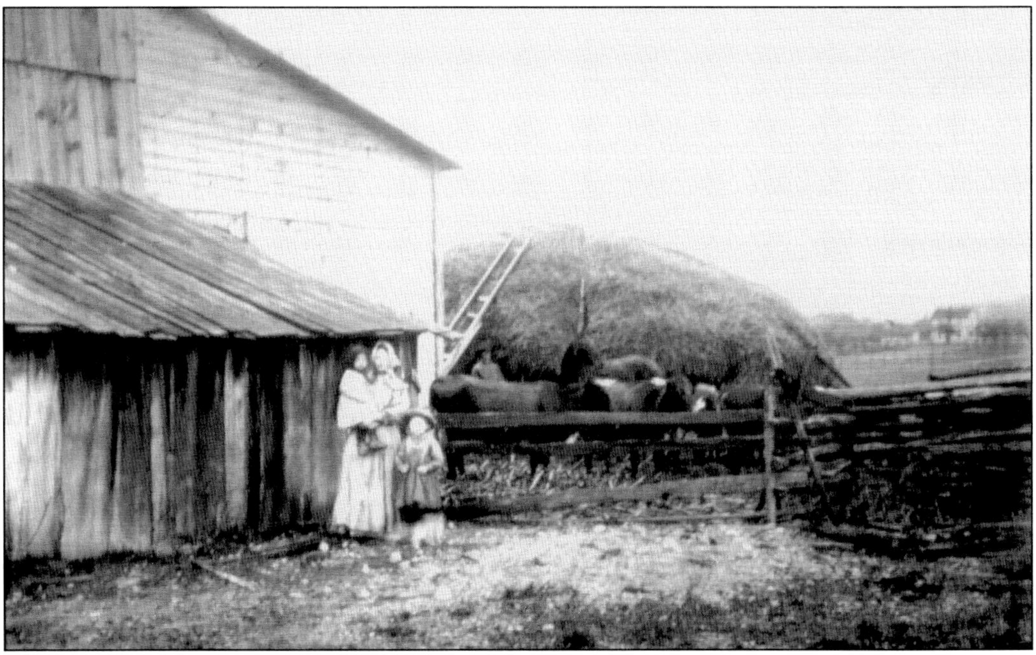

Many farm families, such as this one pictured above, raised dairy cows. In the late 1800s, there were 553 cows living on area farms (compared to 560 horses and mules and 584 hogs). The same report showed that the average Paris Township farm produced an extraordinary amount of dairy products, including up to 400 pounds of butter per year.

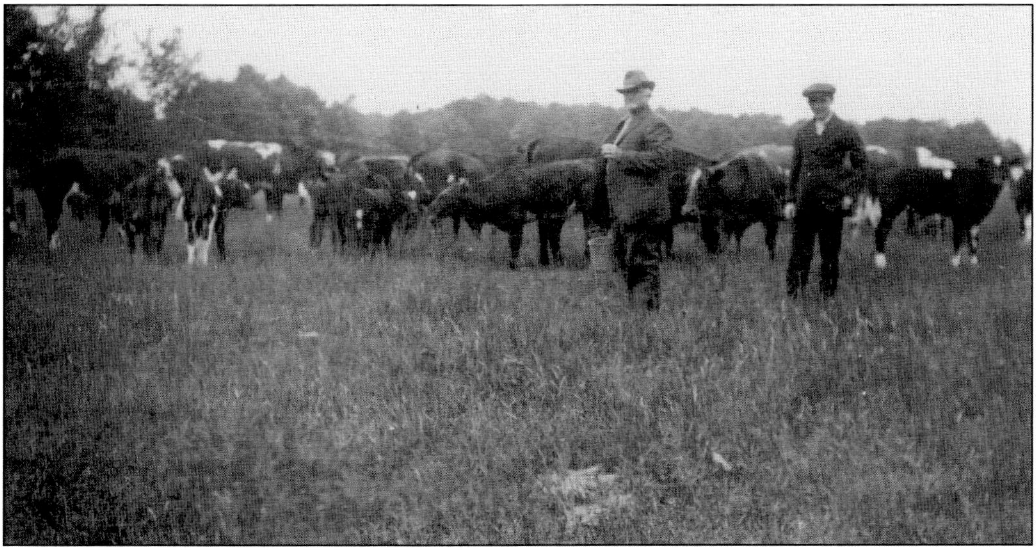

In addition to their family ox team, Jack and Bill, the Bowen family raised a number of cattle on their farm. In this picture, Bostwick and his son, Burr, inspect some of the herd grazing in the field. Many Paris Township farmers raised cattle to be sold in markets in Grand Rapids and then shipped by railroad to customers.

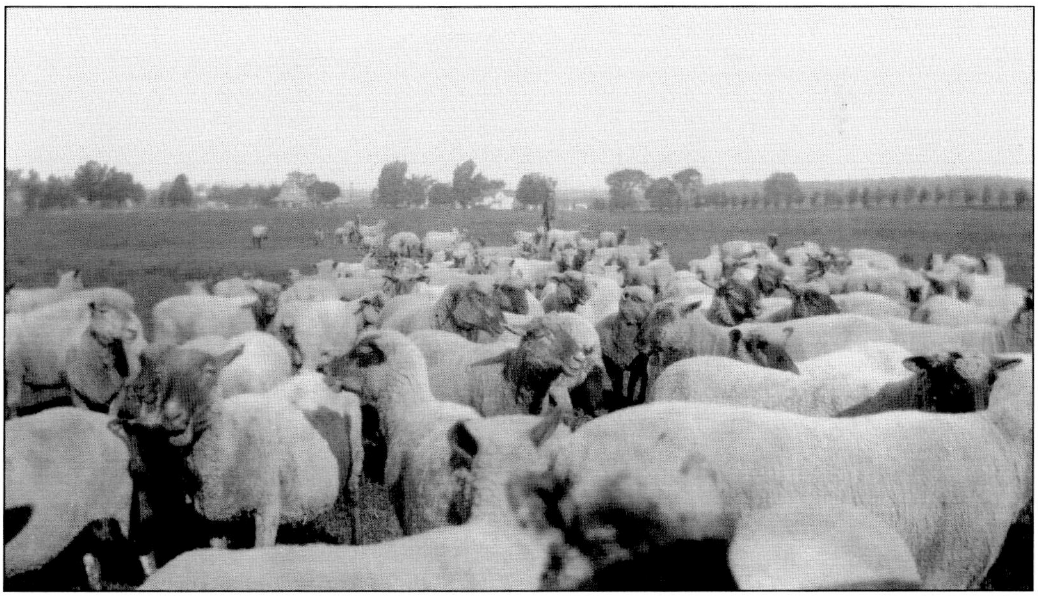

Paris Township had nearly four times as many sheep as cattle. Many farmers used the woolen fleece their sheep produced for clothing and sheepskin to create shoes and rugs. This photograph shows the Bowen family's herd of sheep after the spring shearing. Farmers also butchered young or older sheep to provide their families with lamb and mutton.

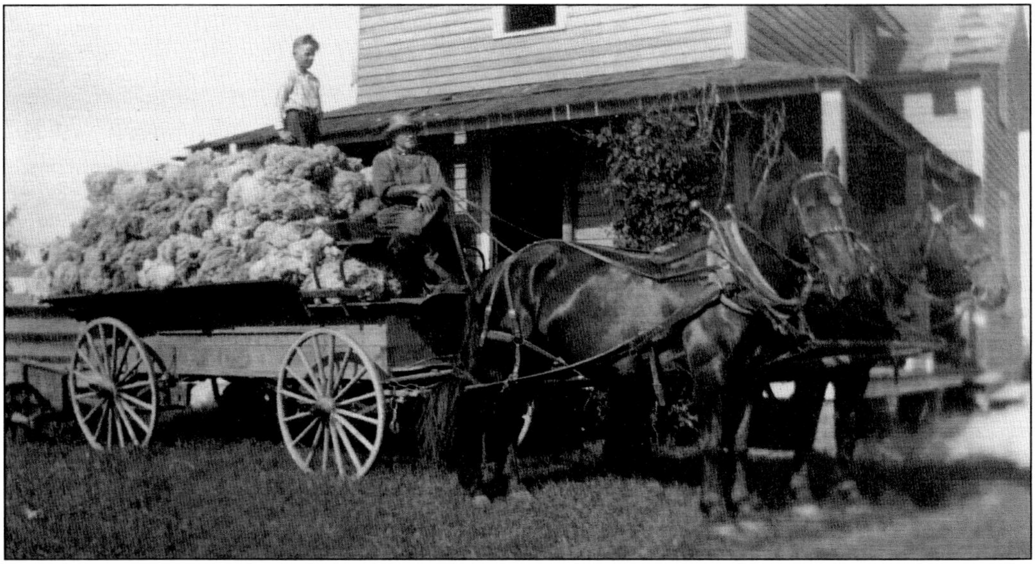

In a cart filled with wool, Bostwick Bowen prepares to lead Maude and Maggie, his team of horses, to market as Max, the Bowen's adopted son, walks on the soft load. At the time, Grand Rapids was quickly becoming the world's center for fine furniture. Manufacturers as well as residents would have been interested in buying the Bowen's wool.

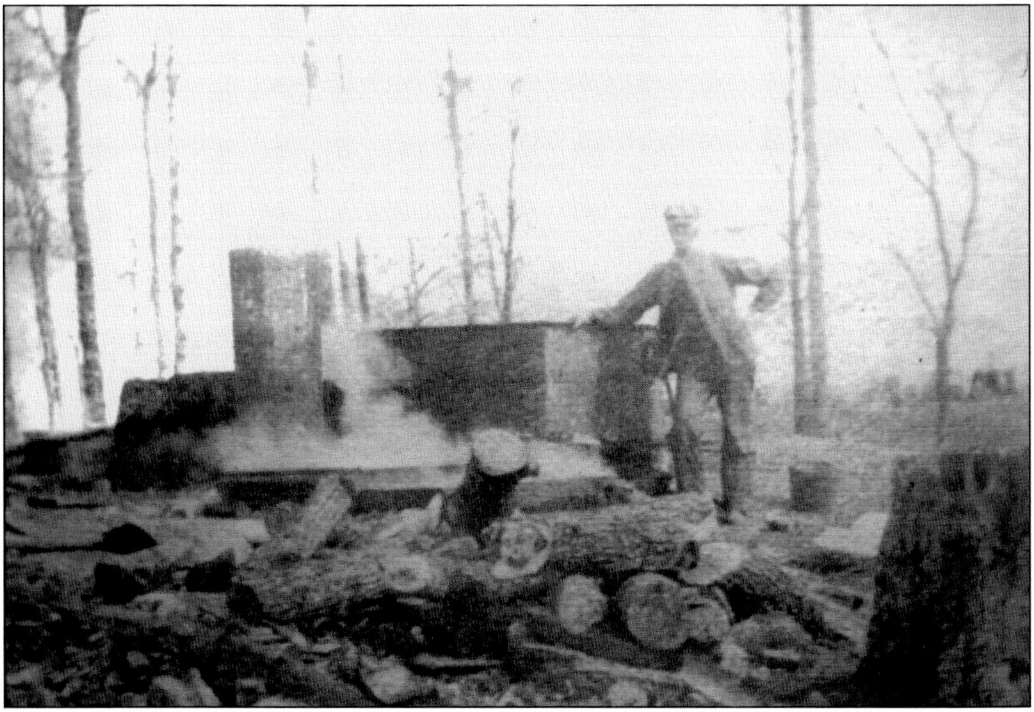

Paris Township was a heavily wooded area, which was known for its abundance of sugar maple trees. From early February until the trees budded, farm families tapped maple trees and collected their colorless sap. This liquid was placed in evaporators (like the one pictured above with a Paris Township farmer) and boiled to remove the water and other impurities. The result was sweet maple syrup.

The Bowen family had a large number of sugar maple trees on their property. Like many Paris Township farmers, the Bowen family collected sap for their own personal use as well as to supplement their farm income. They built this shanty to house their evaporator. To create one gallon of syrup, the Bowens would have had to collect and boil at least 40 gallons of sap.

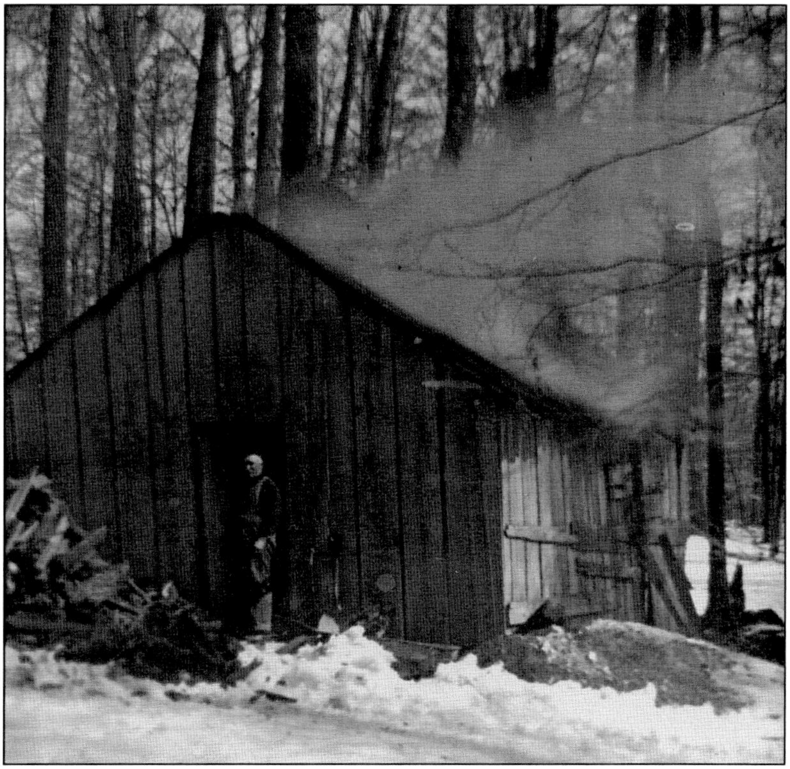

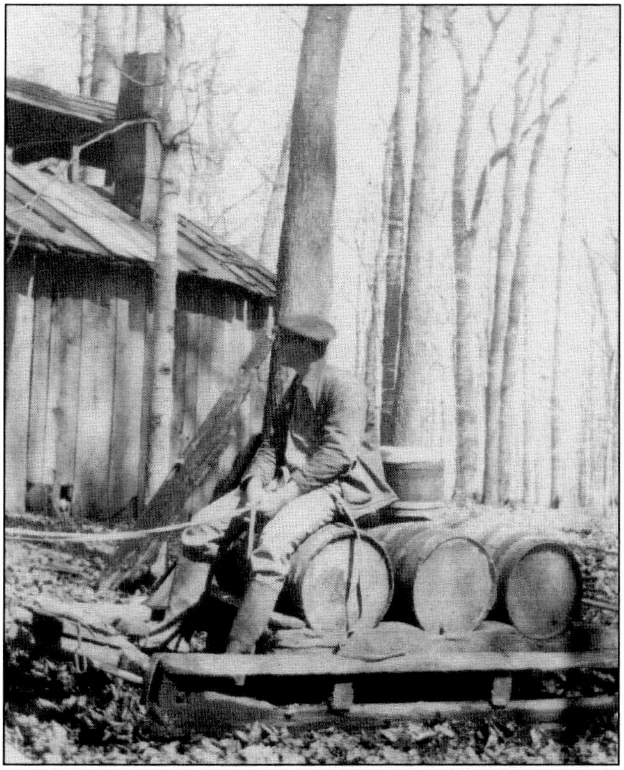

Roy Hutchinson, a longtime friend of the Bowens, sits on a sled loaded with barreled sap for the Bowens' sugar shanty. As Hutchinson's light coat and no gloves suggest, the sap at the time was running (since a sudden warming or freezing would have made tapped maple trees produce sap more quickly). Too much warm weather, however, could end the sugaring season early. Once the trees began to bud, the sap would turn bitter.

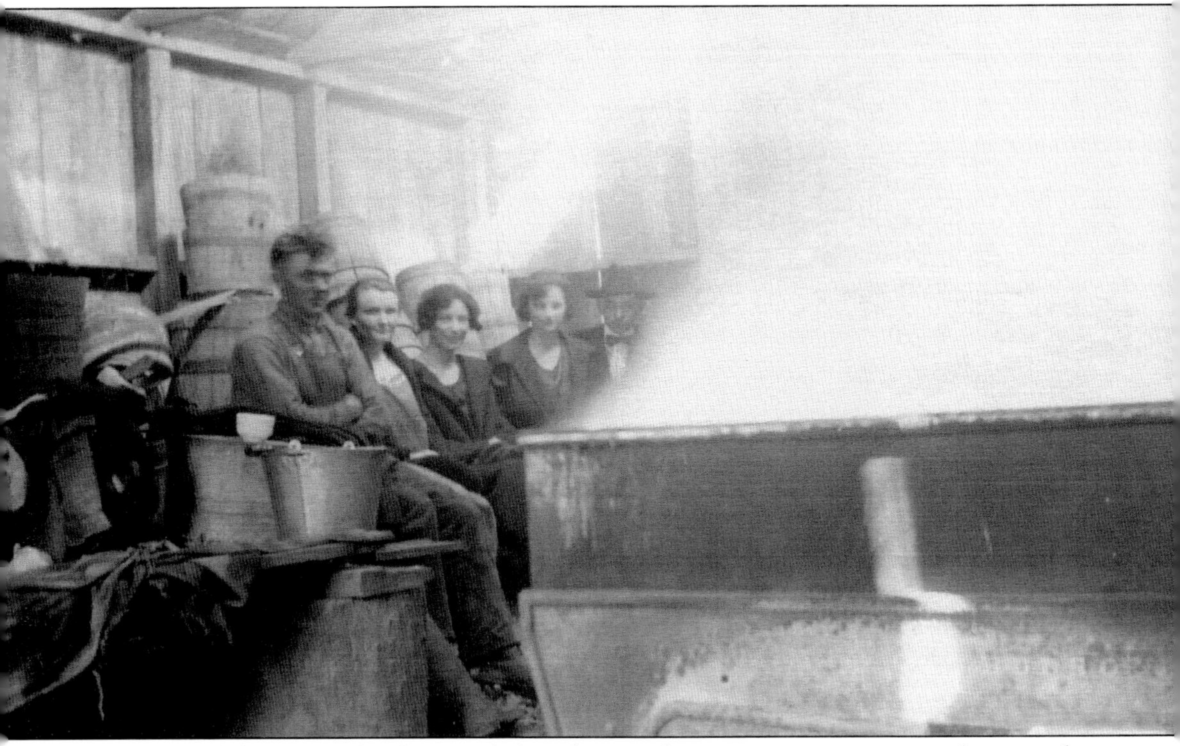

Members of the Bowen family sit with friends around a steaming evaporator in the sugar shanty while it boils the latest batch of maple sap into sugar. Since each tap hole in a maple tree will produce about 10 gallons of sap, collecting it all requires a lot of hands; sugaring time became a natural time for family and friends to get together.

Three

Following Civic Duty

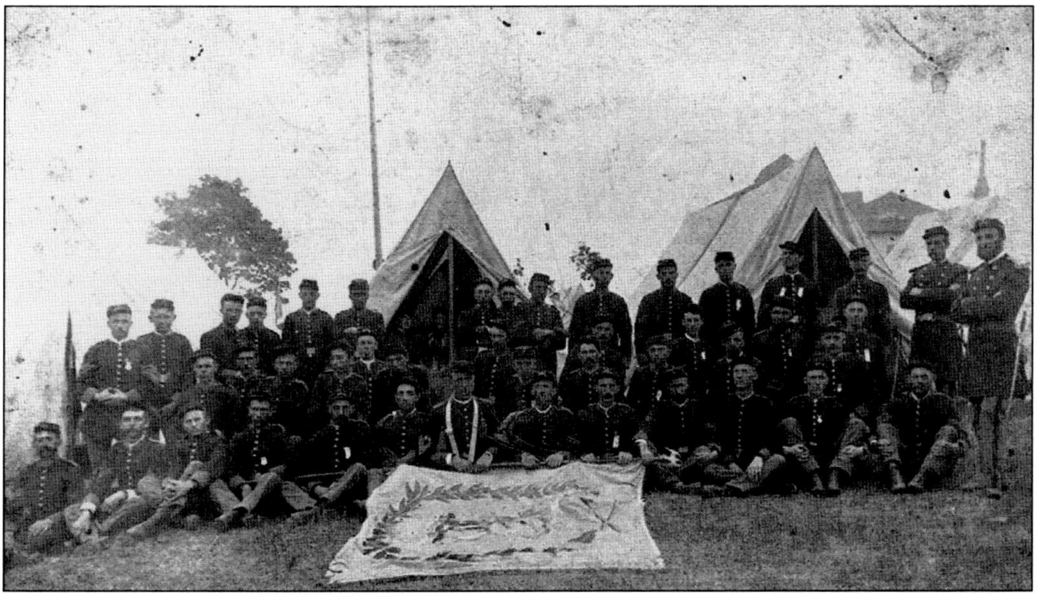

No matter what the era, Paris Township residents frequently put aside their own interests and performed their civic or national duties. Three days after the battle of Fort Sumter, Pres. Abraham Lincoln requested 75,000 volunteers to preserve the Union. Paris Township farmers met the call, leaving their spouses or families to maintain the farm during their absence. At the time, William J. Etten wrote in *A Citizens' History of Grand Rapids, Michigan* that "the war did not come to Grand Rapids, but Grand Rapids went to the war."

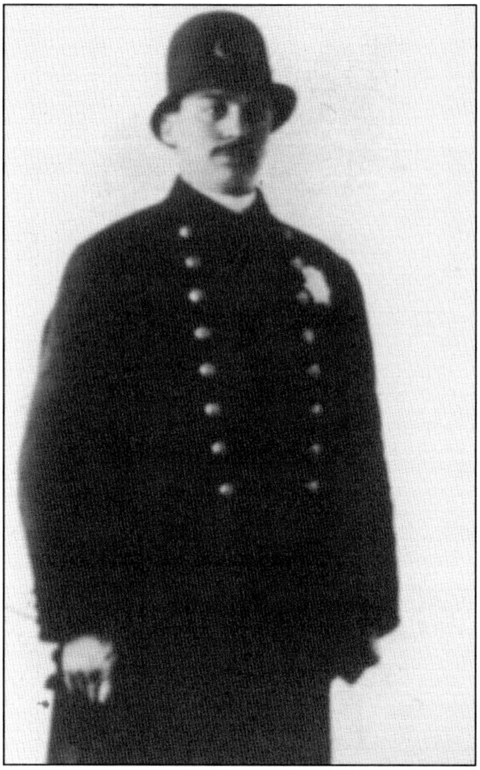

Thomas Slater was just 22 years old when he stood for this photograph in his Grand Rapids Police uniform in 1912. Thomas was the second generation of Slaters, who were from England and Canada, to be born in Paris Township. In 1915, he married Jennie May Patterson, descendant of the Patterson family, one of Paris Township's oldest families. His son Russell later became a police officer for Paris Township.

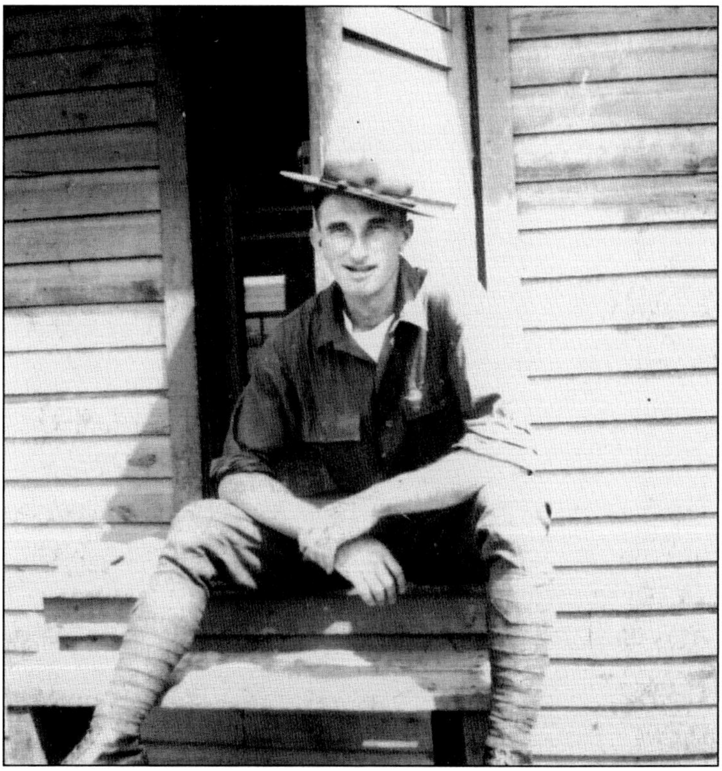

Although the Great War had been raging for several years, it was not until 1917 that events led Pres. Woodrow Wilson to request that Congress declare war. Many young men in Paris Township, like Myron Davis, sitting outside his barracks in his uniform in this picture, were drafted or enlisted into what was then known as one of the bloodiest conflicts in history.

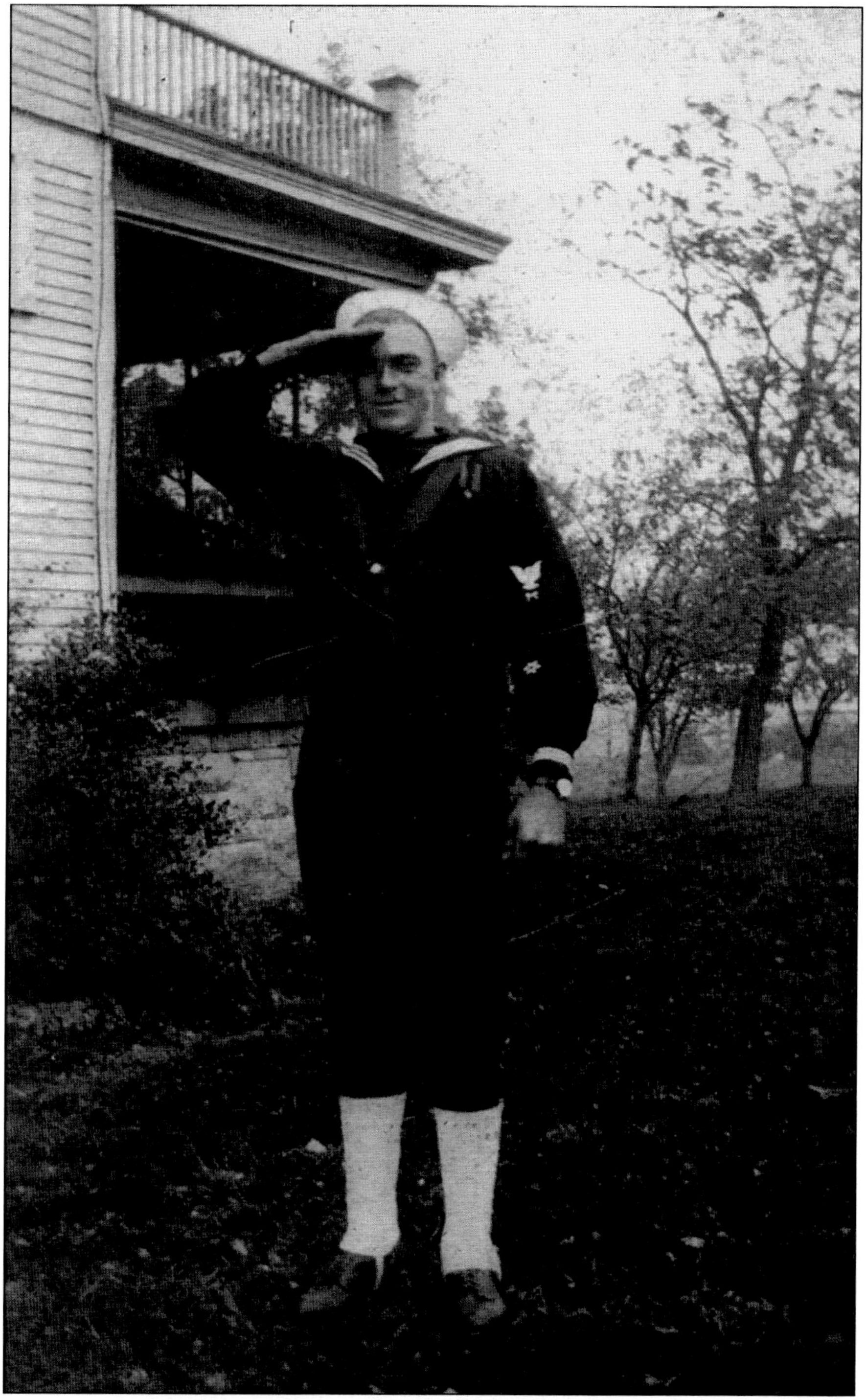

Charlie Feenstra salutes the camera before shipping out. The Feenstra family emigrated from Holland to Michigan and settled in the Paris Township area around 1884. Charlie was born in 1896 as one of seven children on the Feenstra farm. Like Bowen and Campbell, Charlie returned home to the family farm after the war and continued to work there.

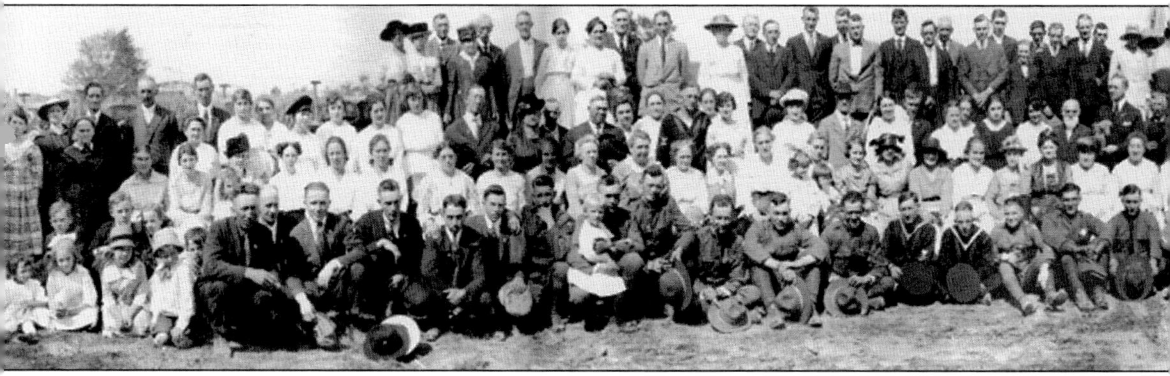

After World War I, Paris Township officials held a special picnic to honor area veterans. Many young men returned, but some, like Alfred Wesley Brake, son of blacksmith Wesley Brake, and Daniel Cassard, a pilot in the nation's early air force, made the ultimate sacrifice. Paris

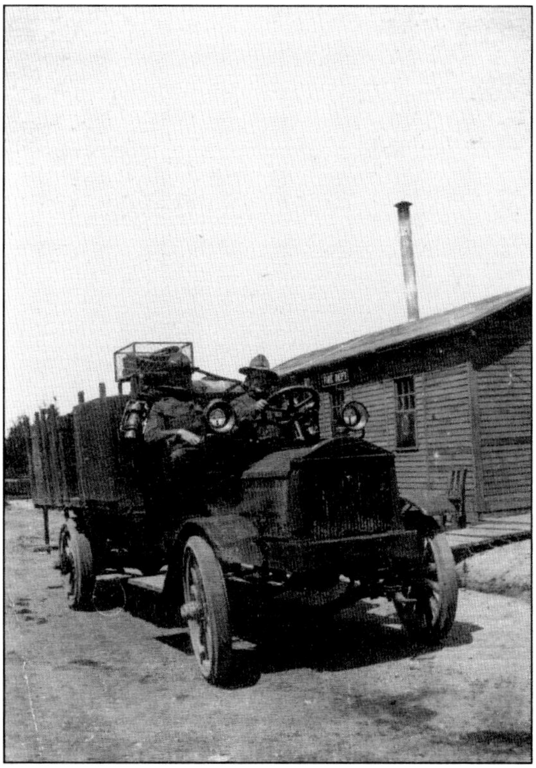

Ralph Campbell and Burr Bowen sit behind the wheel of an army truck during World War I. Campbell moved to the area from Indiana with his family as a boy. After the war, both young men returned home and picked up life where they had left off. Burr helped out on the Bowen farm, while Ralph found a job as a mechanic.

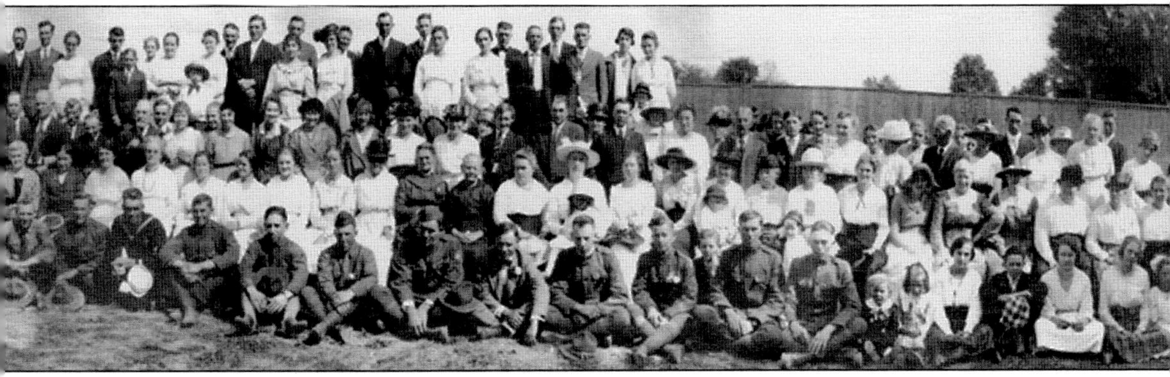

Township residents, like many Americans at the time, thought this war would be the "war to end all wars." Few realized that within a generation another great conflict rooted in this war would require the young men of Paris Township to become soldiers again.

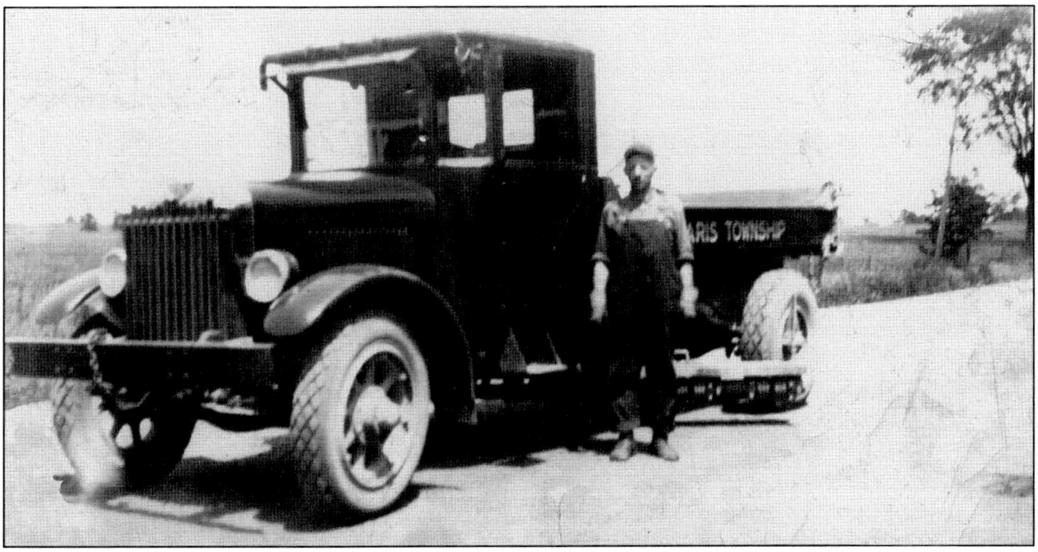

For many years, Paris Township residents rode horses or drove carriages and carts down dirt roads. By the 1920s, automobiles and an ever-growing population soon took their toll on the roads. Paris Township officials knew that they needed someone to maintain the roads. John Kloosterman stands next to the first Paris Township maintenance truck in 1929. The truck had a snowplow for the winter and a grader to keep the local roads level and clear.

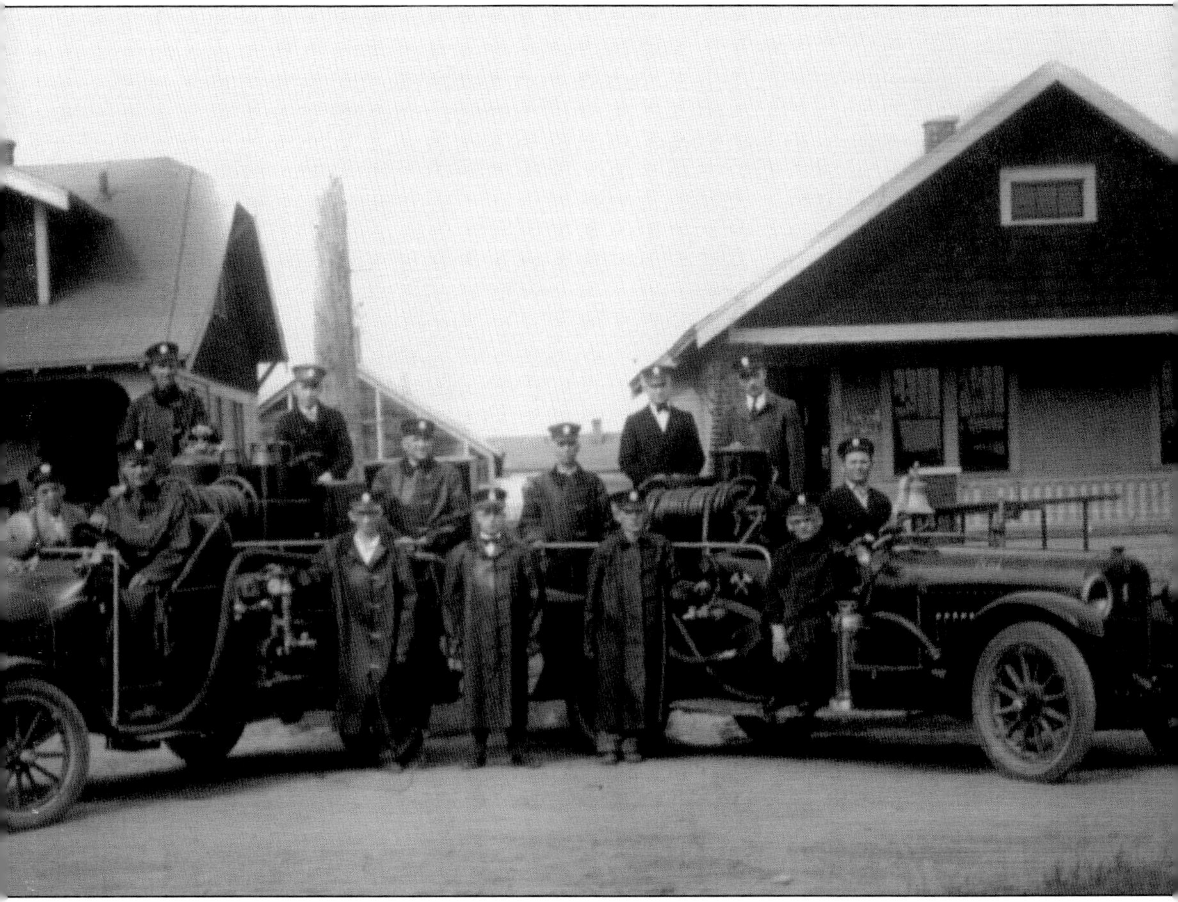

The Godwin Heights Fire Department shows off its fire trucks in 1929. While much of Paris Township was rural, Godwin Heights was a neighborhood of suburban homes and small businesses on South Division Avenue, between Thirty-second Street and Fortieth Street. In the mid-1800s, settler William Godwin owned a tavern called the Godwin House, on Division Avenue, and over time, a thriving neighborhood developed around the tavern.

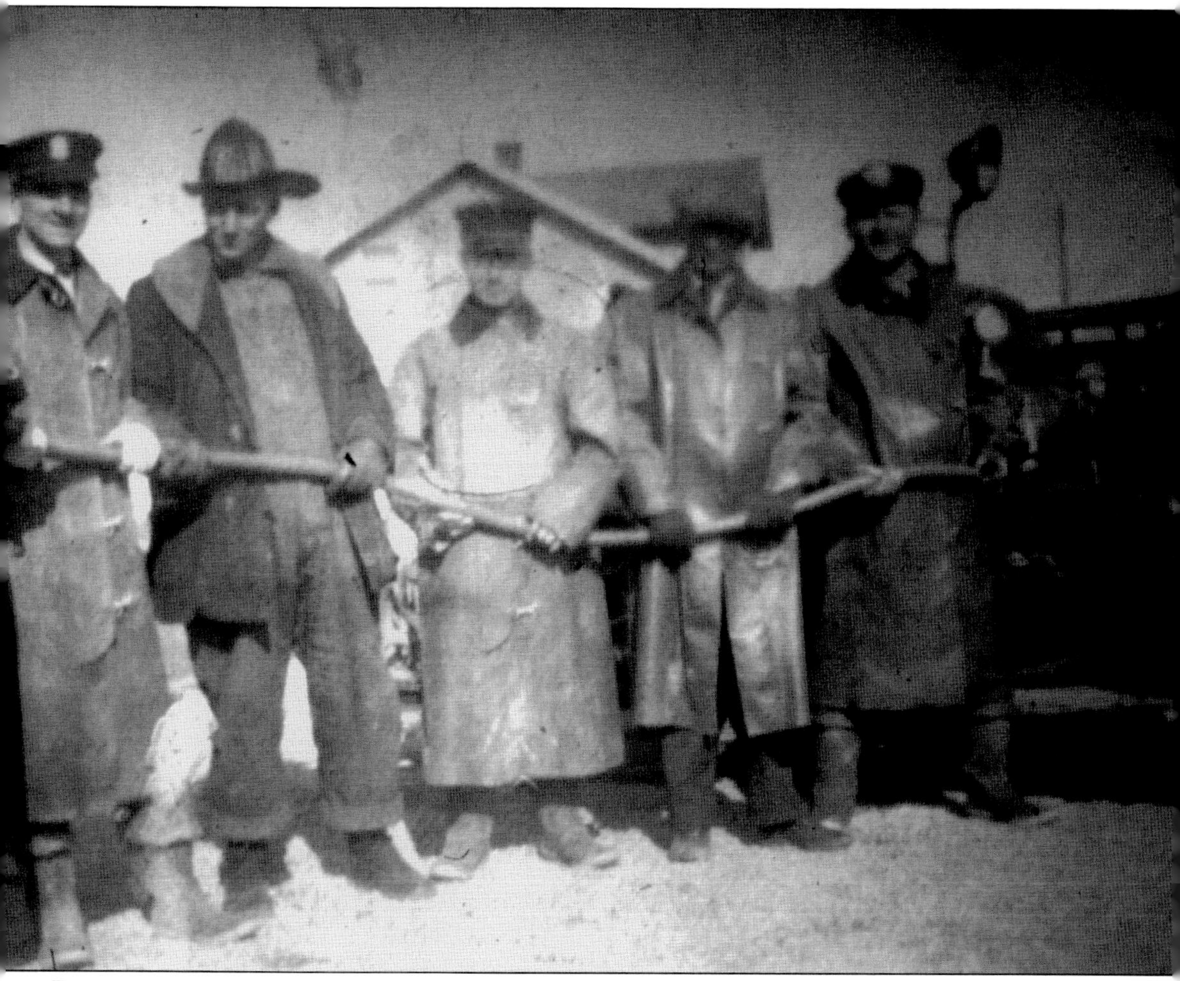

Fire was a constant threat to Paris Township farms and businesses. Although there were fire departments in Grand Rapids, the city was still too far away to help the community. The Paris Township Fire Department was formed and relied on local volunteers to stop fires. In 1929, the Paris Township Fire Department received a new fire truck. Here, the members of the team try out the fire truck hose.

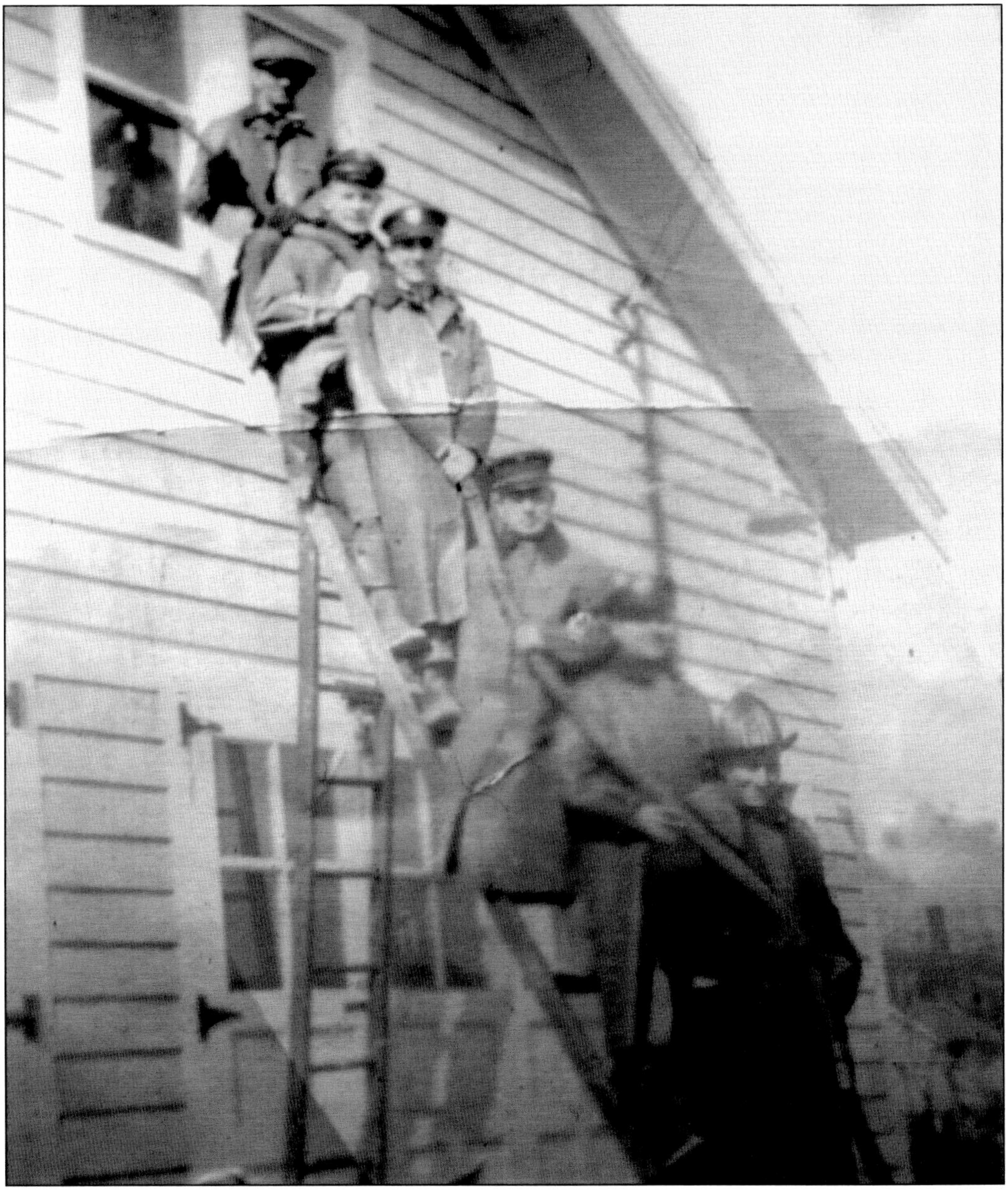

In 1937, Grand Rapids city officials decreed that their fire department could no longer protect property outside of city limits. Paris Township relied on its firefighting team more than ever. Chief Plenis Wolfert and assistant chief Derk VanderLaan (who later became Kentwood's fire chief) began recruiting volunteers like these, who were a step above the rest.

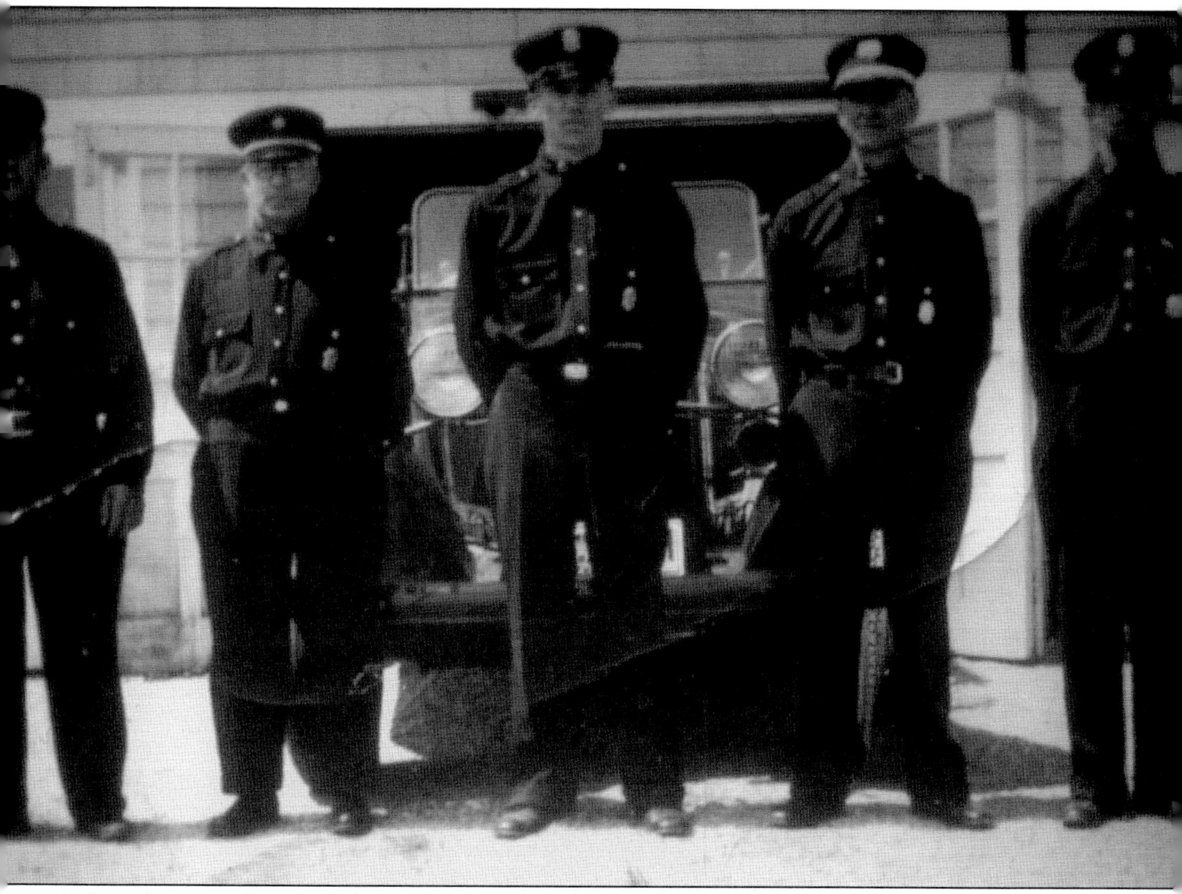

Although constables were elected when Paris Township was first organized, the community had very little need for a police force for years. The Paris Detective Association was formed in 1878 to catch horse thieves and handle local crime. In the 1930s, the Kent County Sheriff Department was formed and deputies were assigned to Paris. By the 1950s, several deputies were hired specifically to protect the community. They became the Paris Township Police Unit No. 721.

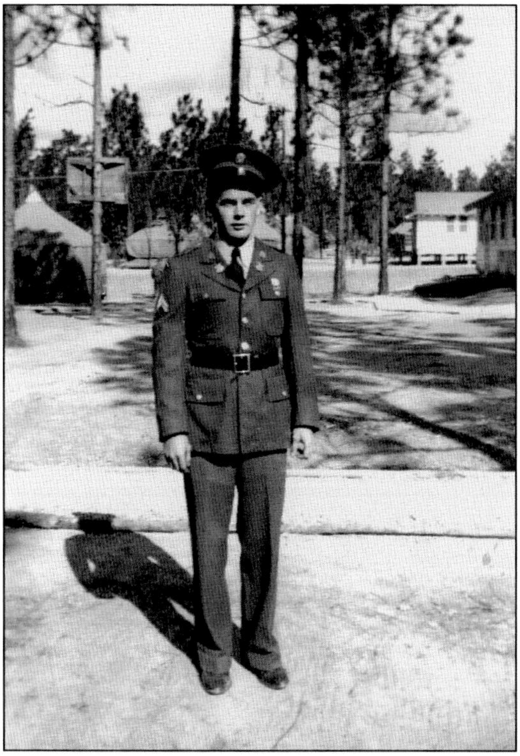

Gene Berridge stands proudly before the camera in his army uniform. Although events leading up to World War II had been culminating for several years, the bombing of Pearl Harbor in 1941 forced the United States into the war. As their fathers before them, many young men from Paris Township signed up to be soldiers.

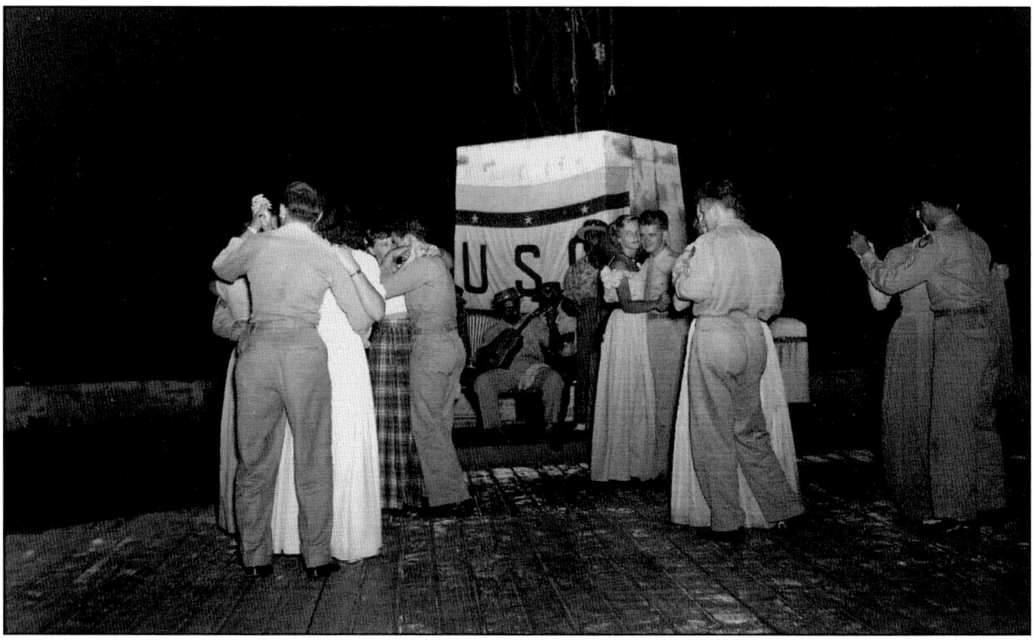

Enlisted men dance with local young women. In 1941, Pres. Franklin D. Roosevelt requested that private non-profit organizations, such as the Salvation Army, provide an on-leave recreation group for U.S. forces. While the United Service Organizations (USO) was best known for bringing camp shows to troops, they also organized activities, such as this outdoor dance, in makeshift centers.

From 1940 to 1944, the number of U.S. troops grew from 50,000 to 12 million. Very few families were untouched by the war. These brothers, standing together in uniform outside their home in one of Paris Township's suburban neighborhoods, were typical of many local families at the time. After the war, these men came home to a Paris Township community that, as always, was rapidly changing.

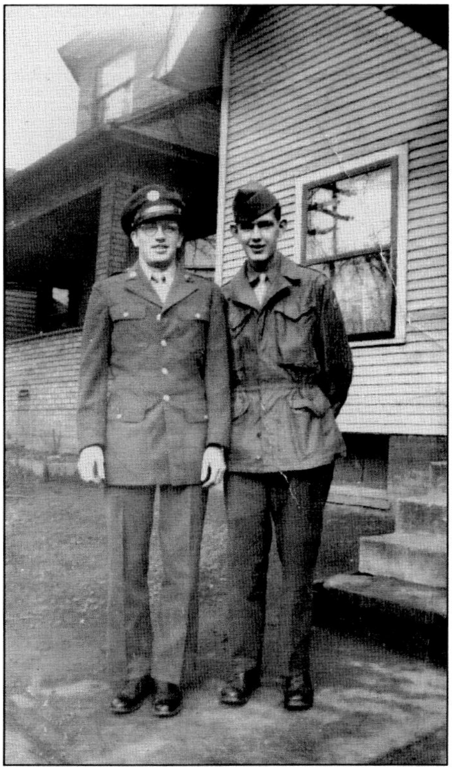

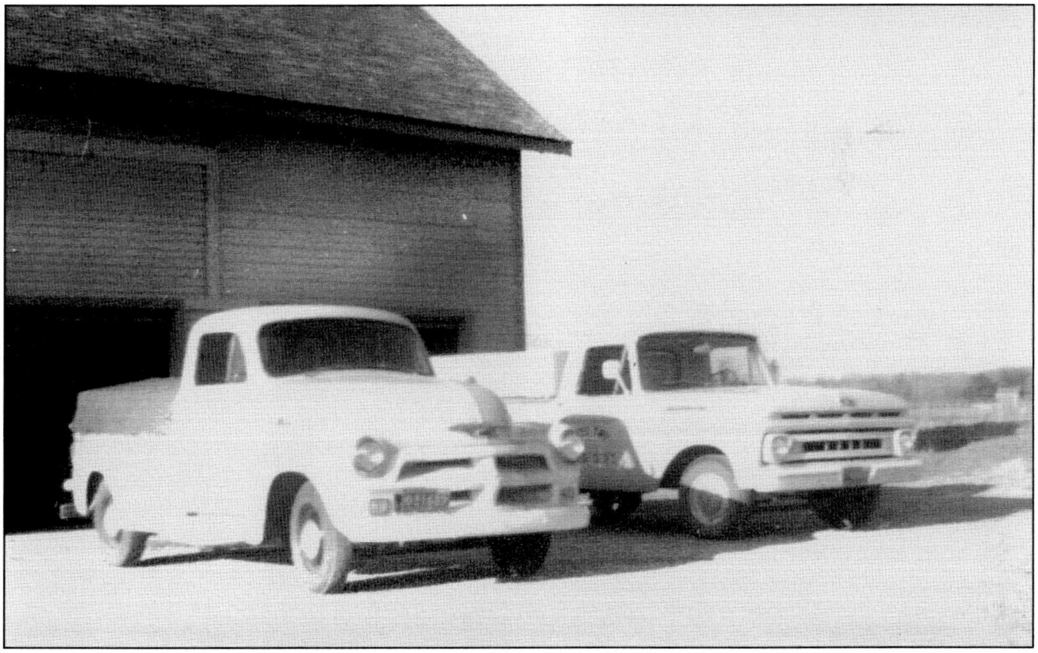

Many farm houses did not have basements because the water table was as high as 13 feet in Paris Township. As the community became more suburban and more businesses moved into the area, many residents became concerned about the availability of clean drinking water. The township organized the Paris Township Water Department. This picture shows their first two trucks.

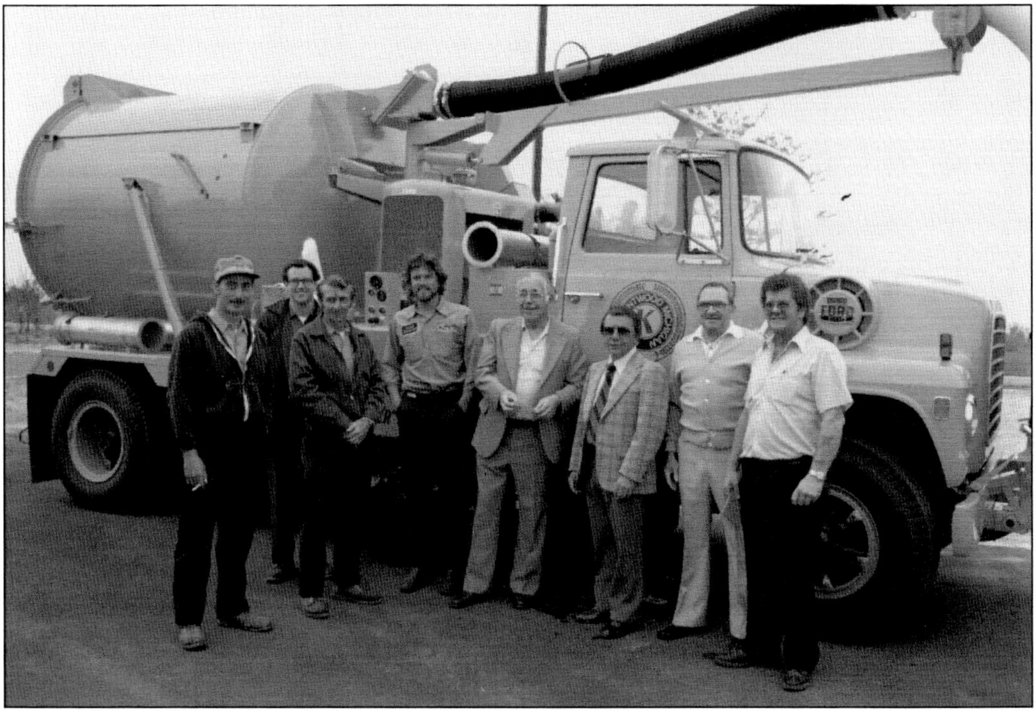

Paris Township became the City of Kentwood in 1967 and Paris supervisor Peter Lamberts became its first mayor. Lamberts stands with the members of the Kentwood Public Works Department in front of one of the city's maintenance trucks. The vehicles were a far cry from John Kloosterman's 1929 truck, plow, and grader. Of course, many area roads at the time were recently paved and intersected by new streets.

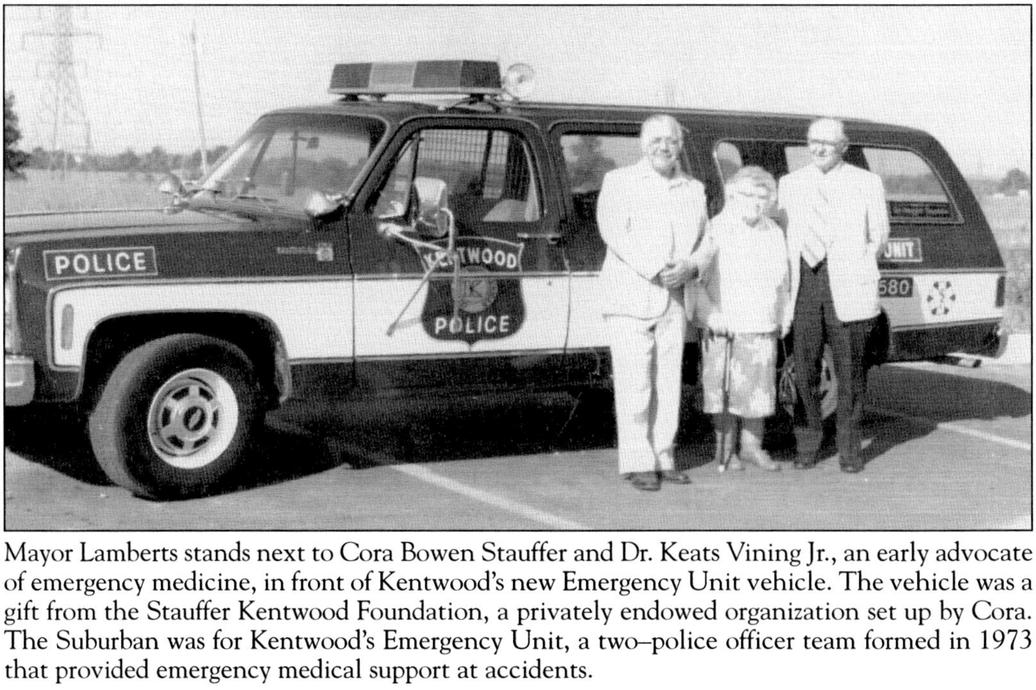

Mayor Lamberts stands next to Cora Bowen Stauffer and Dr. Keats Vining Jr., an early advocate of emergency medicine, in front of Kentwood's new Emergency Unit vehicle. The vehicle was a gift from the Stauffer Kentwood Foundation, a privately endowed organization set up by Cora. The Suburban was for Kentwood's Emergency Unit, a two–police officer team formed in 1973 that provided emergency medical support at accidents.

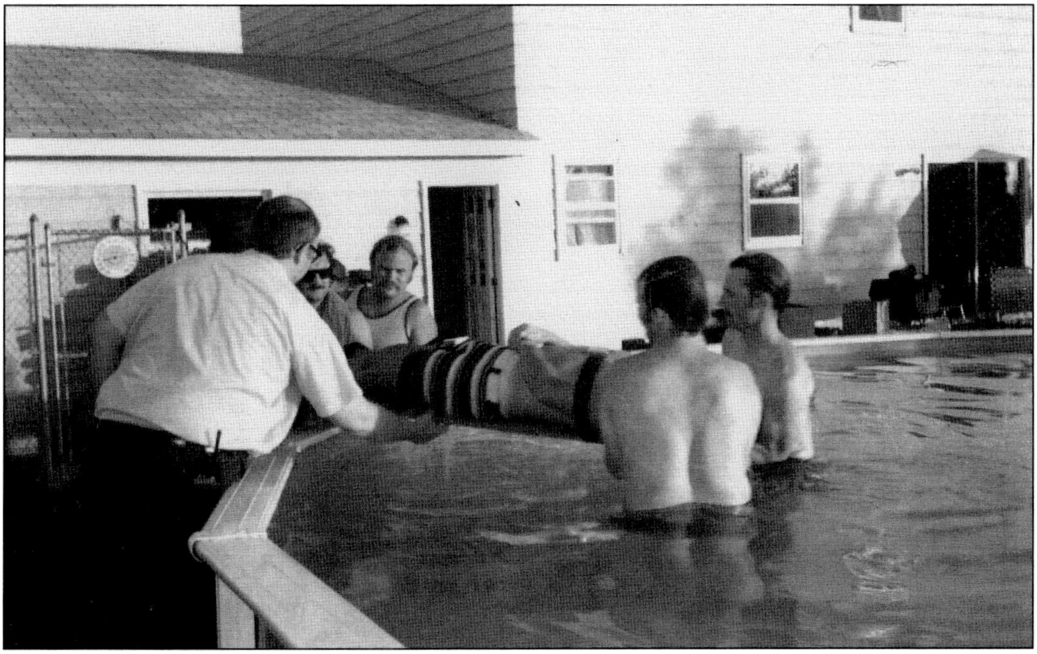

The Kentwood Emergency Unit practices water rescue procedures in a local pool. Emergency medical training for police officers was a relatively new trend in law enforcement. Before the 1970s, medical assistance at an accident usually came from an ambulance driver. Emergency units, like that of Kentwood, eventually appeared across the country and were the forerunners to modern paramedic units.

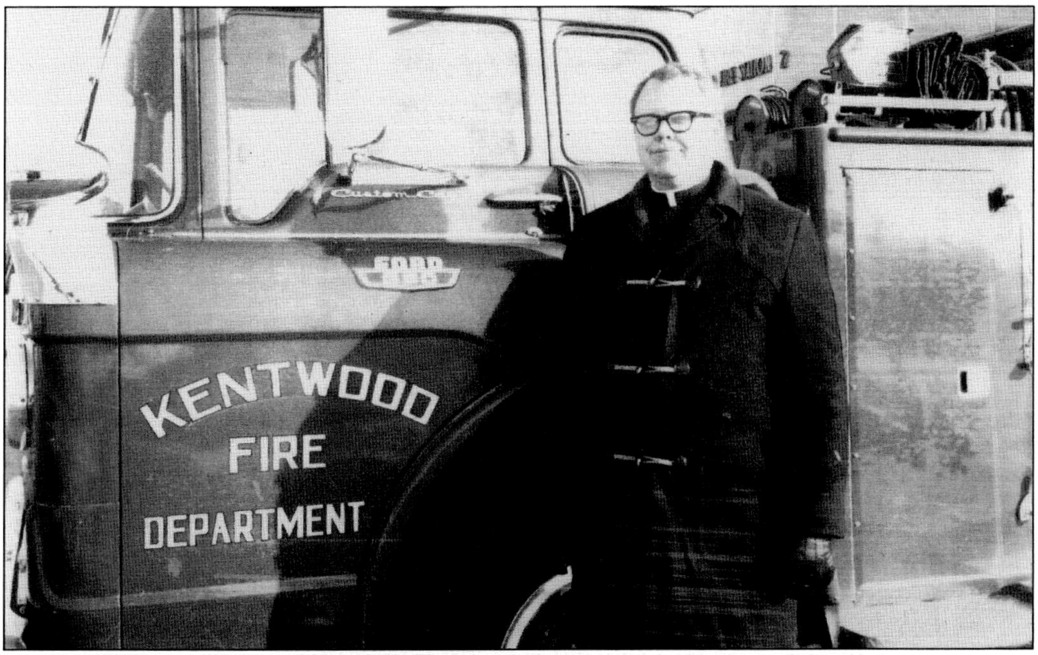

Father Bell stands next to a fire truck at Kentwood Fire Station No. 2. The station was built in 1949 in East Paris. In 1975, the station and its sister stations were modernized with new equipment, such as new fire engines and a pump capable of shooting 1,250 gallons of water per minute.

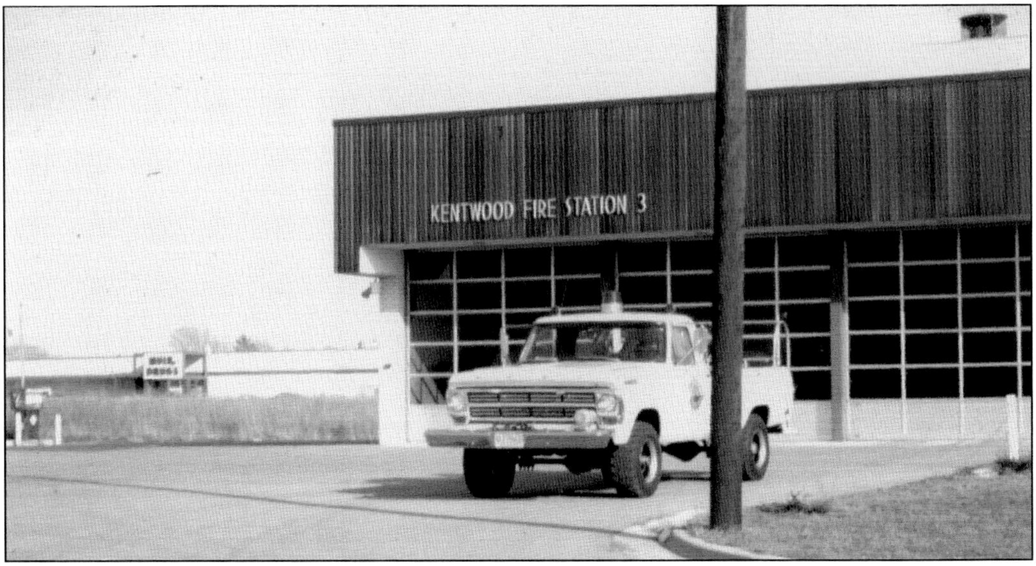

Kentwood Fire Station No. 3 was built on Eastern Avenue to accommodate the continually developing areas of the city. At the time, the Kentwood Fire Department had four full-time firefighters and a staff of 28 volunteers. All three of Kentwood's fire stations were modernized at the beginning of the 21st century.

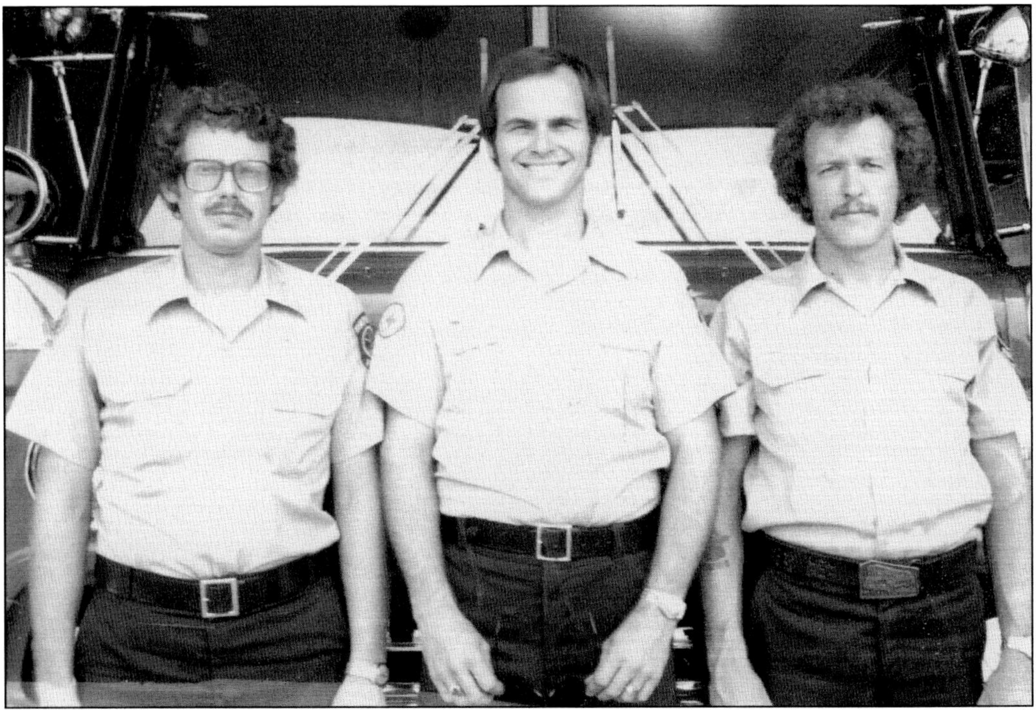

Three Kentwood firefighters stand in front of one of their trucks in the station for a photograph in 1972. Pictured from left to right are Floyd VanHouten, Dick Penning, and Dave Nicholas. Like the police, firefighters at the time were becoming trained to handle problems other than fires. As always, they performed the tasks even if it meant putting their own lives in danger to protect Kentwood residents.

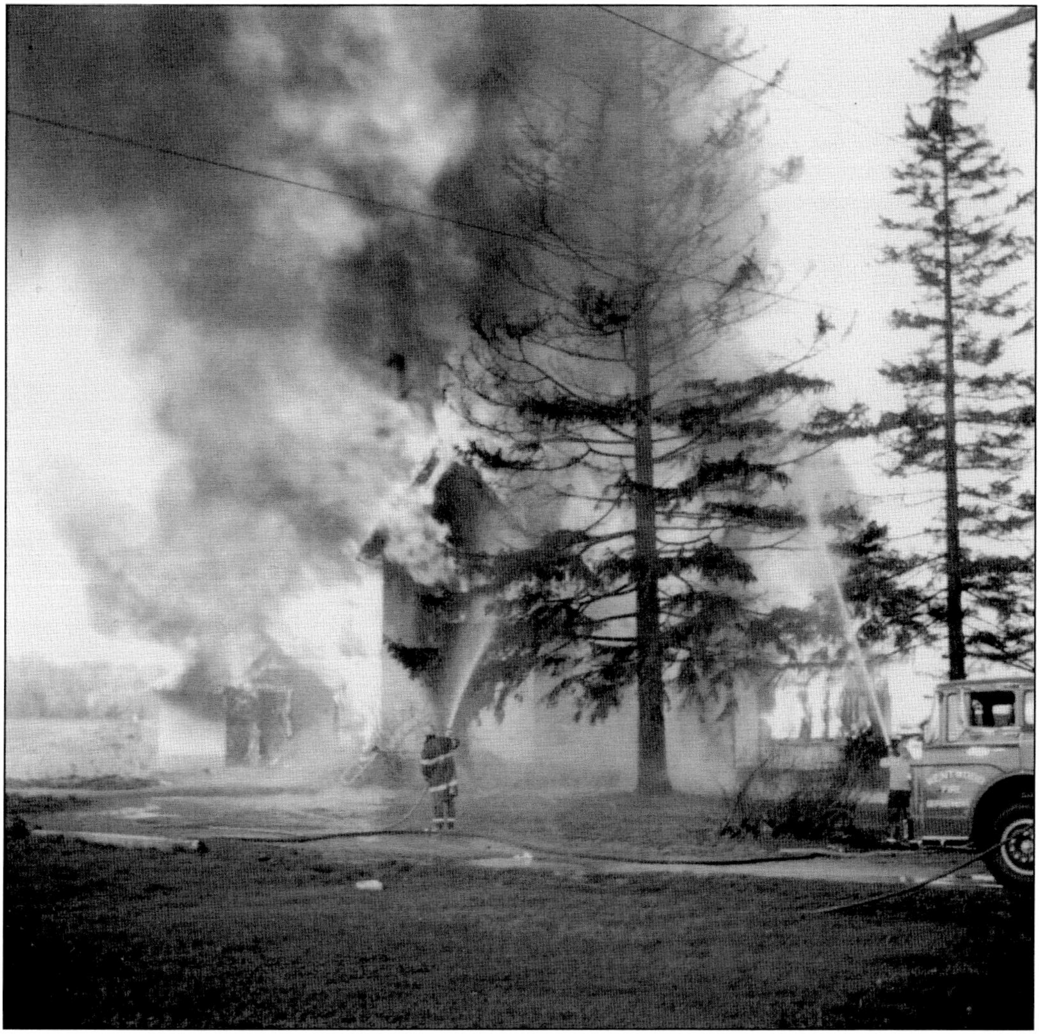

The Kentwood Fire Department is put to the test as a local farmhouse burns. The firefighters tried their best to save the building. The house, which was older and built with material more flammable than some of the newer houses in Kentwood, ultimately burned too quickly to be saved.

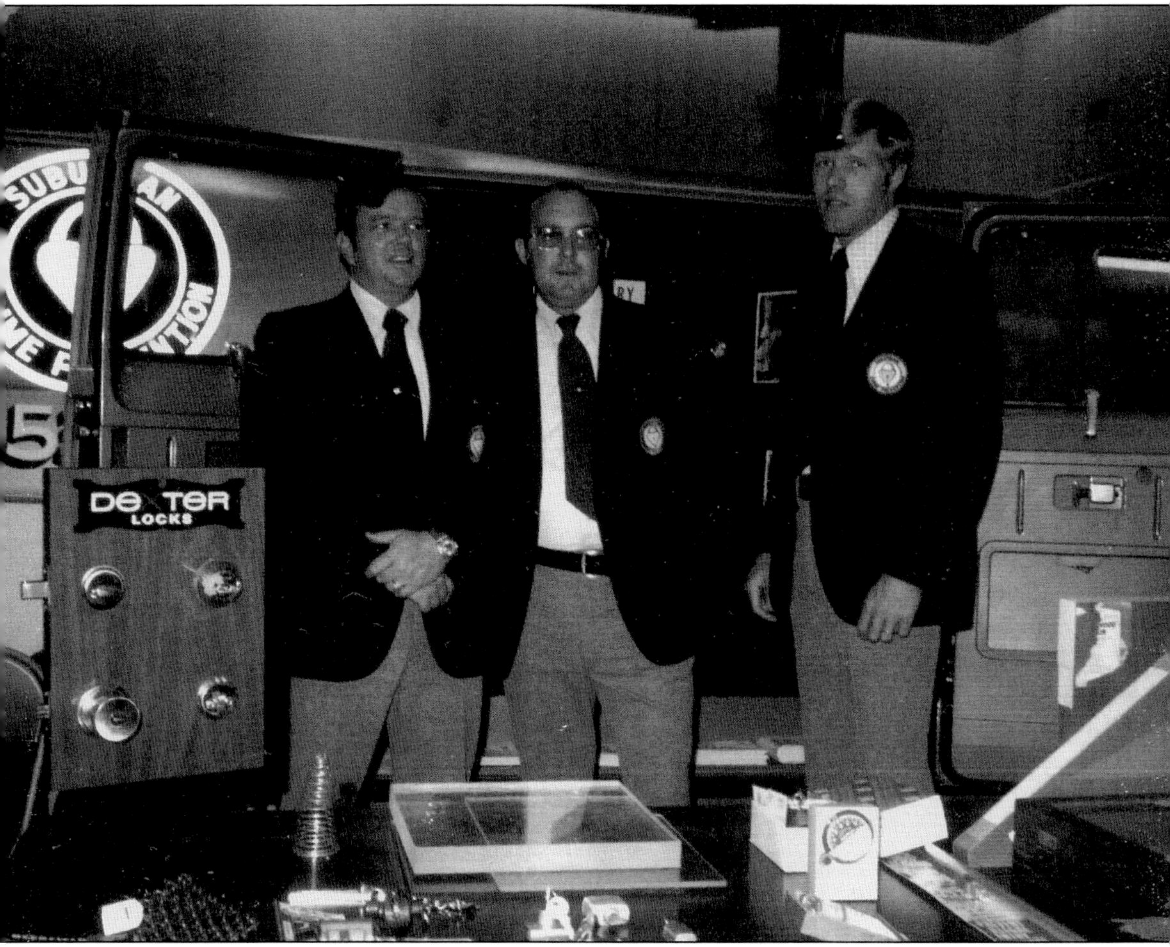

Horse theft was the crime that most early Paris Township farmers worried about. As the Kentwood's Suburban Crime Unit stood together for a photograph of their home safety display at Woodland Mall in 1980, the public's concern was no longer horse theft, but protecting their homes. Thankfully, public education displays like this one have helped Kentwood stay a safe community.

Four

School Days

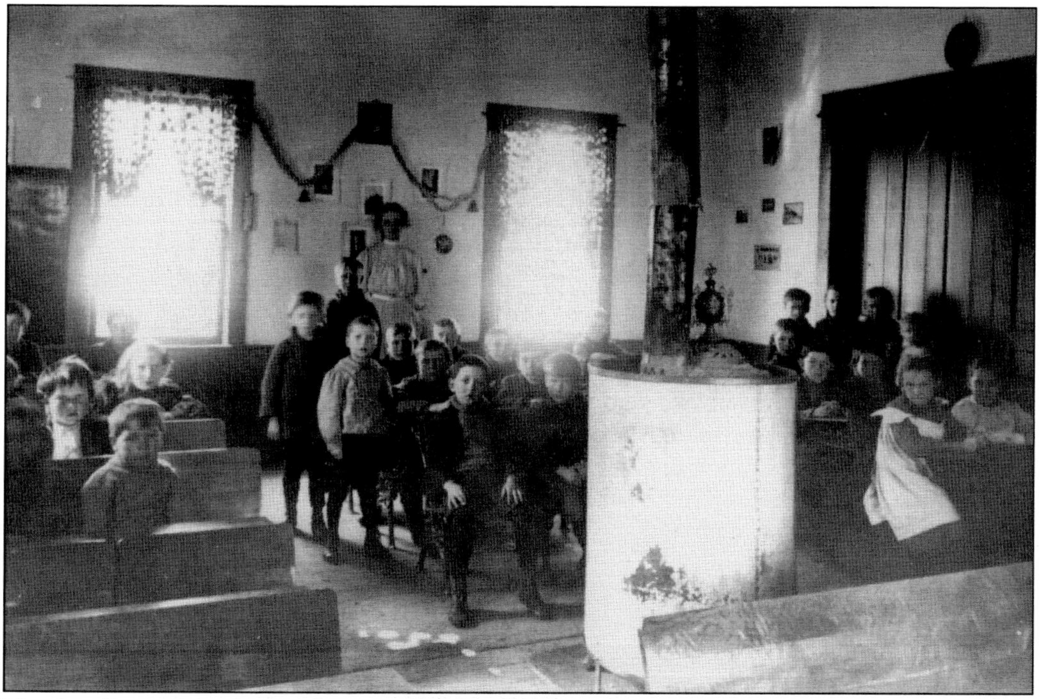

The first Paris Township settlers taught their children at home. This was difficult for large farm families, such as the Clarks, who had 11 children and neighbors five miles away. In 1842, the Clarks built a one-room log cabin to be used as a school for area children (even though their own children were beyond school age). Following the Clarks' example, the Bowen family built the one-room Bowen No. 1 more than a decade later.

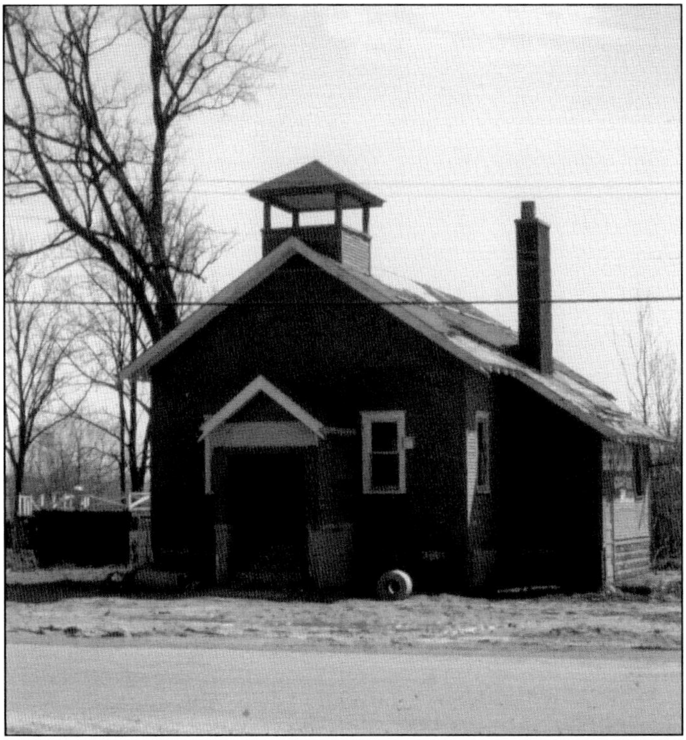

Members of the Shafer family built Shafer Elementary in 1848. Several related families lived on Forty-fourth Street (near the present Shaffer Avenue) and sent their children there for school. Shafer served as one of the first of four schools in Paris Township. The building had fallen into disrepair by the autumn of 1976, when this photograph was taken.

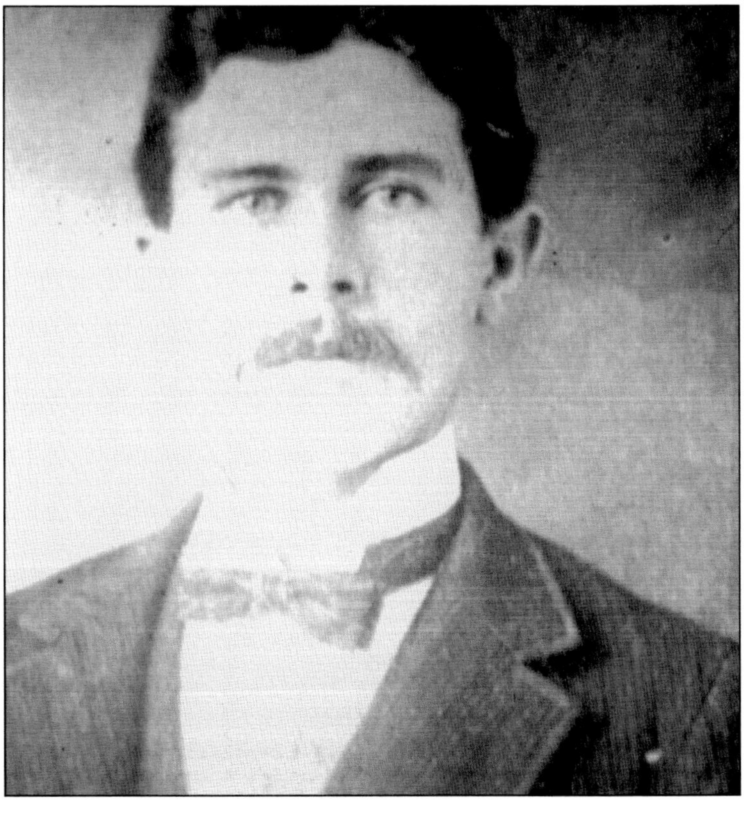

The Cutler and the Young families built the White School around 1850. Members of the Cutler family, including Frank Cutler, pictured on the right in 1907, taught Paris Township children at this school (later called the Townline School) and the Red School. When a new building was proposed, the original White School building was sold and moved to a nearby farm, where it was used as a barn.

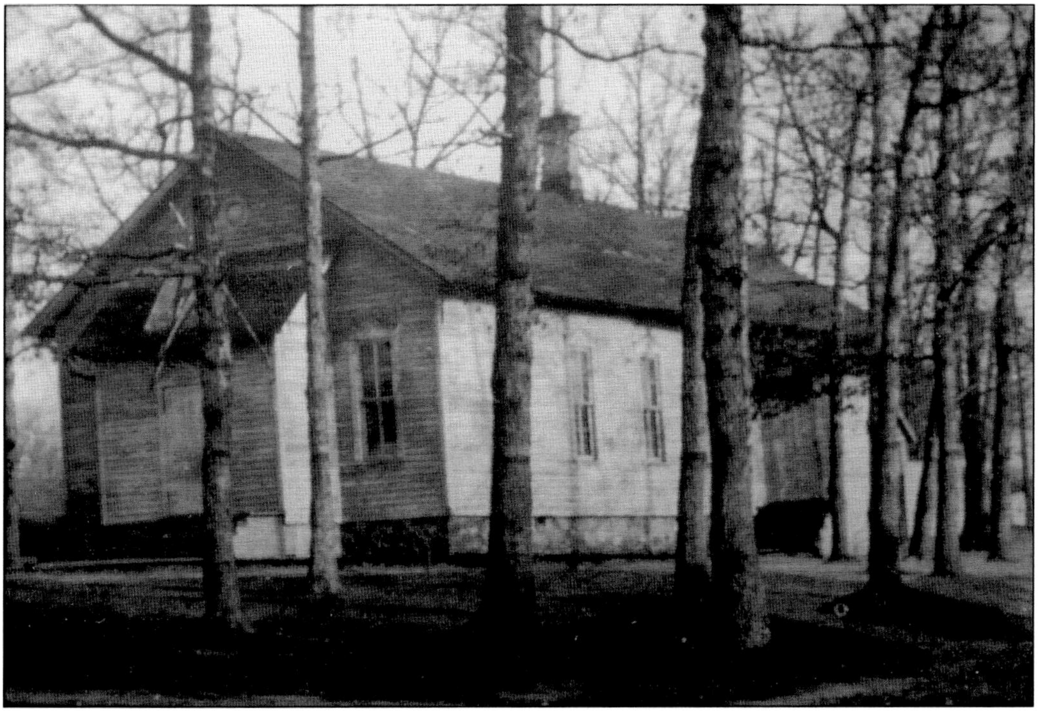

East Paris No. 5 was built in 1900 on the northeast corner of present-day Twenty-eighth Street and Breton Avenue. It was a place of learning until the summer of 1947, when it burned down. A new school, called the Red Brick School, was built in its place. Eventually, that building was replaced by the Hamilton Elementary School.

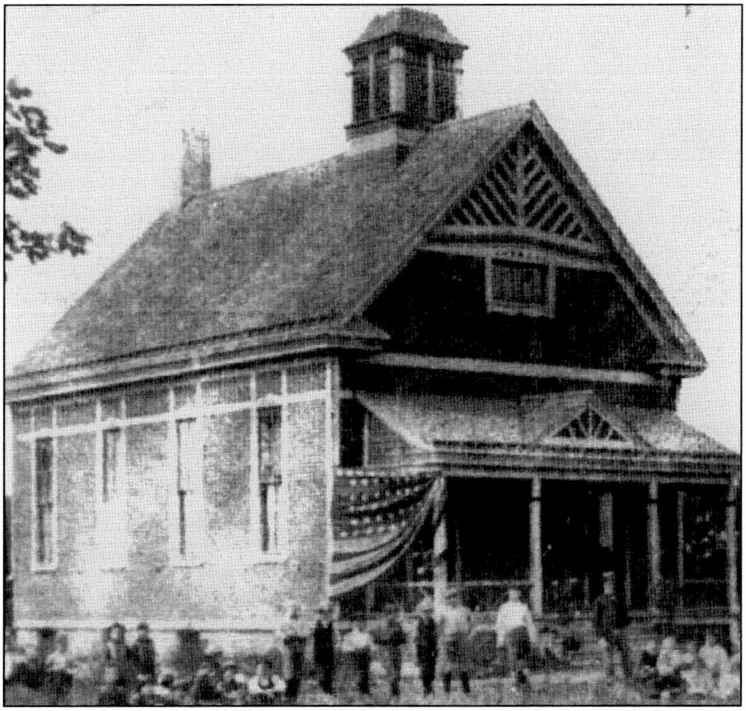

The Bowens felt very passionately about educating area children. They convinced Isaac Davis to donate a section of his land to the township for the creation of a new school. The grand Bowen School No. 2, seen in this picture draped in a flag, was built a short distance away from the first Bowen school.

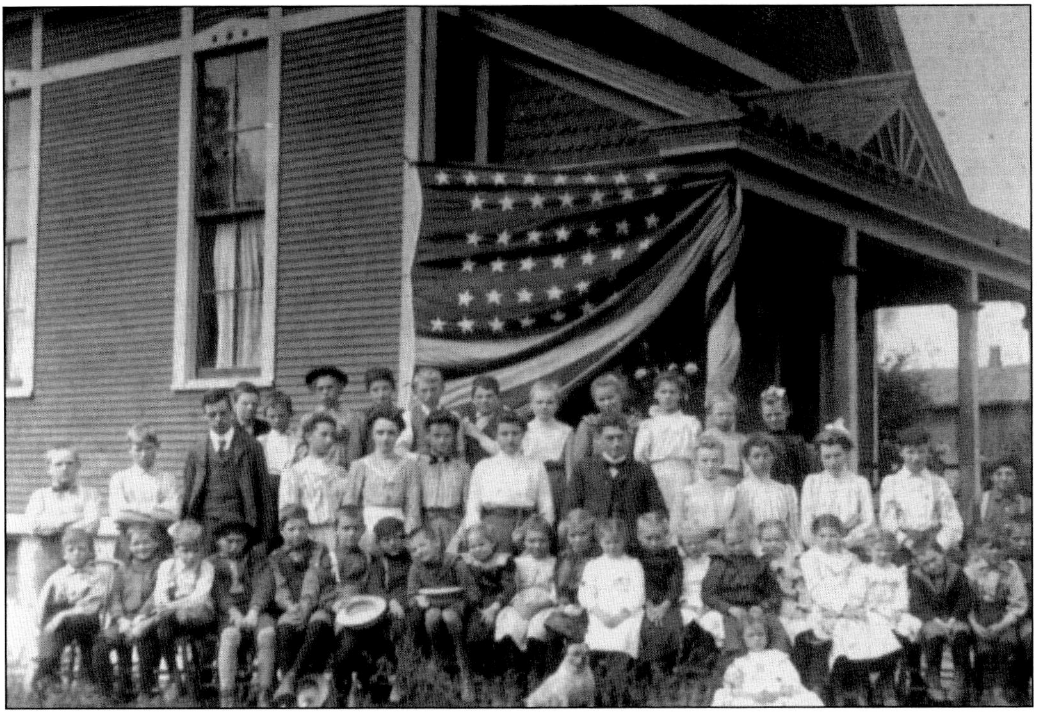

Bostwick and Hattie Bowen's children attended Bowen No. 2 in the early 1900s. Cora's pug dog, Toby, followed her to school every day and even managed to sneak into the class picture with her. Classes were interrupted on Christmas Eve 1904, when a fire broke out and destroyed the schoolhouse.

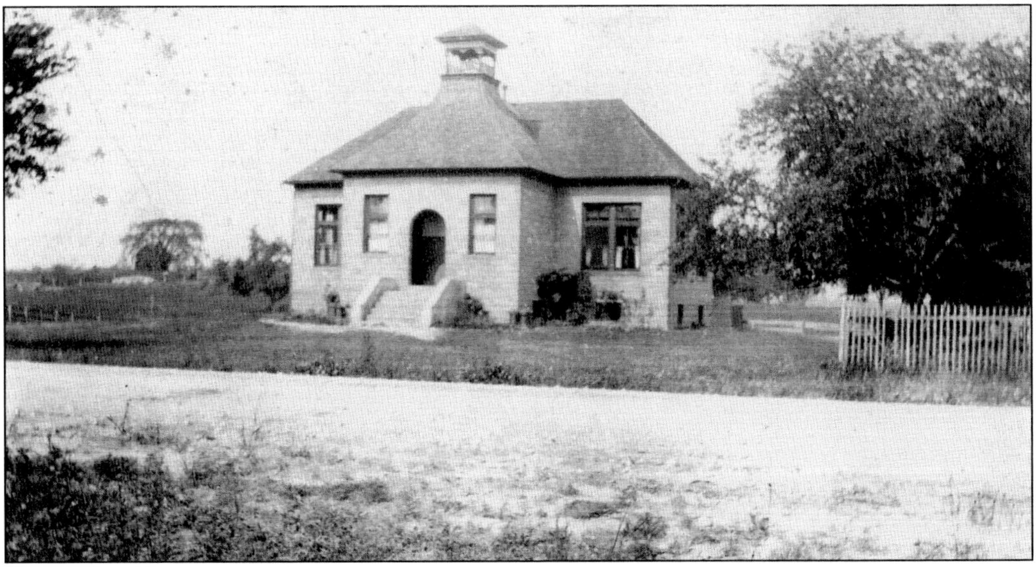

Bowen No. 2 was near Wesley Brake's blacksmith shop and an abandoned train depot. Almost a year before the school fire, the north-bound and south-bound Pere Marquette trains collided in Paris Township. Locals blamed the accident on the railroad company for not maintaining the depot. After the school fire, Wesley Brake donated part of his shop for classes while Bostwick Bowen razed the depot and reused the materials to build the new school.

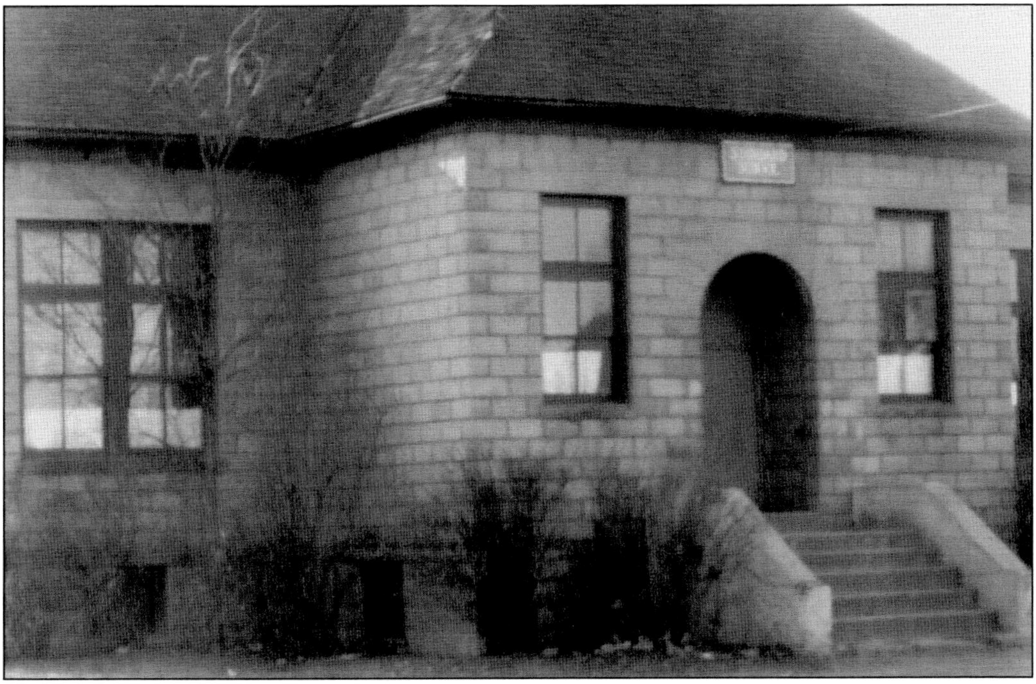

The Bowen School No. 4 was completed in 1905. In addition to its brick exterior, it also had two classrooms—one where younger children could be taught and another for older children. Many Paris Township residents considered the plan controversial, but the Bowen family, who was on the school board, advocated its advantages and eventually won over the public.

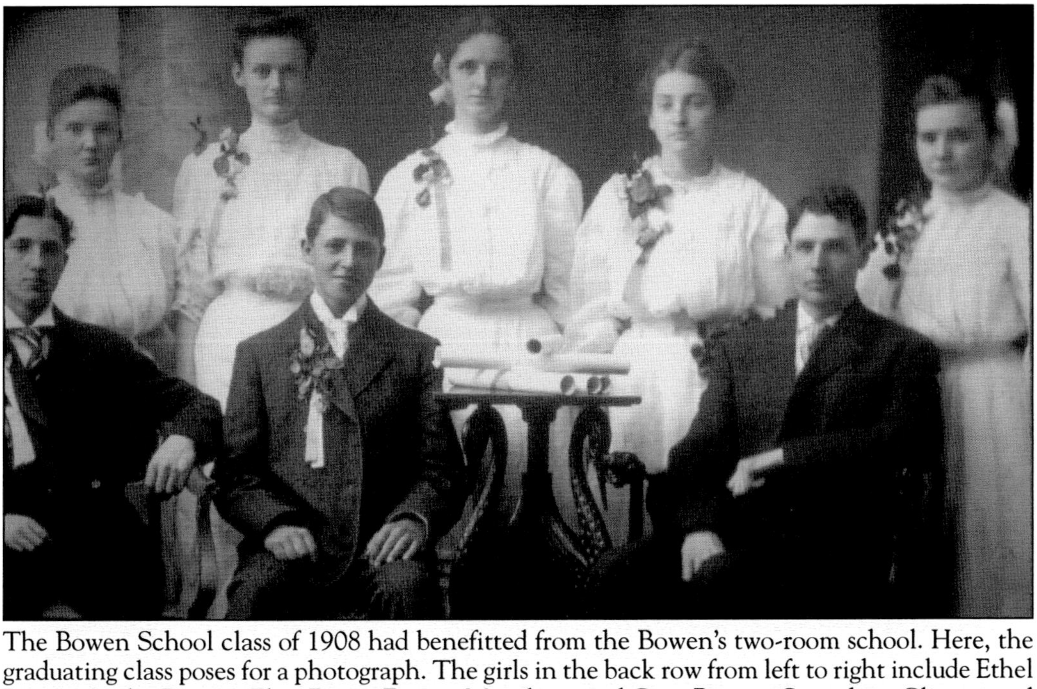

The Bowen School class of 1908 had benefitted from the Bowen's two-room school. Here, the graduating class poses for a photograph. The girls in the back row from left to right include Ethel Bowen, Letha Bowen, Elsia Davis, Fannie Munshaw, and Cora Bowen. Seated are Clinton and Merle Brake with their 12th grade teacher, Robert Compton.

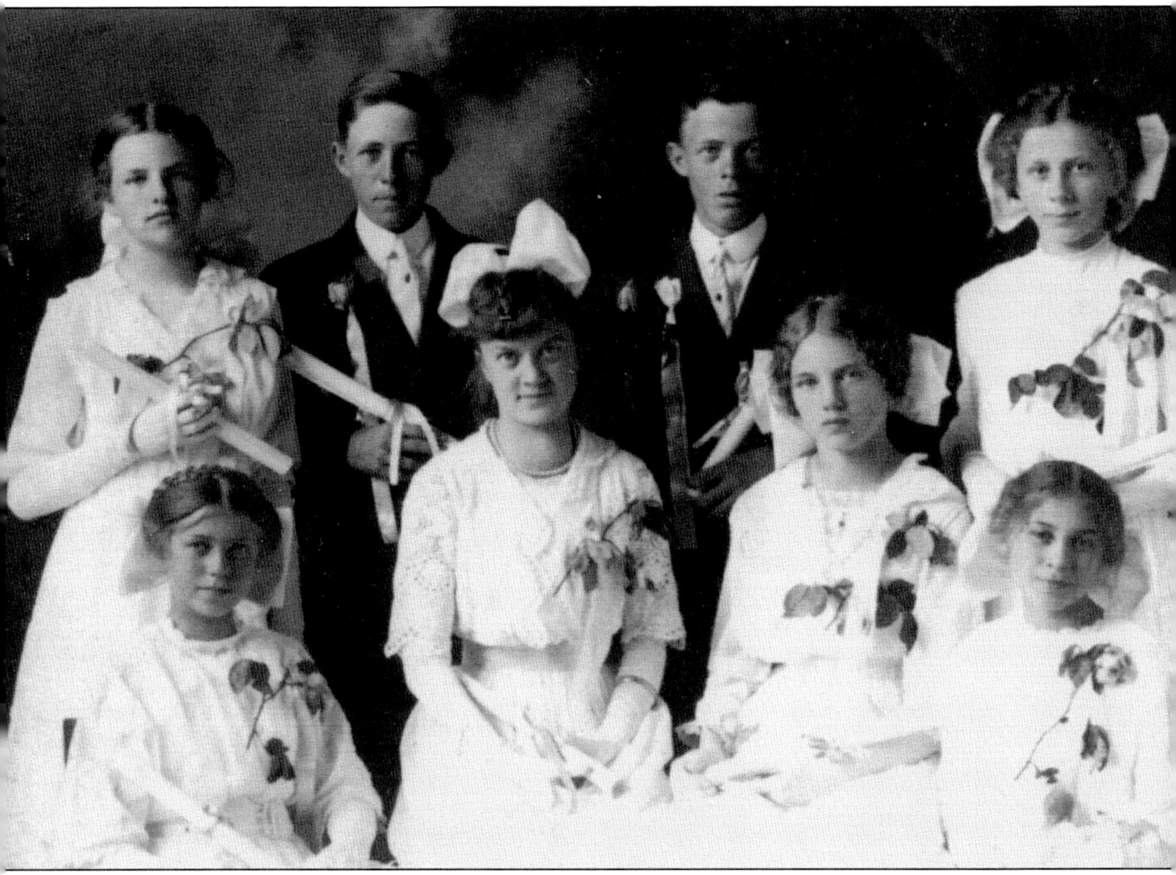

The Bowen School class of 1915 marks their eighth-grade graduation with a group photograph. In the lower right-hand corner, Elsie Randall smiles. Before the Bowen School, many local schools only taught to the eighth grade and sent students on to Grand Rapids, Caledonia, or another local high school to get their degrees

Edith Allen was a friend of Cora Bowen. Like Bowen, she was a descendant of one of Paris Township's early settlers (Hiram Allen) and her family had been very active in the development of the community. Following her forefather's example, Edith eventually became a teacher at the Bowen School and taught a generation of Paris Township residents.

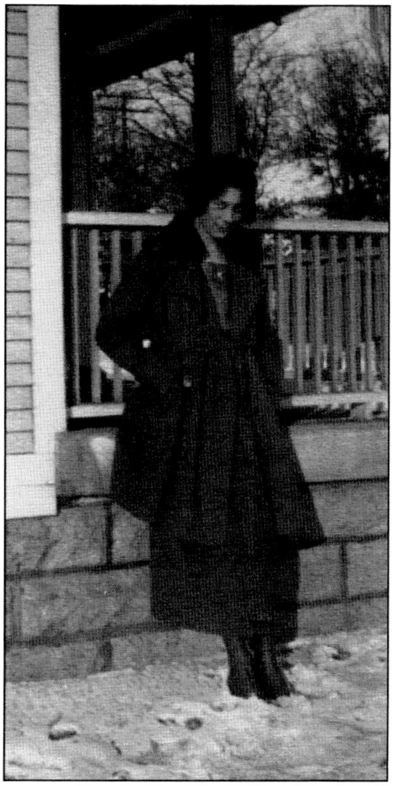

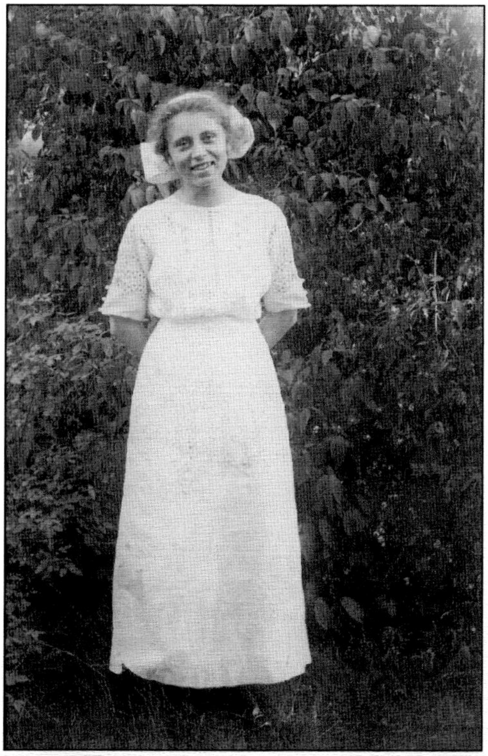

Many parents with daughters that were Elsie Randall's age in 1915 felt that high school was no place for a girl. Fortunately for Randall, she had parents who let her continue her studies at one of the area's high schools. After receiving her diploma, she attended college. Here, Randall smiles for her college photograph.

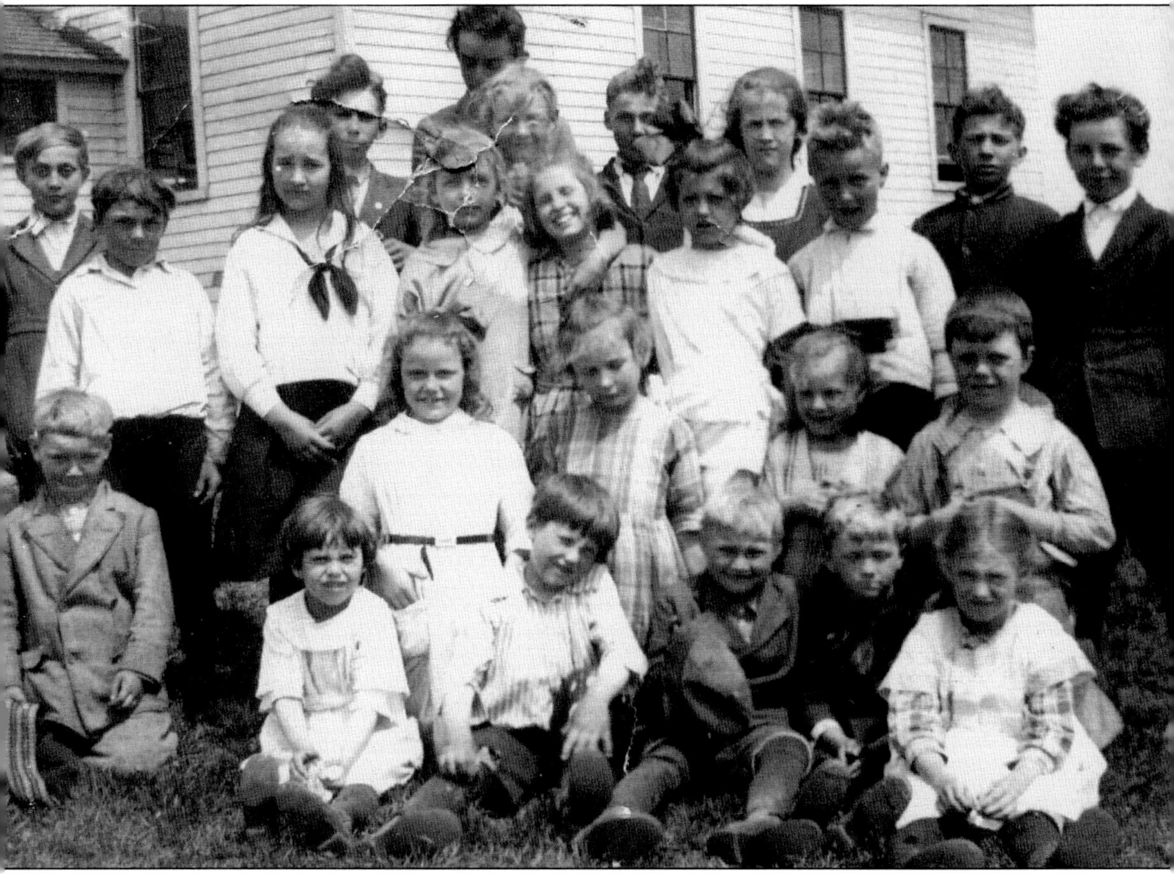

The 1922 class at East Paris School No. 8 gathers for a group picture. As one of the first four schools in the area, the original East Paris Schoolhouse was a log cabin on Twenty-eighth and Patterson Streets. When fire struck in the late 1890s, a new one-room wooden structure for the students was built on East Paris Avenue.

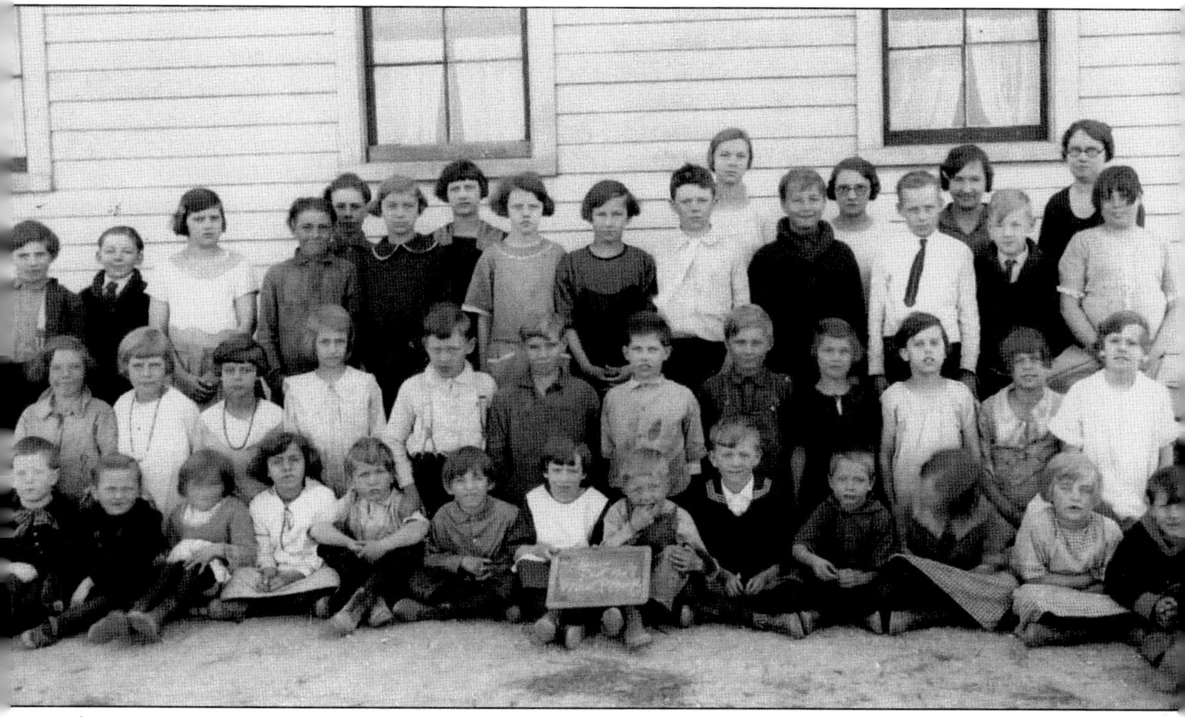

The 1925 class at East Paris School No. 8 poses for the camera. This wooden schoolhouse was an extremely well-constructed building. Some Paris Township families, like the Darlings and Slaters, sent generations of children to No. 8. Aside from repair work performed by the Works Progress Administration (WPA) during the Depression, the building housed the school until 1967 and then became the headquarters for the Kentwood Jaycees.

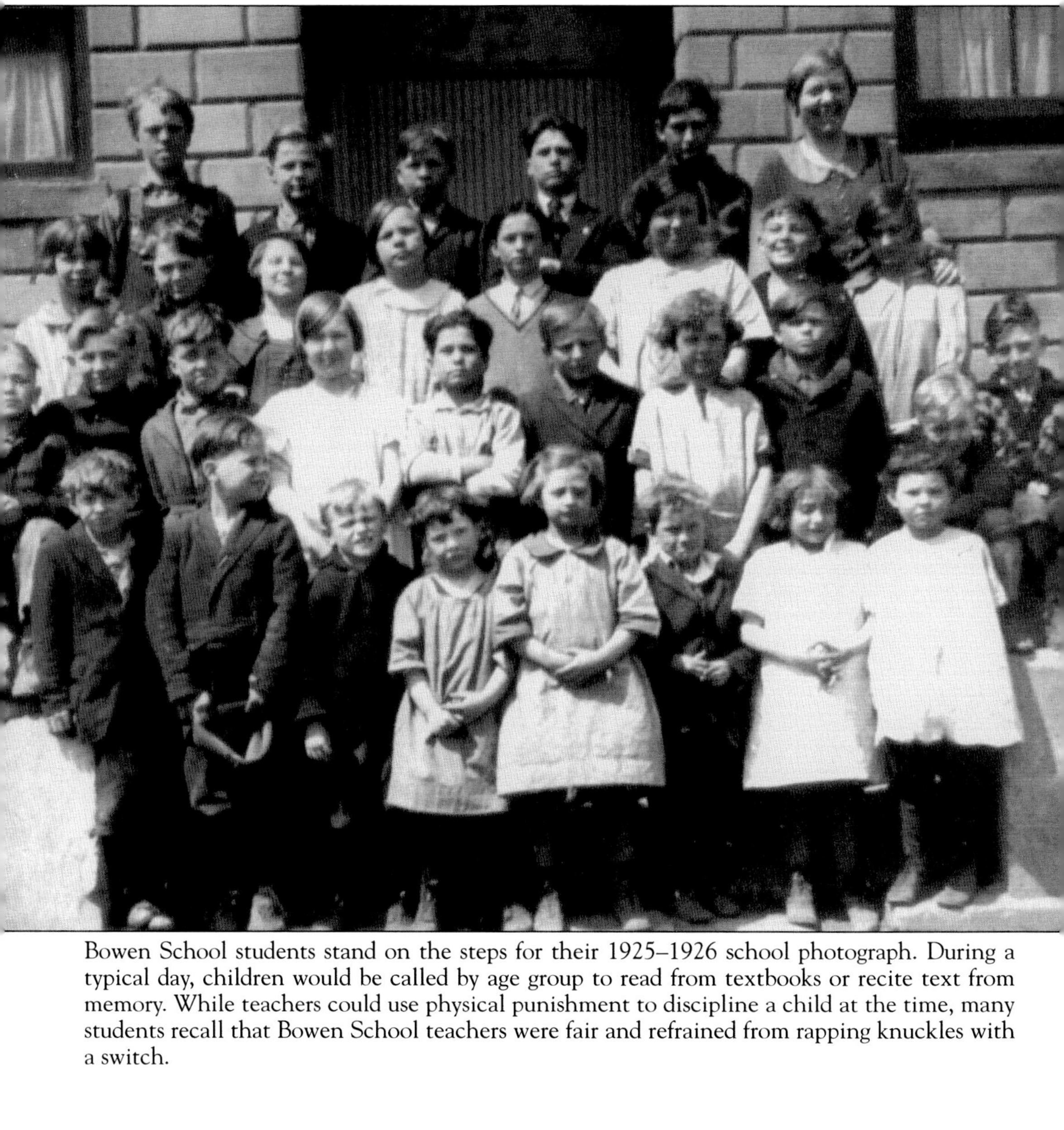

Bowen School students stand on the steps for their 1925–1926 school photograph. During a typical day, children would be called by age group to read from textbooks or recite text from memory. While teachers could use physical punishment to discipline a child at the time, many students recall that Bowen School teachers were fair and refrained from rapping knuckles with a switch.

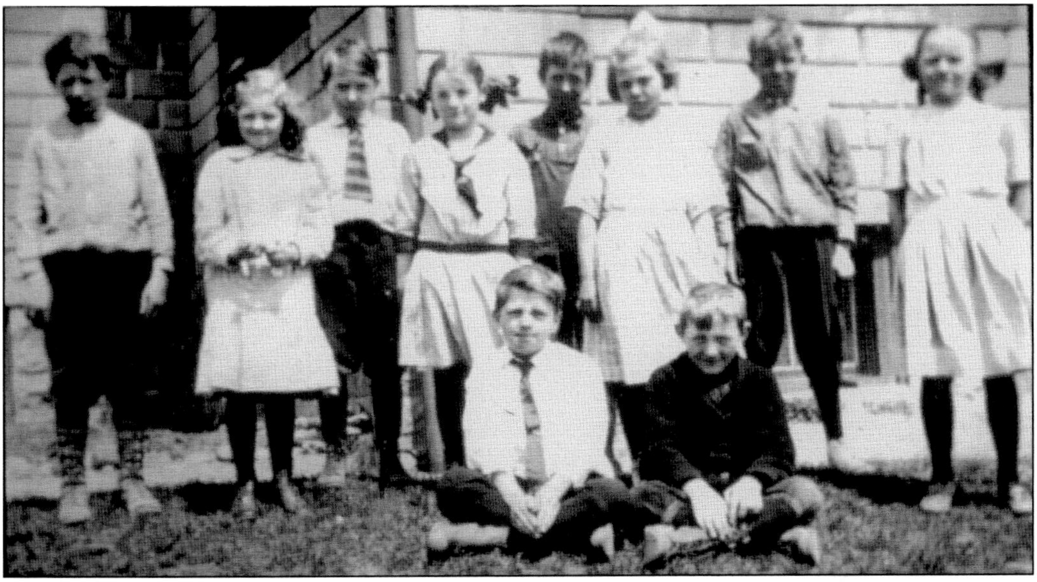

Children at the Bowen School take a break from learning to play and socialize with friends outside. Some of the children in this photograph are Cornelia Feenstra, Max Bowen, Marie VanDyke, and Julius Post. They may have played with marbles, played a game of tag, or enjoyed other activities before returning to their lessons.

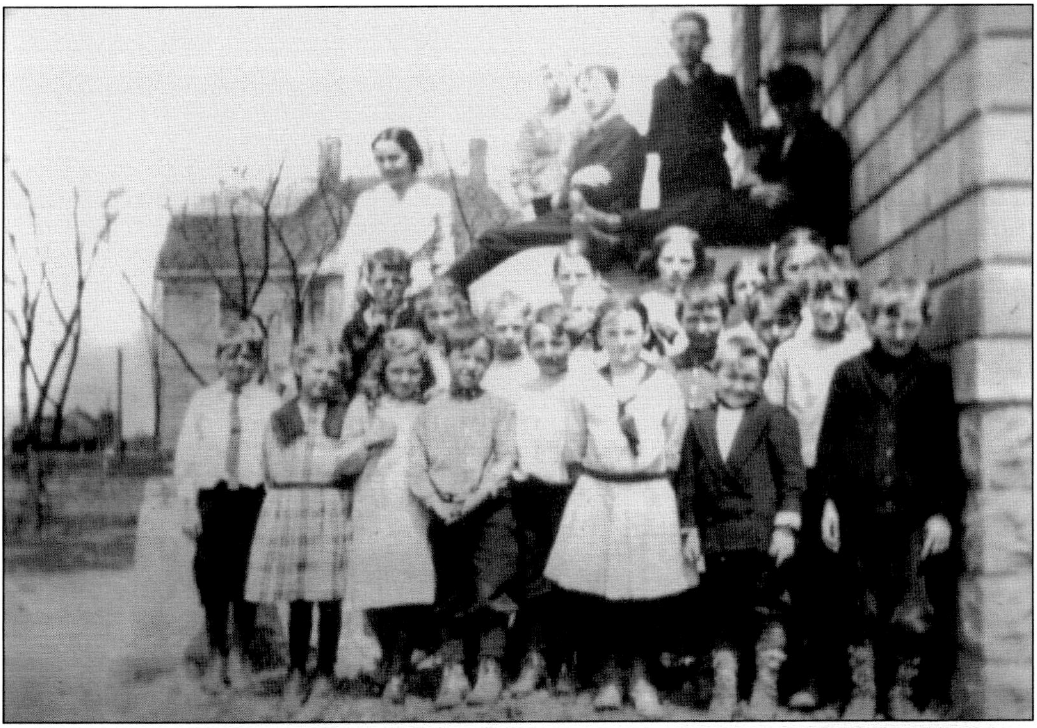

Bowen School students gather on the steps of the schoolhouse with their teacher, Miss Hutchinson. Some of the children present in this picture are Leonard and Hiram Troost, Margaret VanDyke, and Julius and Augustus Post. Schools frequently changed teachers. Many teachers simply moved to a new post or married and left teaching to raise a family.

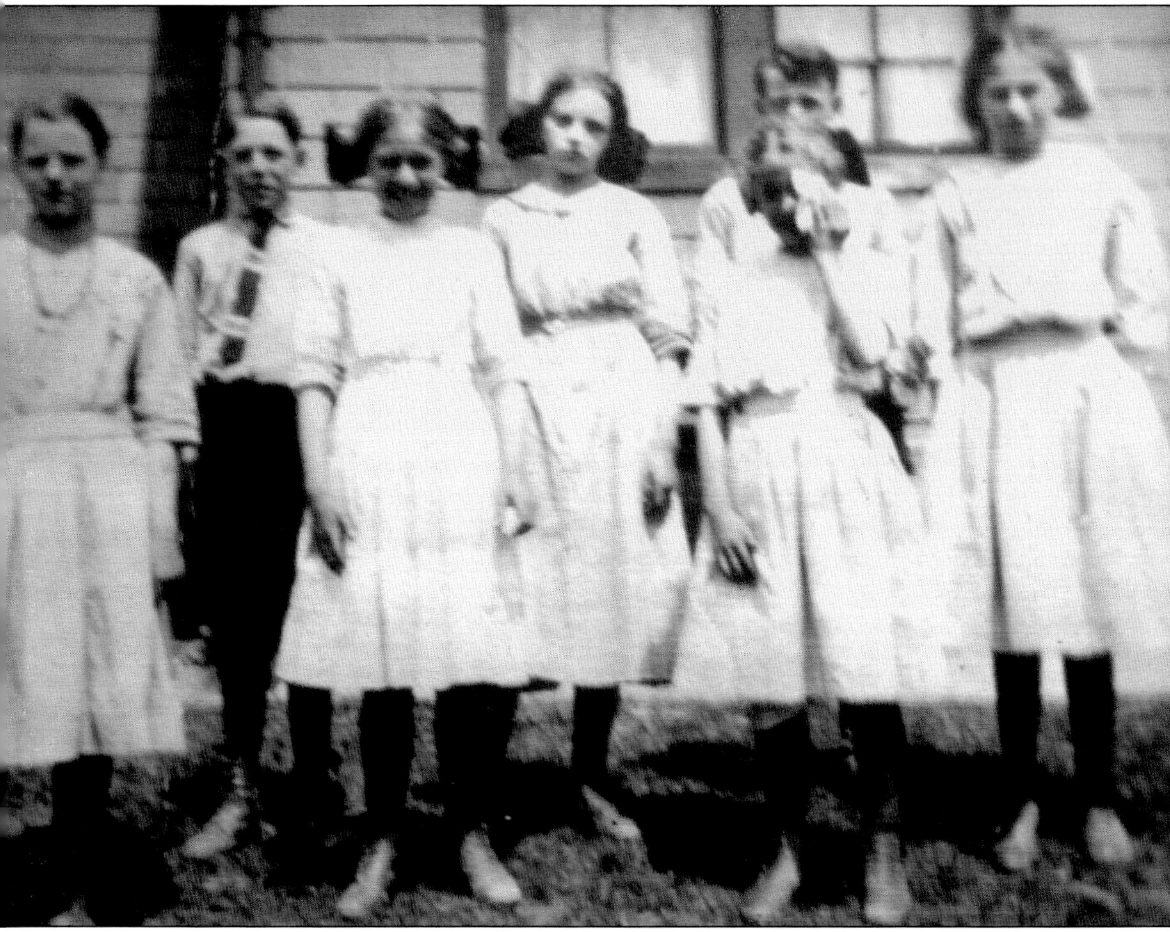

What a difference a few years can make. Bowen School students in this picture include (from left to right) Rosie Oosterhouse, Hiriam Troost, Isabell Feenstra, Margaret VanDyke, Clara Feenstra, Leonard Troost, and Marie Burns. In a few short years, these students would be expected to make their mark on the community, and many succeeded in doing so.

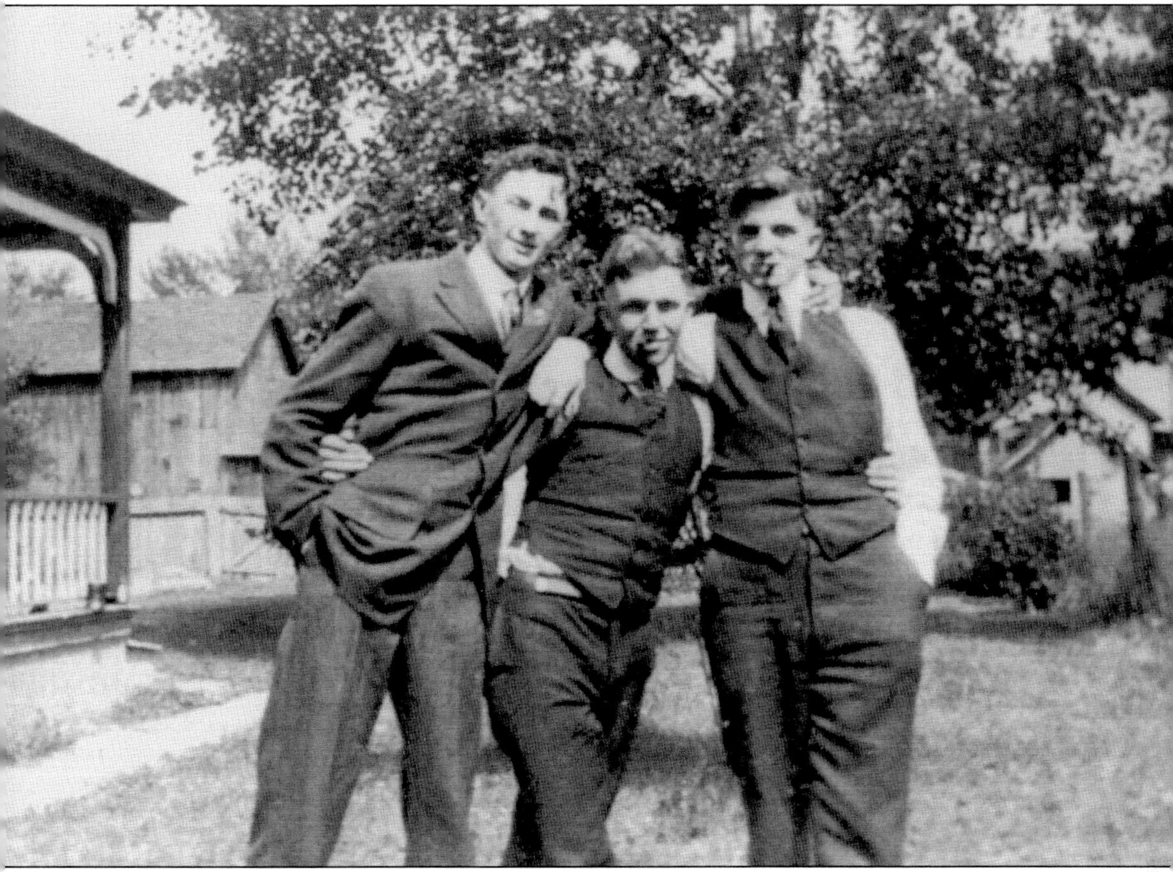

Once graduated, adults remembered their time at the Bowen School fondly. Reunion picnics for Paris Township students were frequently held in the summer. Many turned out to reminisce with old friends and catch up on the lives of their fellow classmates since school. In this photograph (from left to right), Rollin Davis, Don Carnck, and Walter Buck pose together.

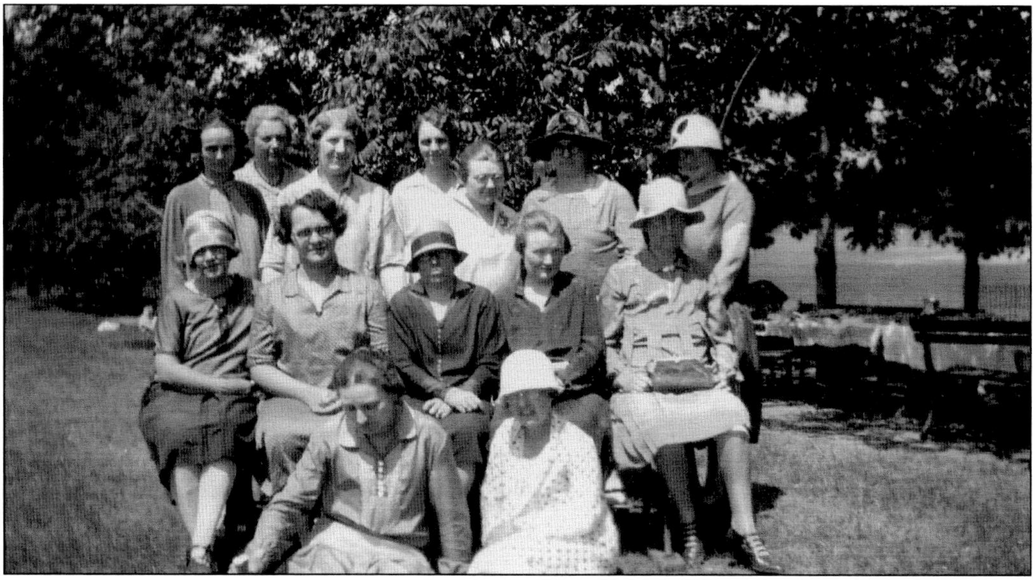

Ladies pose in Garfield Park for the 1927 Bowen School reunion. Pictured from left to right are the following: (front row) Letta Bowen Burridge and Katie O'Riley; (second row) Irene Corcoran (Balding), Theresa Esbaugh Shears, Ina Witters, Ethel Bowen, and Carrie Bankley Darling; (back row) Fannie Patterson, May Blodgett Sills, Agnes Hoekstra Whitford, Elsie Davis, Cora Bowen, Marnie Esbaugh Troost, and Jessie Bowen Lawrence.

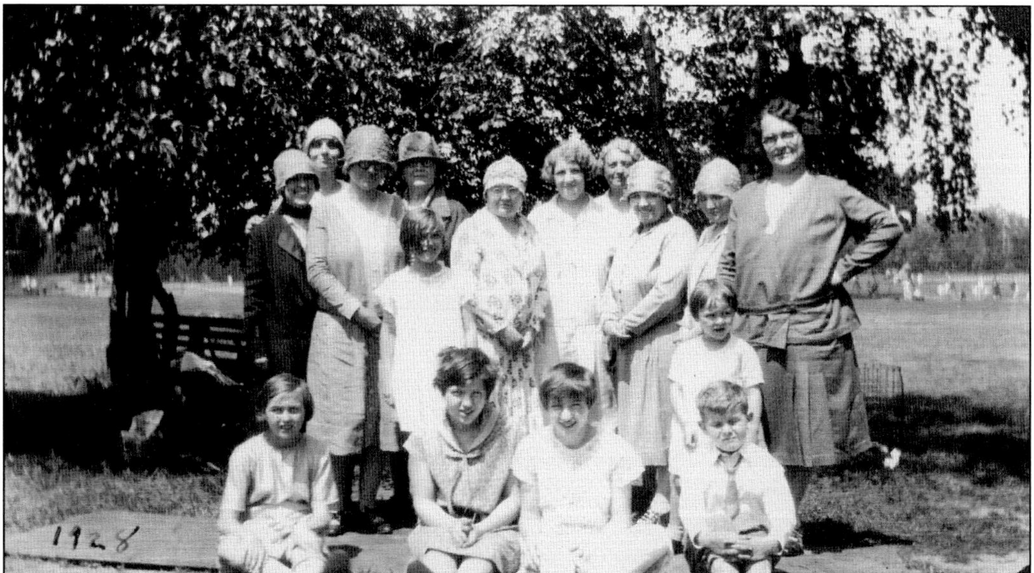

The 1927 reunion was so much fun that many of the Bowen School alumni met again the following year. In this picture, two generations of students stand together for a photograph. Incidentally, the park the reunion was held in was named for Charles Garfield, a banker, horticulturalist, and civic leader who was a prominent graduate of Paris School No. 5.

The congregation at the East Paris Christian Reformed Church had longed to send their children to a Christian school. In 1923, they formed a committee to start one. By 1927, the East Paris Christian School opened with Herbert Husselman, at the top of the stairs in the middle, as teacher. Husselman received $125 per month to teach reading, writing, and arithmetic. (Photograph courtesy of Heritage Hall at Calvin College.)

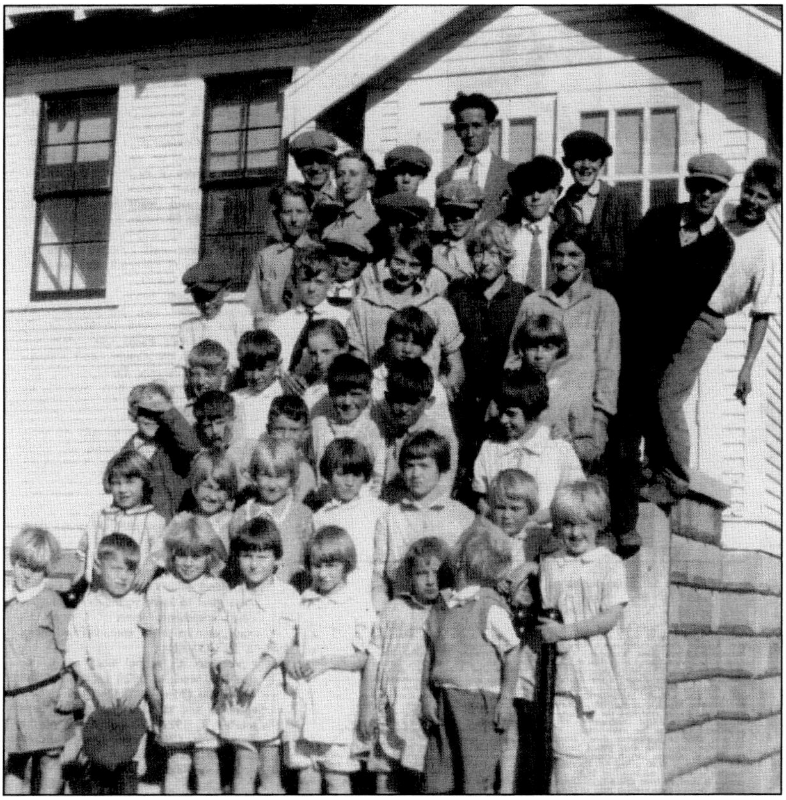

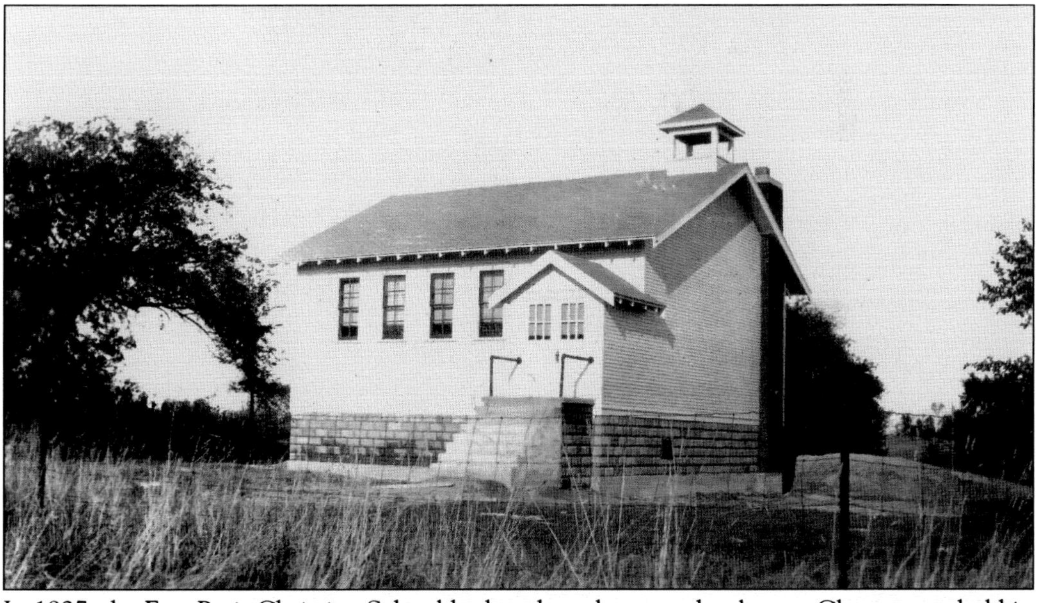

In 1927, the East Paris Christian School had students but no schoolroom. Classes were held in the chapel beside the church. In November of that year, the Christian School Society donated a large section of land to the east of the East Paris Christian Reformed Church. Construction on the one-room school was completed in 1928.

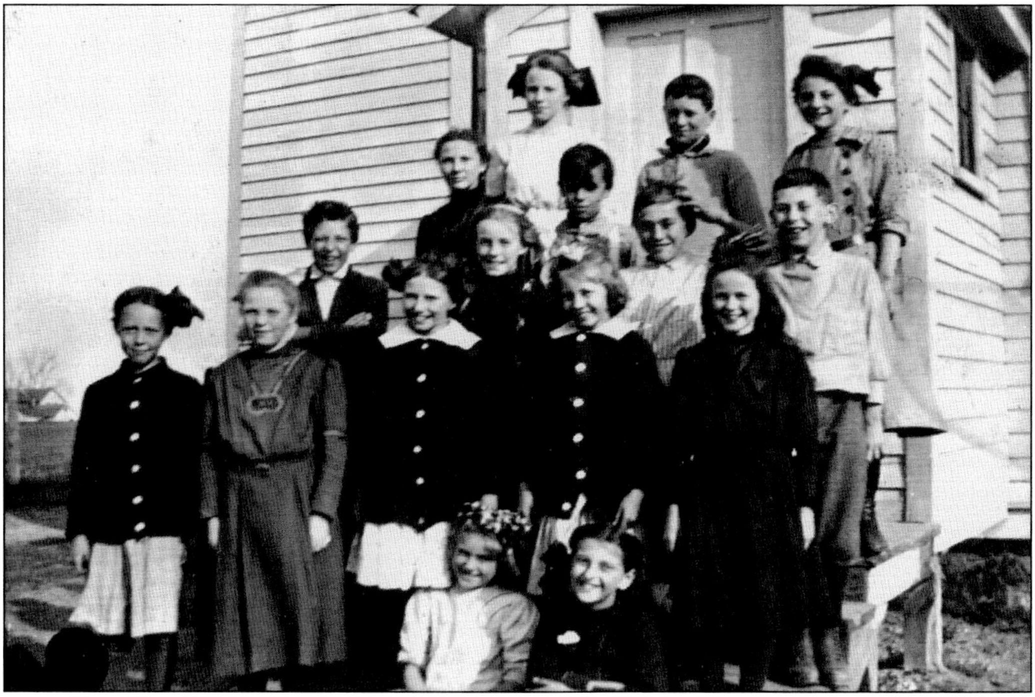

The East Paris Christian School students at the time read from class books like *History of Our Nations* and the *Elson Reader*. Although Paris Township residents paid to send their children to this school, the institution was also supported by charitable contributions from groups like the Ladies Aid Society. Other Christian schools in the area included Kelloggsville Christian School. (Photograph courtesy of Heritage Hall at Calvin College.)

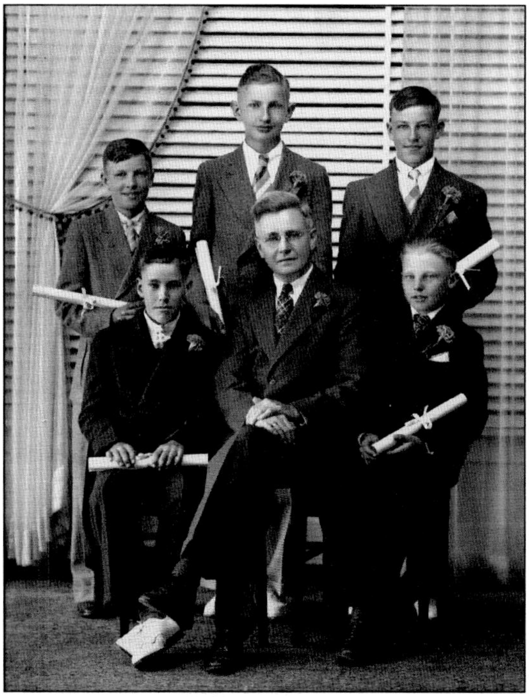

The East Paris Christian School had come a long way in a decade. The 1936 graduating class of eighth graders from East Paris Christian School sits for a photograph with principal Richard Kass. These boys, like all students at the school, could enroll in one of the area's public high schools or another private Christian school. (Photograph courtesy of Heritage Hall at Calvin College.)

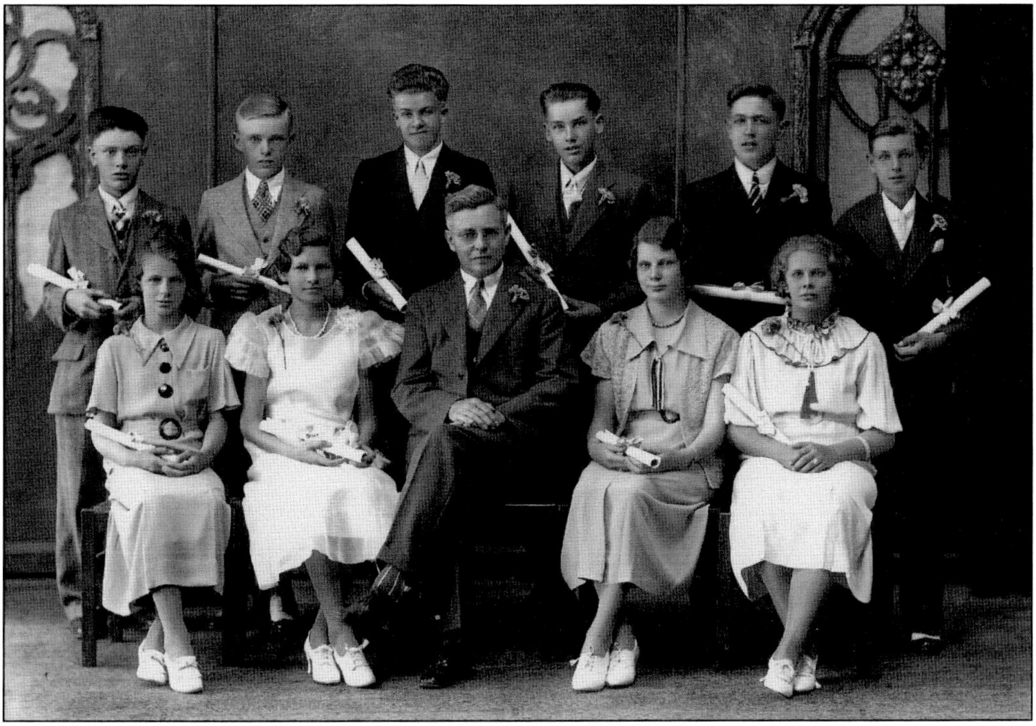

Principal Richard Kass proudly sits with the 1937 graduating class of eighth graders from East Paris Christian School. After high school, many of these students would continue their education at Calvin College, located in Grand Rapids on Franklin Street between Benjamin and Giddings Avenues. At the time, Calvin College offered teaching and pre-professional courses with a religious basis. (Photograph courtesy of Heritage Hall at Calvin College.)

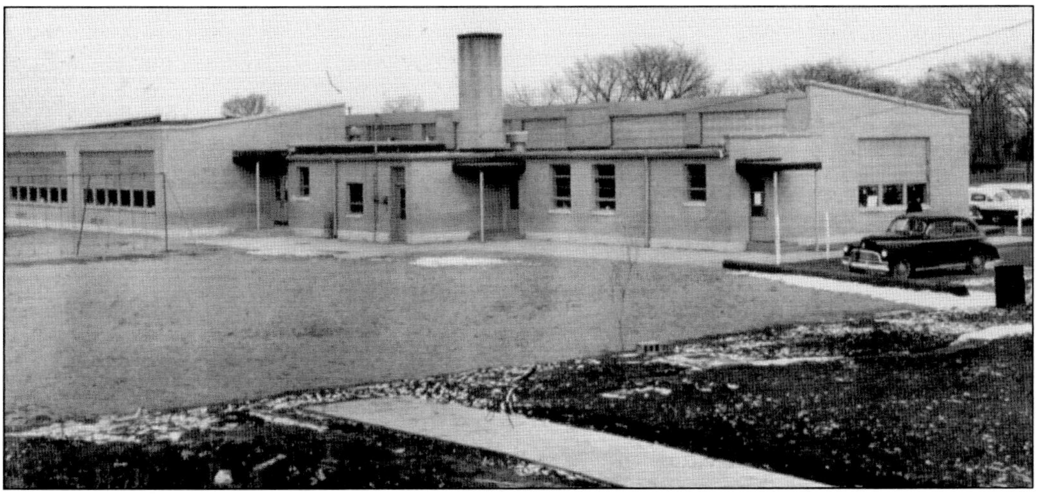

By the 1950s, attitudes about education had changed. In 1958, the Kentwood School District was developed. This was the first time the name was associated with Paris Township, and a decade later, residents chose it for their new city. The district began consolidating and updating existing Paris Township schools. In 1962, the Bowen School was also rebuilt into a multi-classroom school where children were divided up by grade.

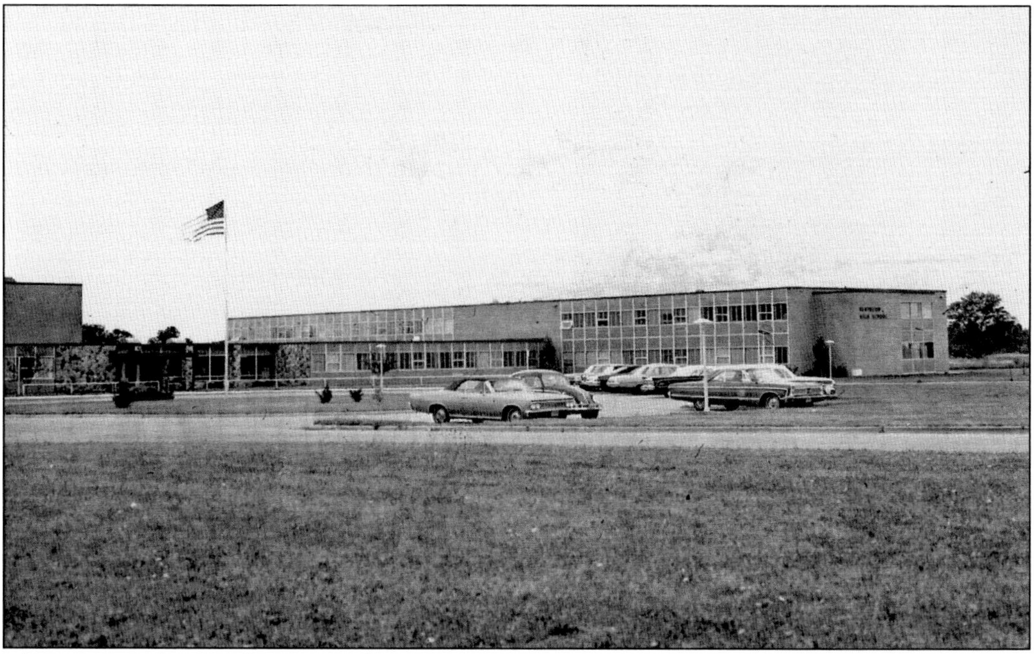

The Kentwood School District also began to add new facilities to accommodate the growing population. In 1960, the Kentwood Public High School, pictured here, was built. Within a decade, however, the population of Kentwood grew. This facility became Crestwood Middle School, and a new facility, the East Kentwood Public High School, was built in 1969.

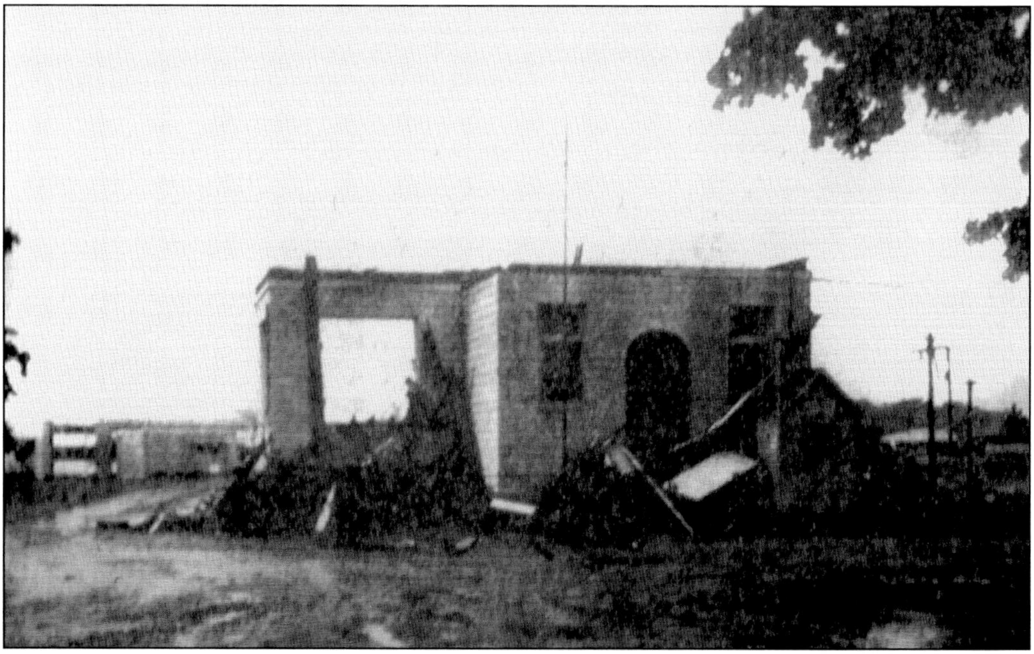

In 1962, the Bowen School No. 4 was unused but still standing. The new Bowen School can be seen in the background of this picture. When No. 4 was razed in 1965, it signified the end of a way of life in Paris Township. The Kentwood School District would be the first to usher in a new quality of life for the entire community.

Five

A Township at Play

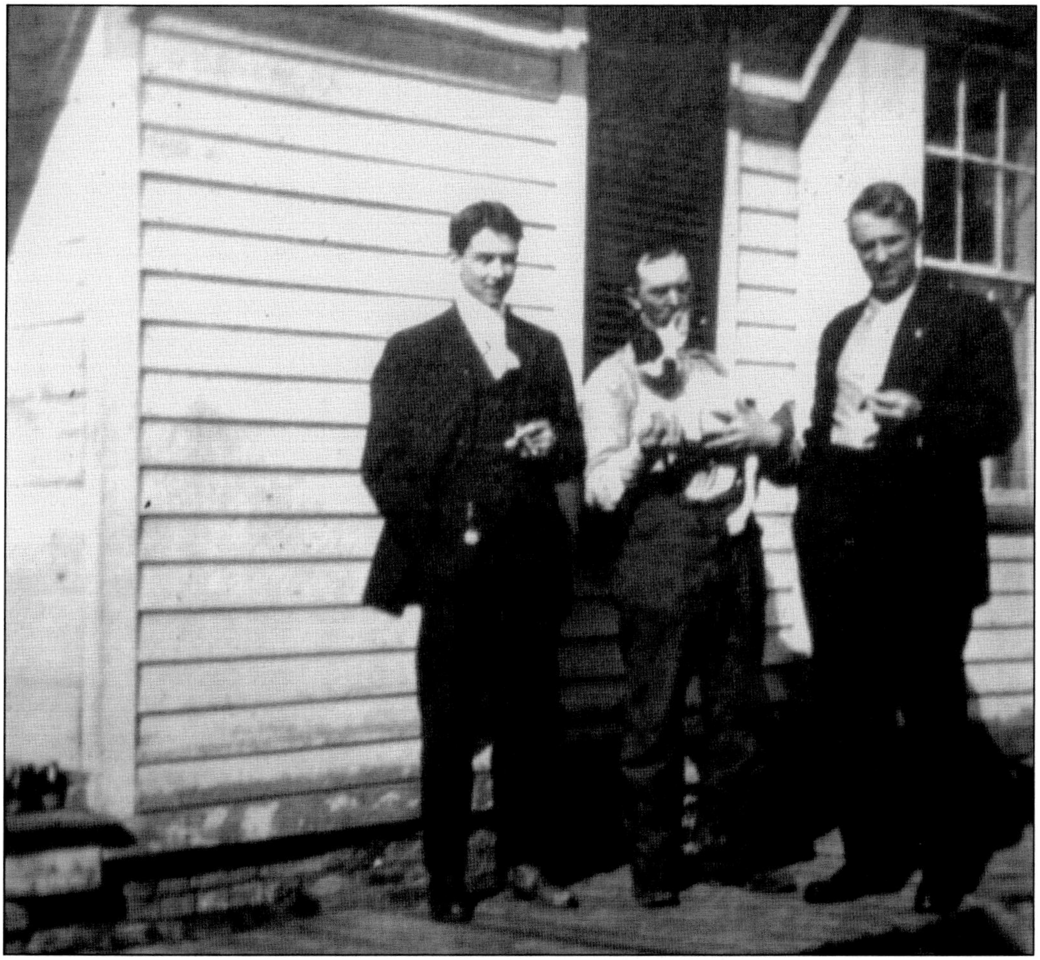

While the early settlers of Paris Township worked hard to survive, they also took any opportunity to get together with family and friends. As their farms became established and thrived, many of the children of the original settlers established a unique and almost unbreakable bond. In this photograph (from left to right), Stewart Darling, Lincoln Patterson (holding a dog), and Ralph Darling step outside for a smoke.

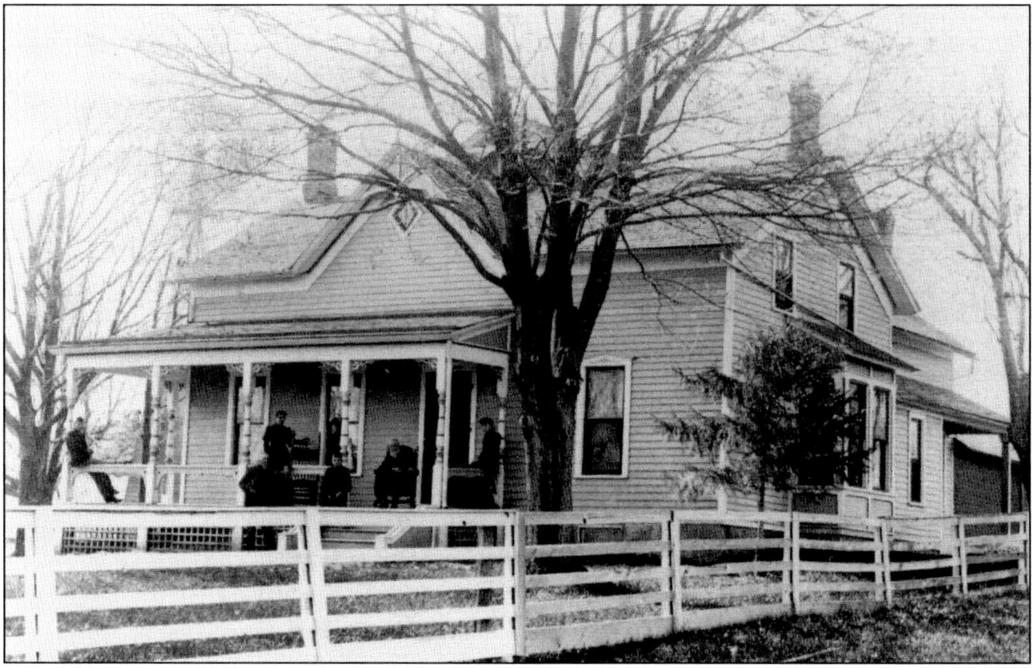

The Martin family was an early Paris Township family. During the Civil War, Marion Martin, daughter of settler Thomas Martin, married M. A. Shafer, a cavalry surgeon and son of settler John Shafer. In this photograph, members of the Martin family pose on the front porch of their Breton Avenue and Twenty-eighth Street farmhouse. Some of the people pictured here are Thomas Watson Martin, James Henry Martin, Arthur Randall Martin, and Cora Martin Davis.

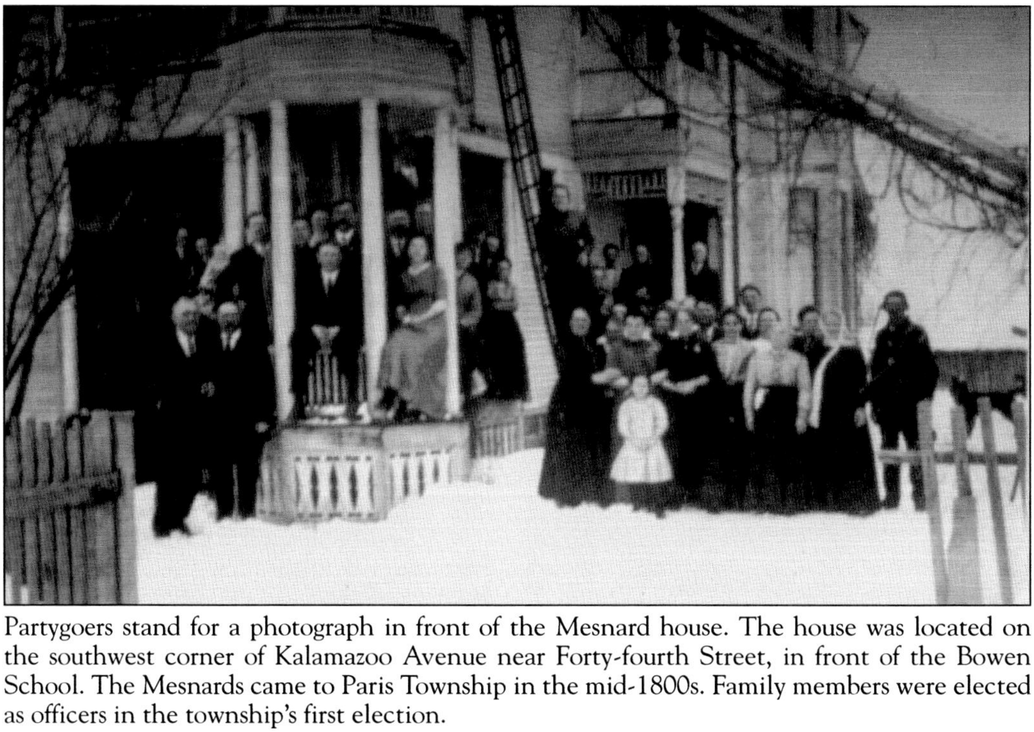

Partygoers stand for a photograph in front of the Mesnard house. The house was located on the southwest corner of Kalamazoo Avenue near Forty-fourth Street, in front of the Bowen School. The Mesnards came to Paris Township in the mid-1800s. Family members were elected as officers in the township's first election.

Members of the Fitch family take a step on a ladder in front of their house. In this photograph, from left to right, Norine Bennett, Harold Fitch, and Ruth Fitch stand on the ladder while Myrtie Fitch provides a little support. George Fitch, believed to be taking the picture, lived in Paris Township for a number of years.

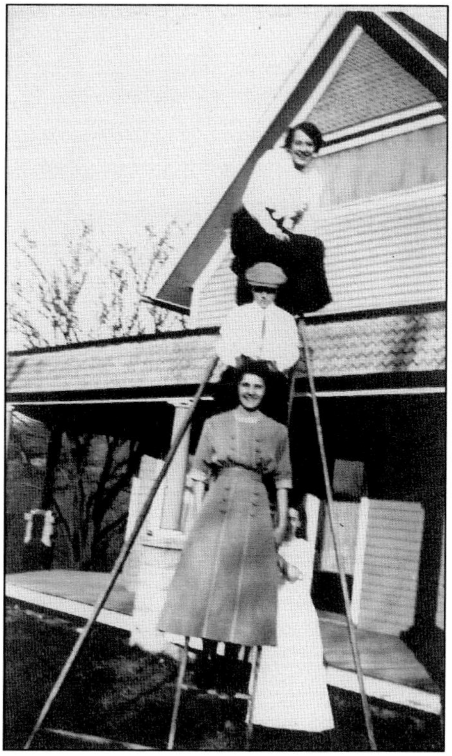

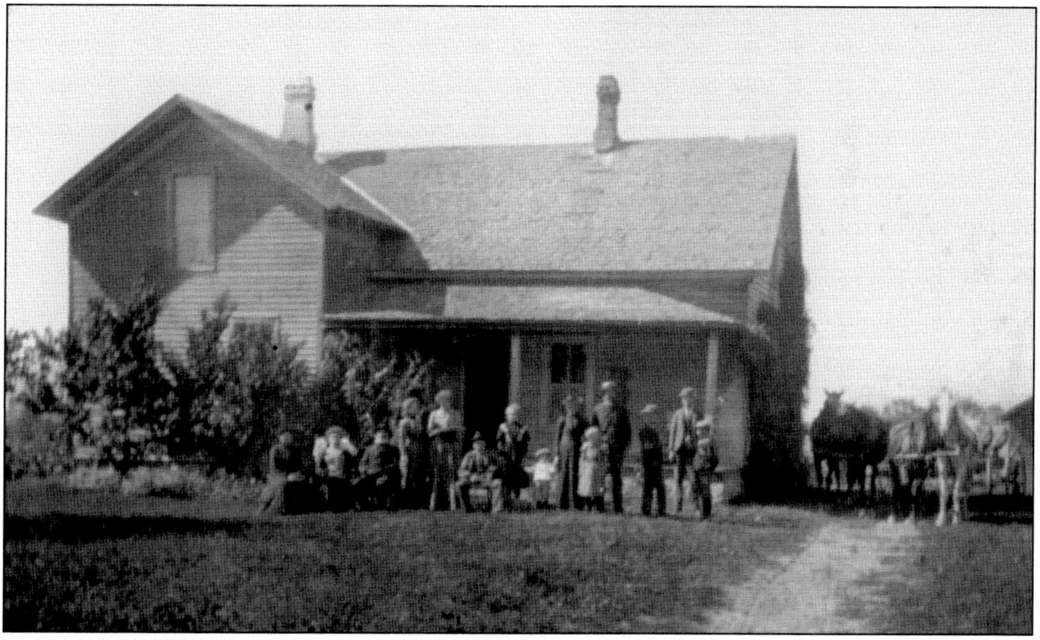

The Oosterhouse family visits the Slater house. While the Slater family was one of the first settlers of Paris Township, the Oosterhouses were Dutch immigrants who settled in the area in the late 1870s. The two families met frequently to talk about their farms and share other events in their lives.

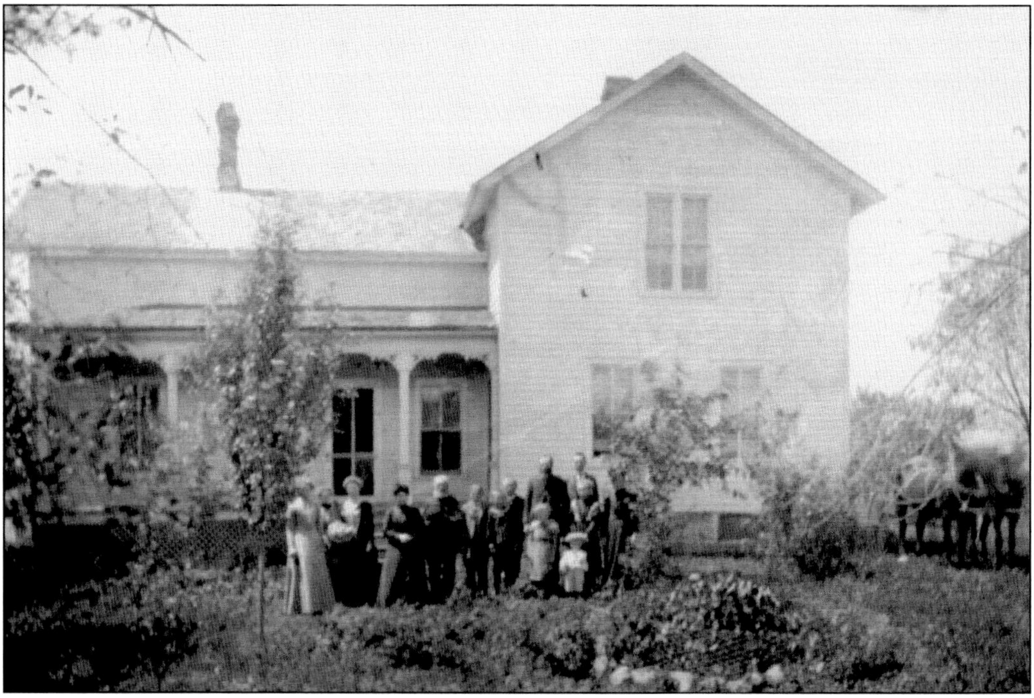

Henry Oosterhouse; his wife, Alice; and their seven children stand with friends in front of one of their houses. Oosterhouse purchased this house on Fifty-second Street and Wing Street from Eli Buck. The Dutch immigrant was an excellent farmer and was good with his profits. Over time, he was able to buy a number of properties throughout Paris Township.

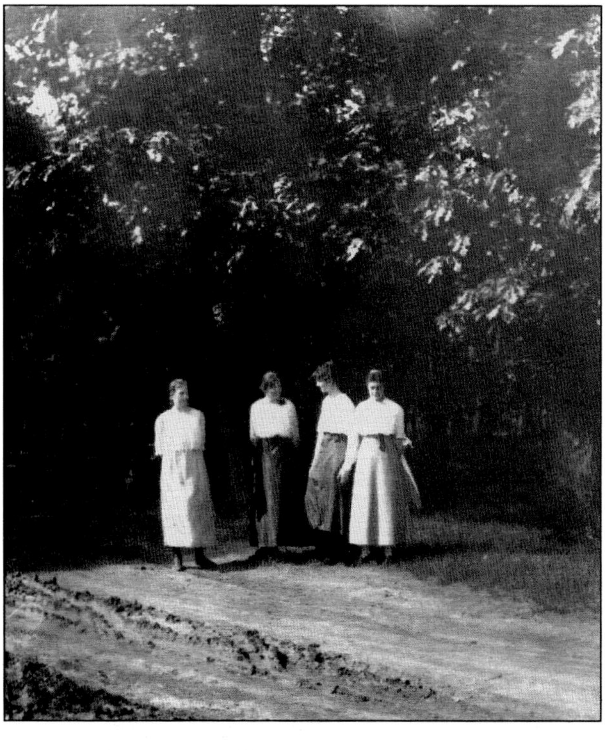

Helen Randall and Elise Davis were part of a close circle of friends for years. In this photograph (from left to right), friends Gladys ?, Inez Manthe, Elsie Davis, and Helen Randall stand together on a sunny afternoon outside the Davis home. The four ladies stayed in contact with each other for many years, even after Elsie and Helen went to college.

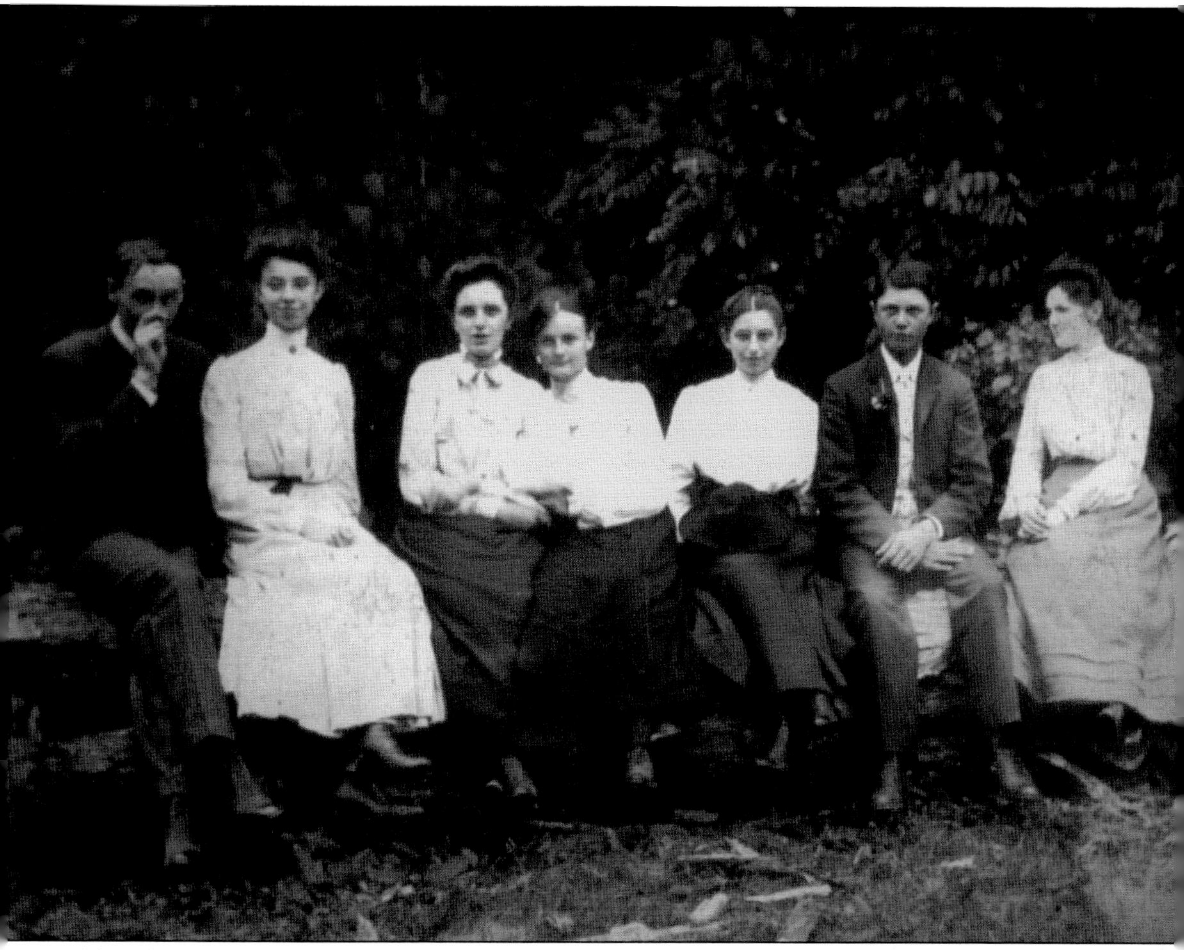

Although much was required and expected of young adults, changes in agricultural technology at the time and the abundance of the community enabled the children of many farm families to spend more time socializing with friends. Young men and women (some of whom are in the Bowen School Class of 1908 photograph on page 57) pose together on a log.

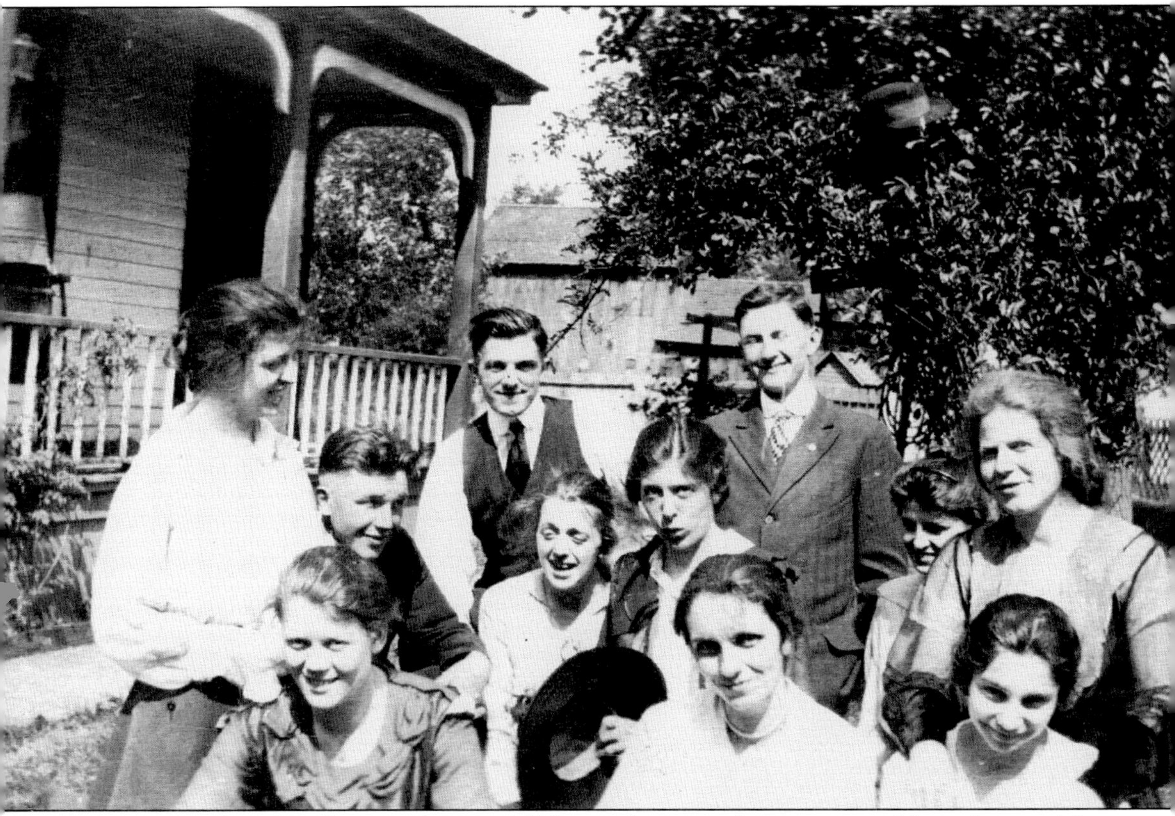

A group of friends gathers on the Randall farm. The young ladies were grabbing the men's hats and throwing them into the tree. One hat hangs in the tree, while another hat, held by the woman in the middle, probably made it into the tree after this photograph was taken. Some of the people in this photograph are Elsie Davis, Maude Randall, and John VanderVeen.

Helen Randall strikes a shy pose in a college picture (similar to the one of her sister, Elsie, on page 59). She sent copies of the photograph out as postcards to friends like Elsie Davis. "My dear Elsie," the back reads, "I received your picture and was so glad to get it. I am sorry I haven't a better one of myself to send, but I am going to have some later, Your loving friend, Helen R."

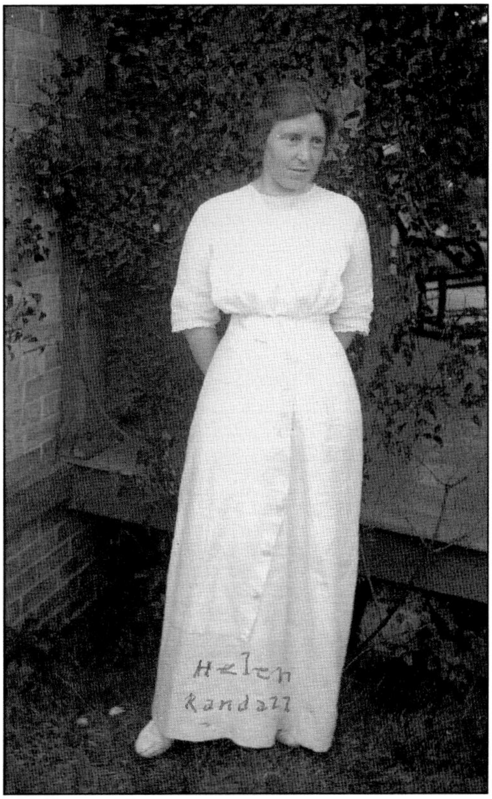

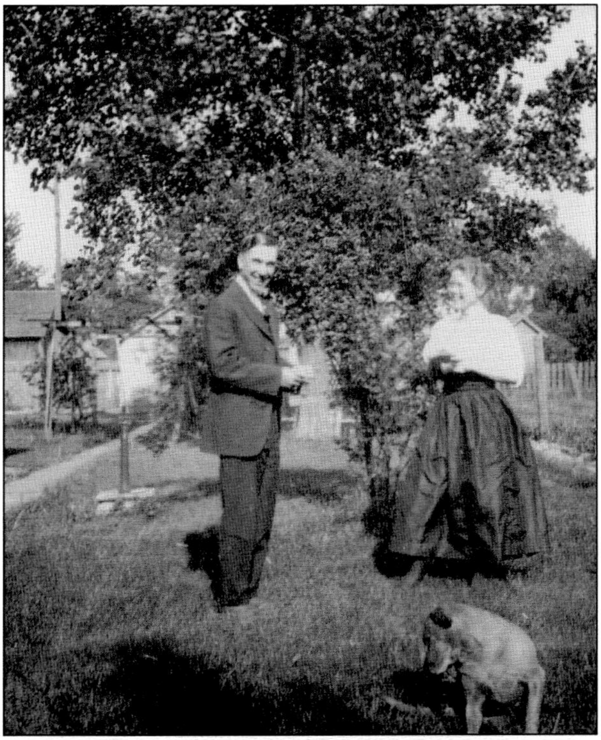

Al Kiemle and Maude Randall Pearsall share a laugh and a picture as the family dog, Ginger, plays in the grass. This picture, which was taken late in the second decade of the 20th century, offers a view of the Randall's side yard. Behind Al and Maude, the cattle field and outbuildings of the family farm can be seen.

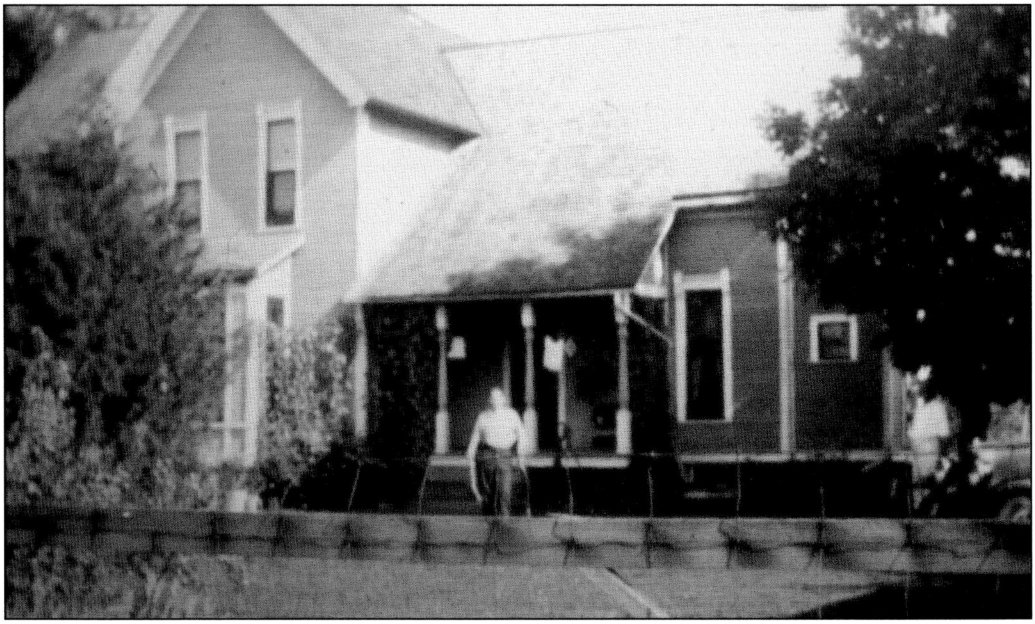

Young adults were not the only ones having fun. This farm had a tennis net and court installed on its property. At the time, tennis as a popular sport was a fairly young game. It was patented in 1874, and tennis clubs were slowly spreading across the country in the late 1880s. Tennis was probably a way for this Paris Township resident to get exercise and relax after a long day of work.

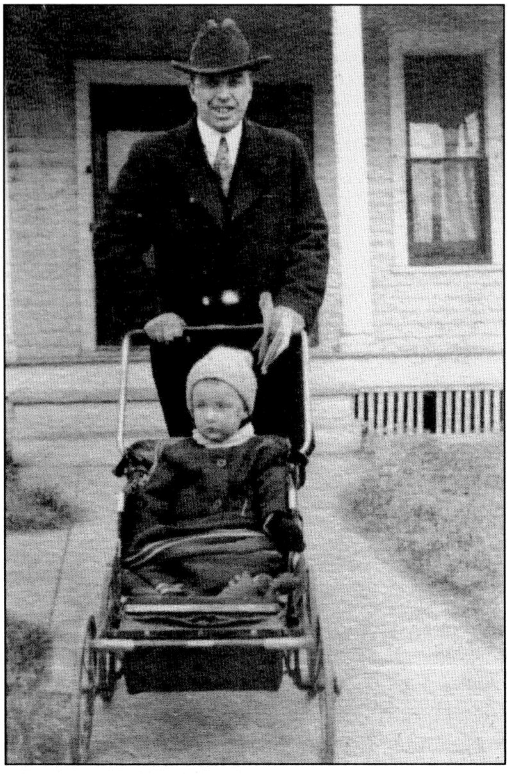

Even if residents were not second or third generation farmers, but someone who moved into one of Paris Township's growing suburbs, they found that the community was a warm and friendly place to live. In this photograph, James Gould proudly shows off his young daughter as he pushes her in a stroller for a walk on a chilly, but pleasant, Michigan afternoon.

Margaret Gould, James's wife, shares a laugh and a swing with her daughter and newborn at a Paris Township park. Residents living in one of the area's suburban neighborhoods had the best of both worlds. Everything a person needed was usually available in one of the neighborhood stores and Grand Rapids was just a trolley or bus ride away. At the same time, children could grow up in a safe area away from the hustle and bustle of the city.

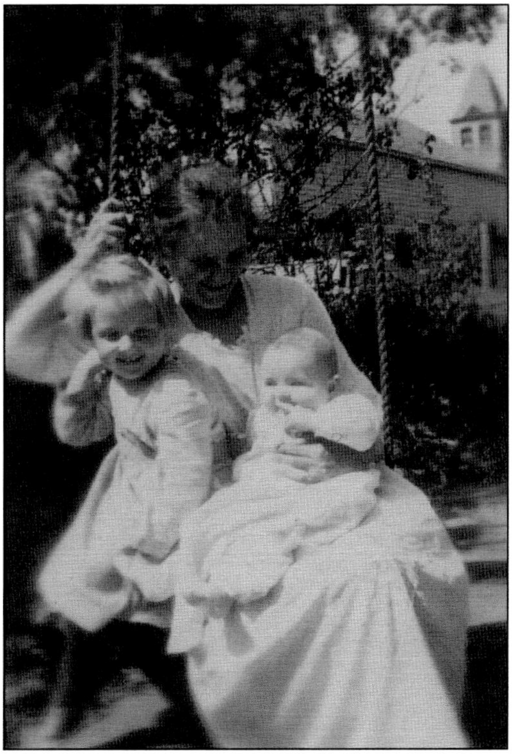

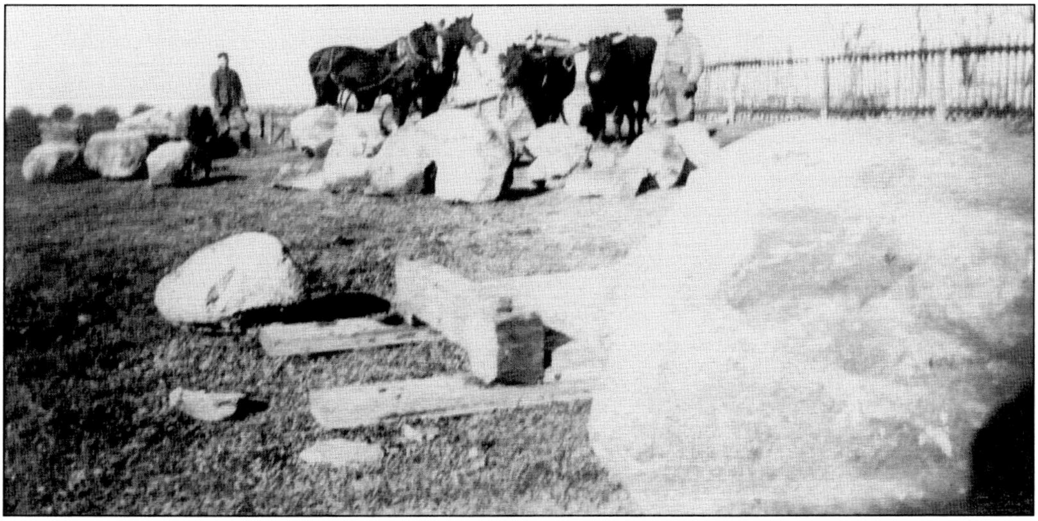

While the Bowens lived a very abundant life in Paris Township, fire burned down their original home in 1910. Afterward, the Bowens decided to rebuild. In this photograph, Burr Bowen, with his horses, Baldie and Billie, and Bostwick Bowen, with oxen Jack and Bill, haul boulders to be used for the foundation of the house to their property. Some of the boulders were too large and needed to be broken down with dynamite.

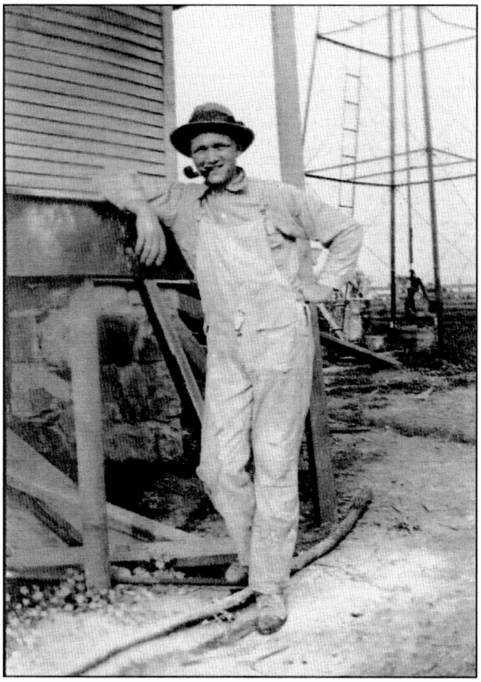

Clark Bowen takes a break from helping Bostwick build the new house to smoke his pipe and pose for a picture. Behind Bowen, the frame of the farm's windmill can be seen. Before electricity was brought to rural areas, many Paris Township farmers constructed windmills, such as this one, to pump water out of ground wells.

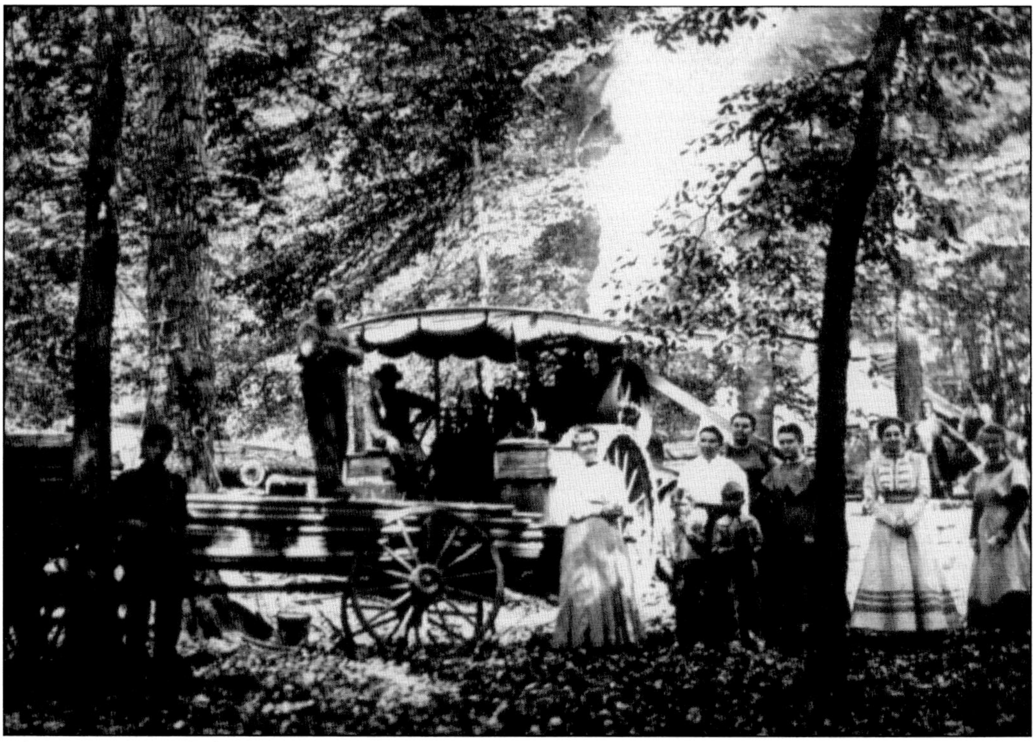

The Bowen family hired many laborers and housed them on their property. After a fire struck their house in 1910, the Bowens moved into the labor quarters. In the meantime, Bostwick set about building a new house. In this photograph, the family stands in the woods on their property as their steam engine, previously used for threshing wheat, cuts lumber.

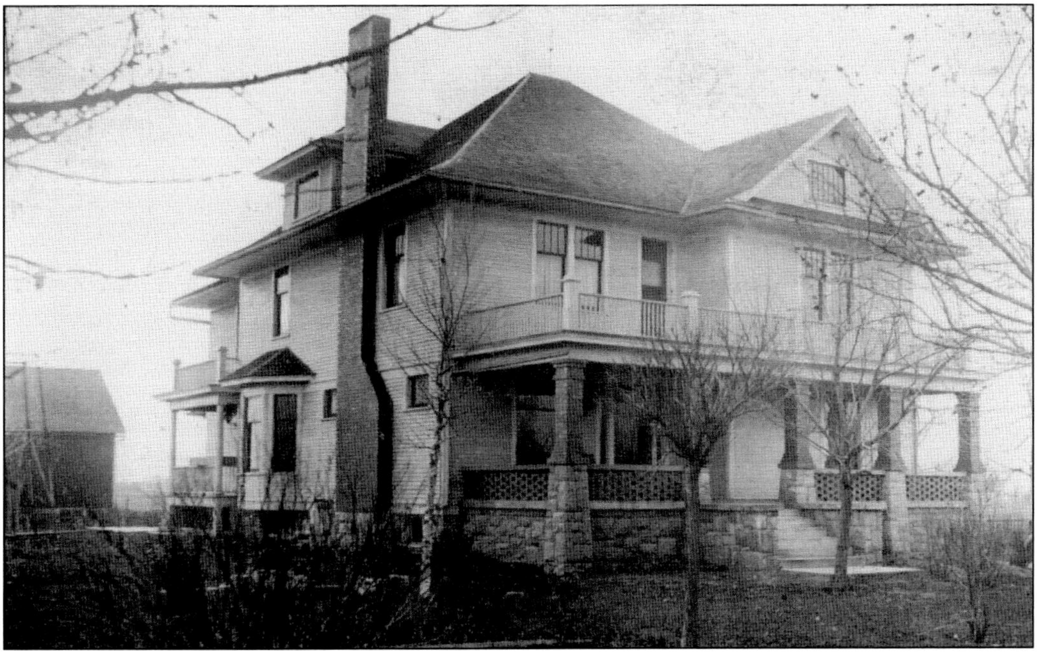

Construction was completed on the new Bowen home in 1912. The white frame house Bostwick had built was quite different from the house that Philonzo Bowen had erected in the 19th century. The Bowens had even carefully selected a variety of flowering plants, shrubs, and trees to beautify their front yard.

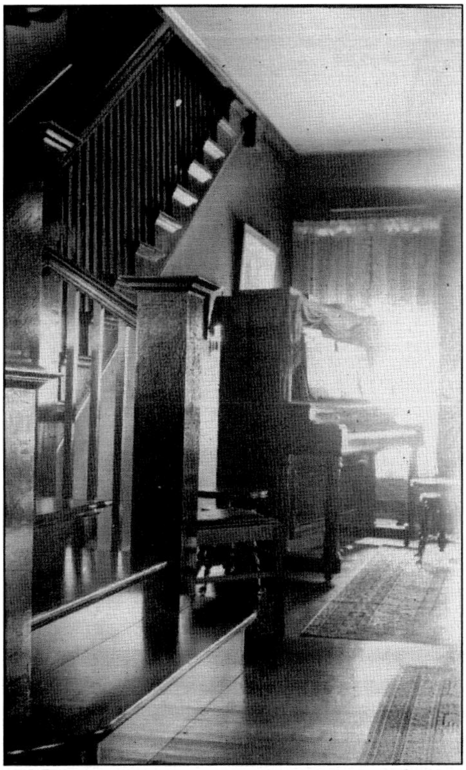

Inside the Bowen house, the living room had quarter-sawed wood, and each room in the upper level had a different type of wood. The house featured a speaking tube between the upstairs and downstairs and a dumb waiter. At the time, the house was not wired for electric lights because the Bowens never believed that electricity would reach Paris Township.

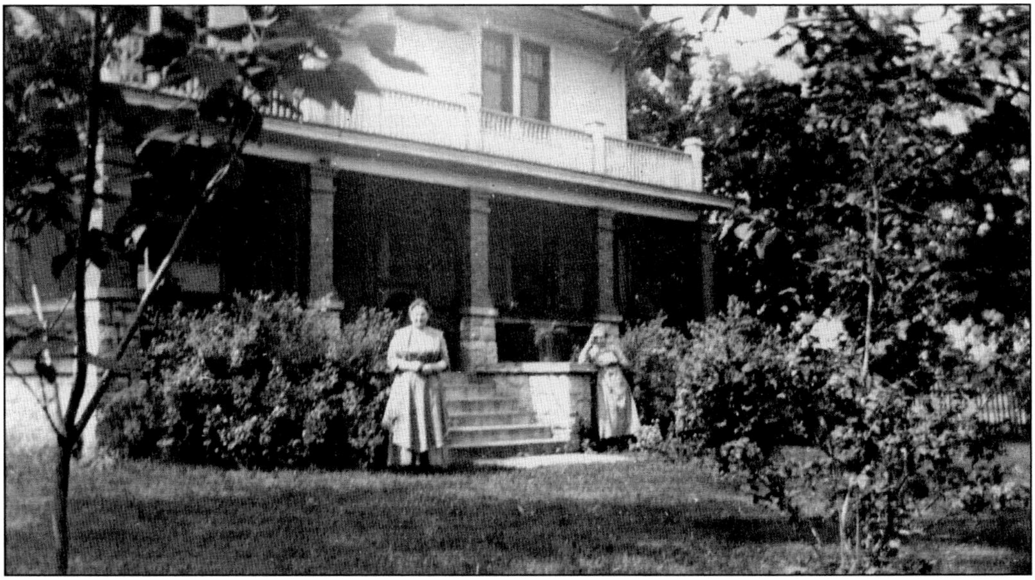

Hattie Bowen and her daughter Ethel stand in front of the steps of their newly constructed house. Although Ethel never married, she remained active in the community, often granting local interviews on her family's history. Until her death in 1973, Ethel lived in the house with her widowed sister, Cora.

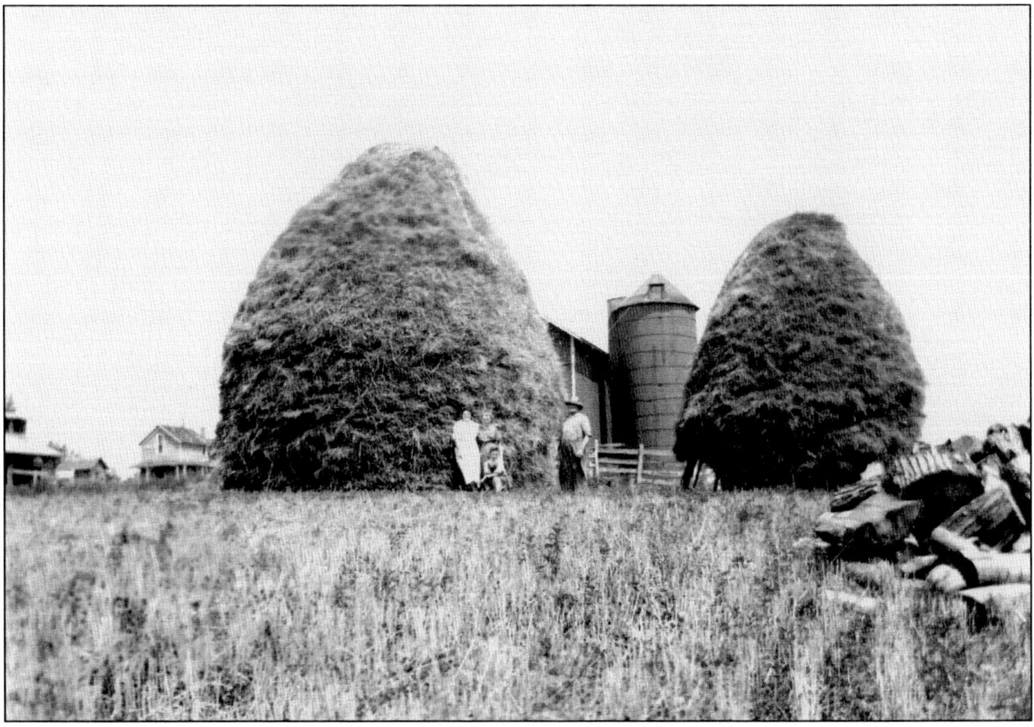

During threshing time, Florence Rogers, a cousin of the Bowens, stands next to a recently threshed mound of hay with her arm around Hattie Bowen. Bostwick and his nephew Jack (the one pictured on the binder on page 28) watch on after a hard day of work. Harvest time meant a lot of work for family and friends, but after the work was done, people gathered together and celebrated.

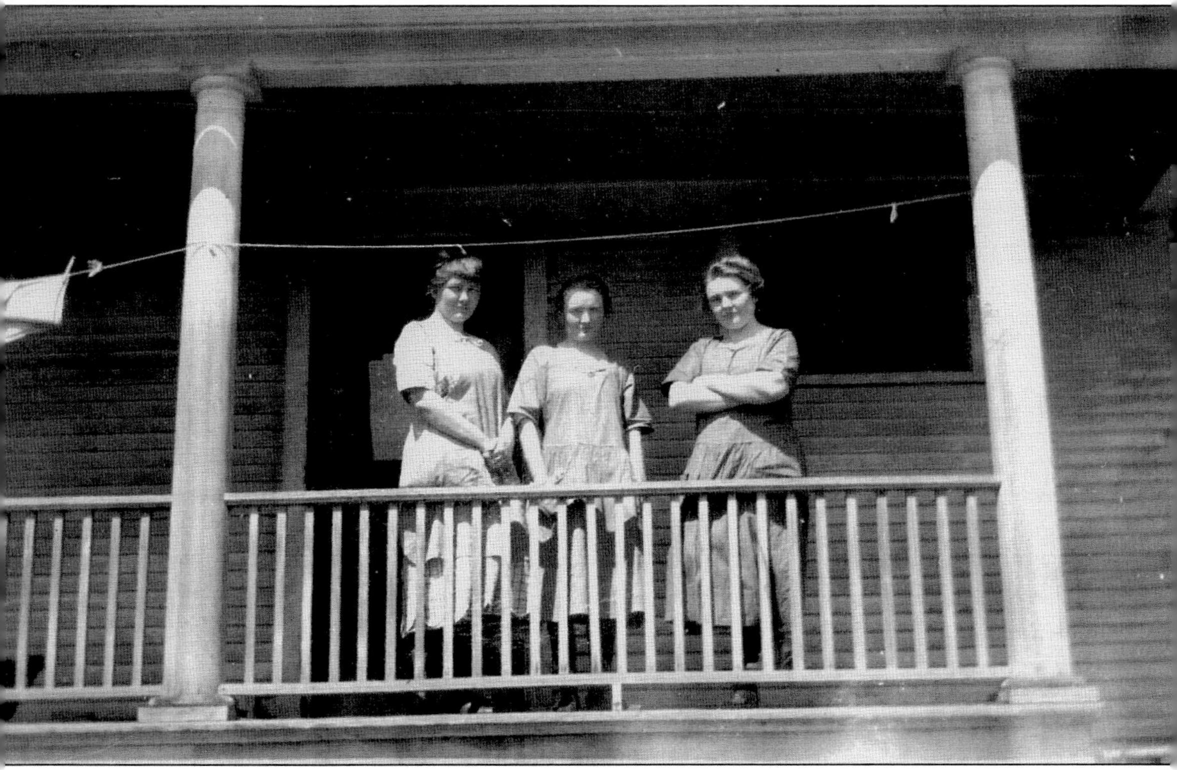

Jessie, Ethel, and Cora (from left to right) stand on the back porch of the Bowen house on laundry day. Without electricity, the Bowens probably used a hand-powered washing machine to clean their clothes. Washed clothing was later placed on a clothesline like this one hanging across the back porch, and was held down with wooden clothespins to dry.

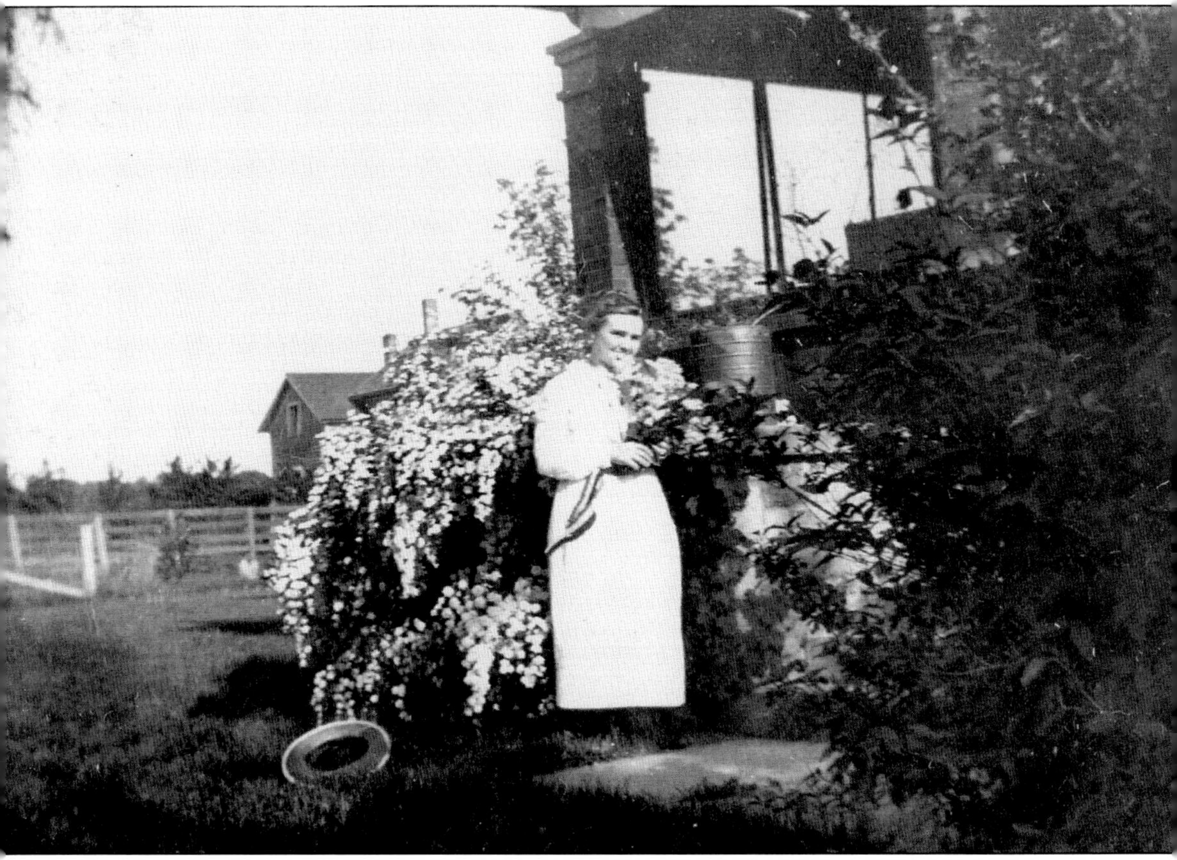

Cora Bowen takes a moment to smell an armful of spirea flowers in the front garden of the Bowen house. While the difficulties of farm life required farmers to focus on function over form, the Bowen family worked hard to make sure their house and property were attractive and neat.

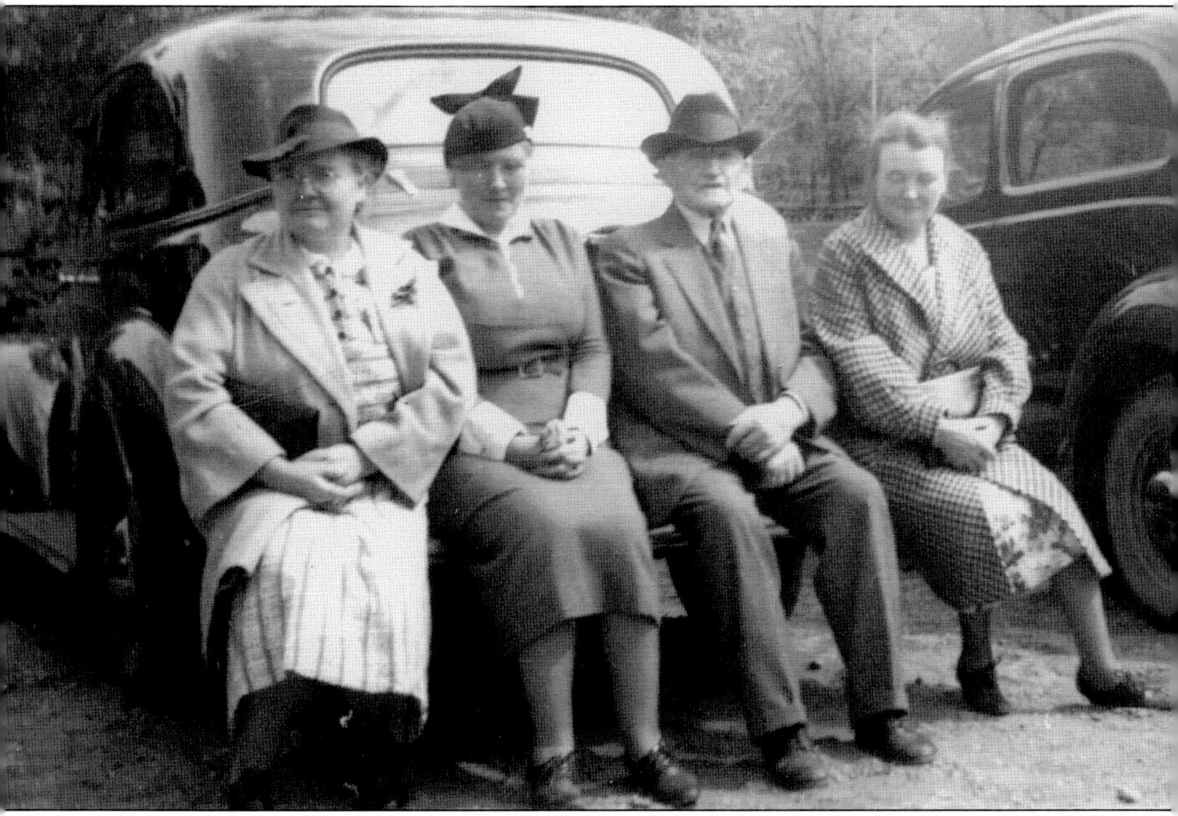

From left to right, Cora, Jessie, Bostwick, and Ethel Bowen sit on the bumper of David Stauffer's car for a group photograph. The Stauffer and Bowen families were good friends and looked forward to getting together. Cora even married Archie Stauffer in 1930. Although the couple never had children, they maintained a good marriage until Archie's death in 1947.

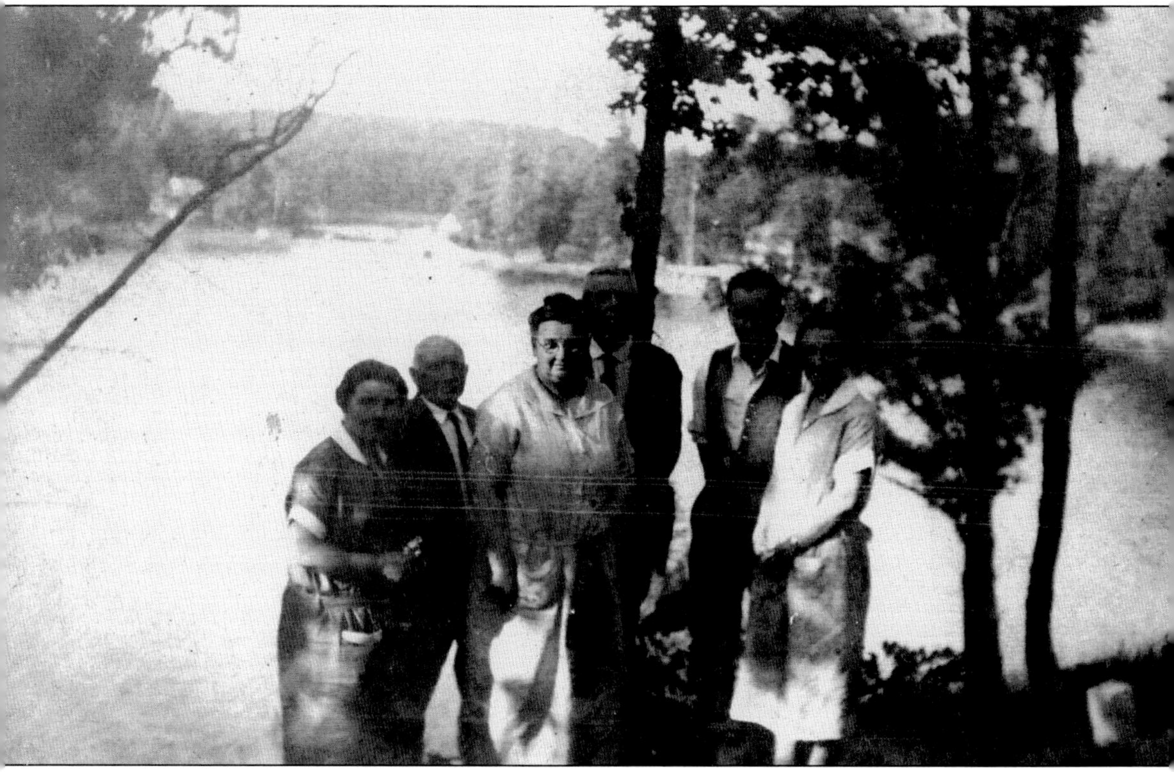

The Bowen family visits the Slawsons at Baldwin Lake. Pictured from left to right are Cora, Bostwick, Hattie, Will Slawson, Kent Slawson, and Ethel. The area, as it is today, was known as a vacation spot for West Michigan residents and offered a variety of relaxing activities, including canoeing, fishing, and boating.

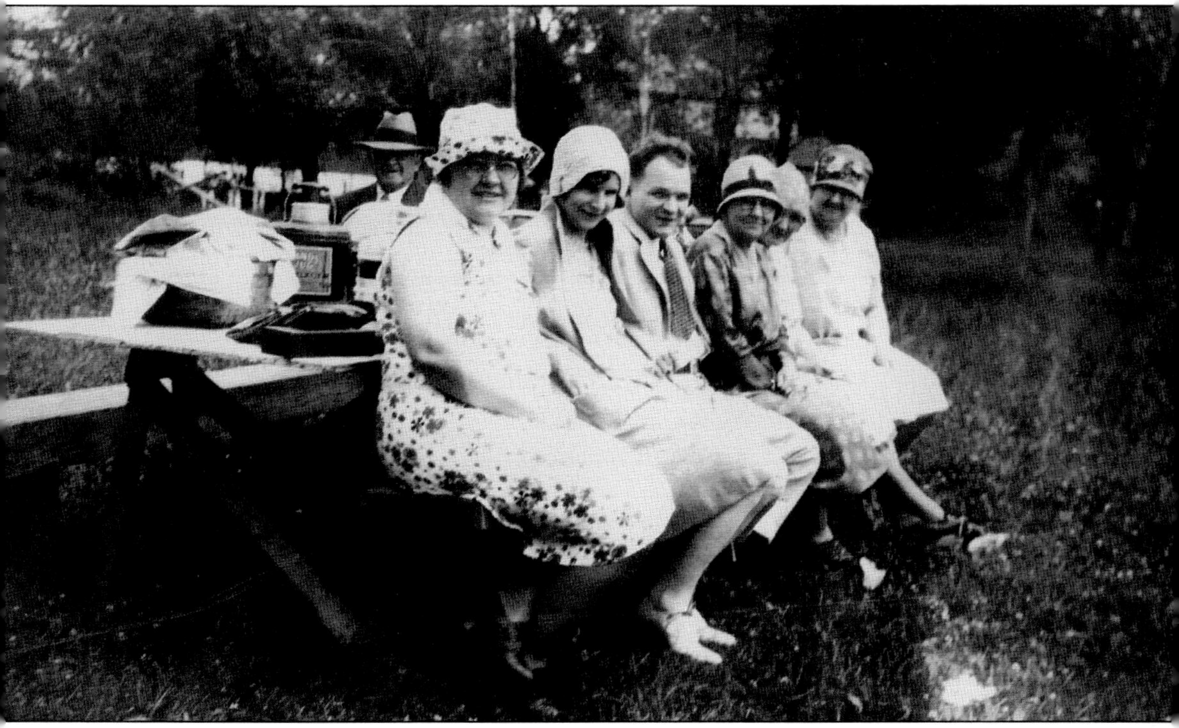

Reeds Lake was another popular spot for Paris Township residents to relax. The lake was located in East Grand Rapids, just beyond the borders of the township. The lake bears the name of the Reed family, who settled in the area. In this photograph, the Bowen and Reed families share a picnic table on the shore. Pictured here from left to right are Bostwick Bowen, Cora Bowen Stauffer, Lucelle and Collins Reed, Cora Reed, Ethel Bowen, and Hattie Bowen.

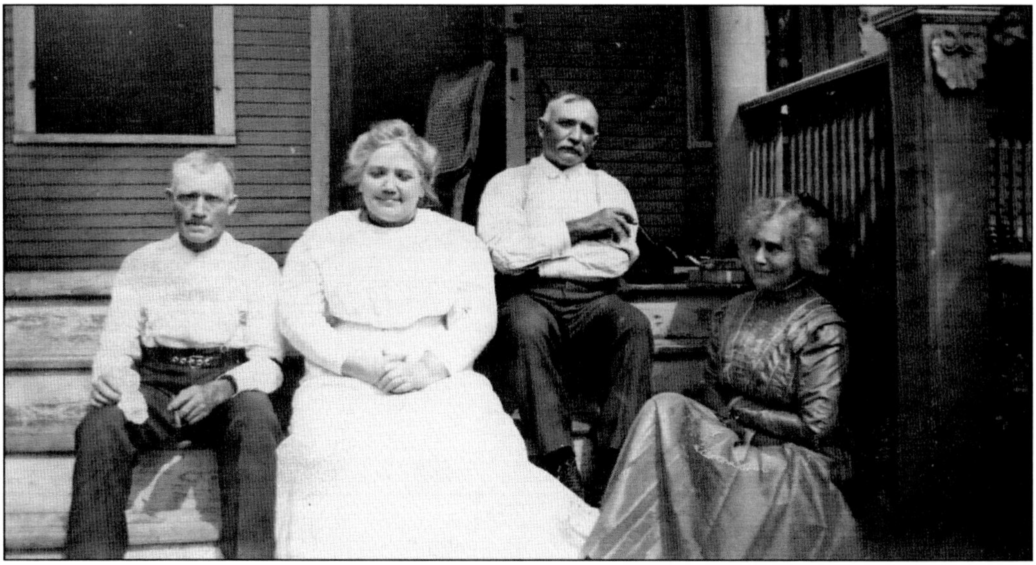

Orson Bowen and his wife, Mary, sit on the front porch of their house on Horton Avenue while Bostwick sits near his sister, Lora Bowen Tanner. In the mid-1800s, the Tanner family owned a mill at the intersection of Forty-fourth Street and Kalamazoo Avenue near the Bowen farm. Over the years, the two families maintained a close friendship. Lora Bowen was a dance instructor who married into the Tanner family.

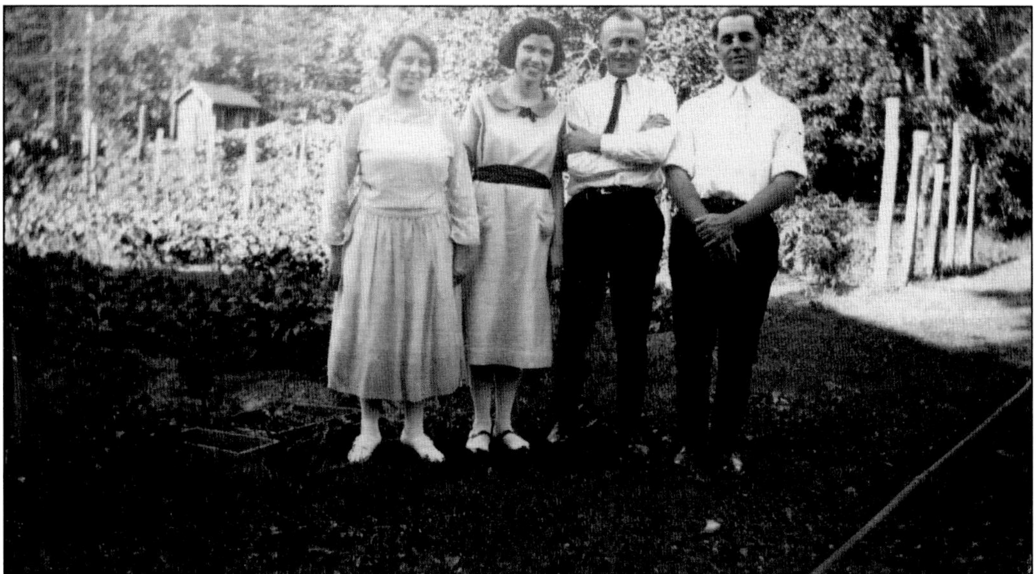

Don and Margaret Lakie stand in the garden of their Francis Avenue home with friends Laura Schuman and Ralph Rockwell in a picture taken in the 1920s. In an area where farming was a business, the Lakies' garden was a bit unusual. Don and Margaret grew vegetables and plants mainly for themselves and cultivated flowers and other plants on their property for beauty, not produce.

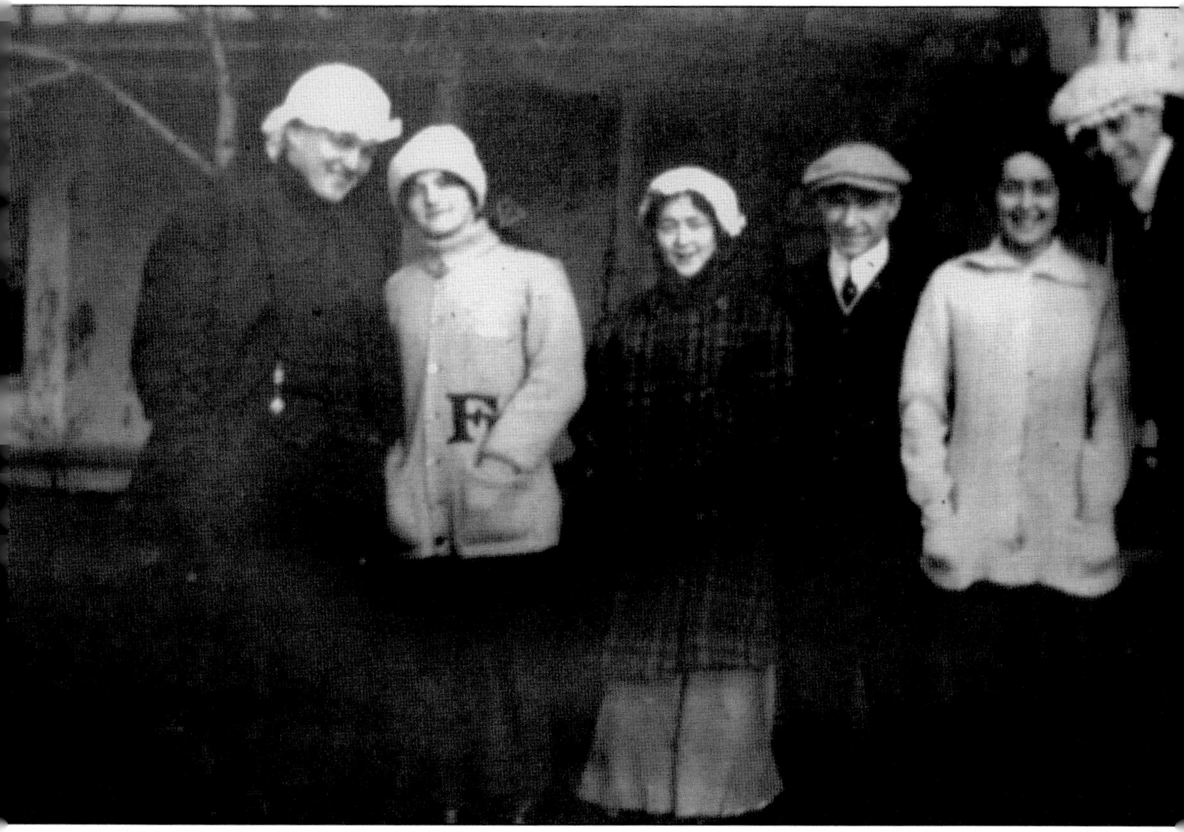

Friends gather together for a photograph outside of the Octagon House on an autumn evening. From left to right are Byron Cook, Genevieve Sears, Margaret Cook, Norton Warren, Fern Cook, and an unidentified male friend.

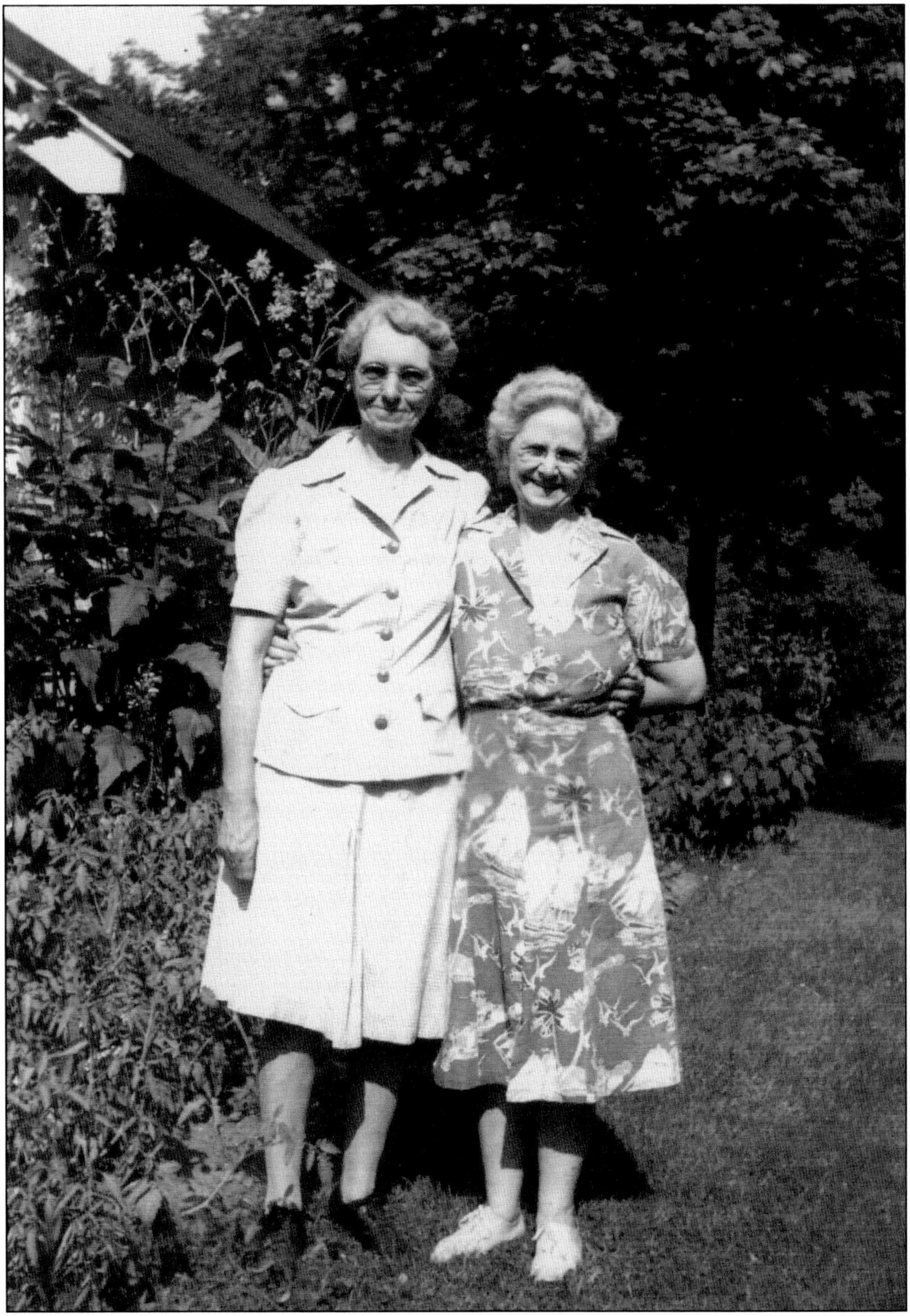

Even after years of being apart, many families in Paris Township made an unbreakable connection with friends. Friends Elsie Davis and Inez Manthe stand arm in arm in the garden outside the Davis house for a photograph together. Elsie Davis remained in contact with her friends until her death.

Six

A Community of Faith

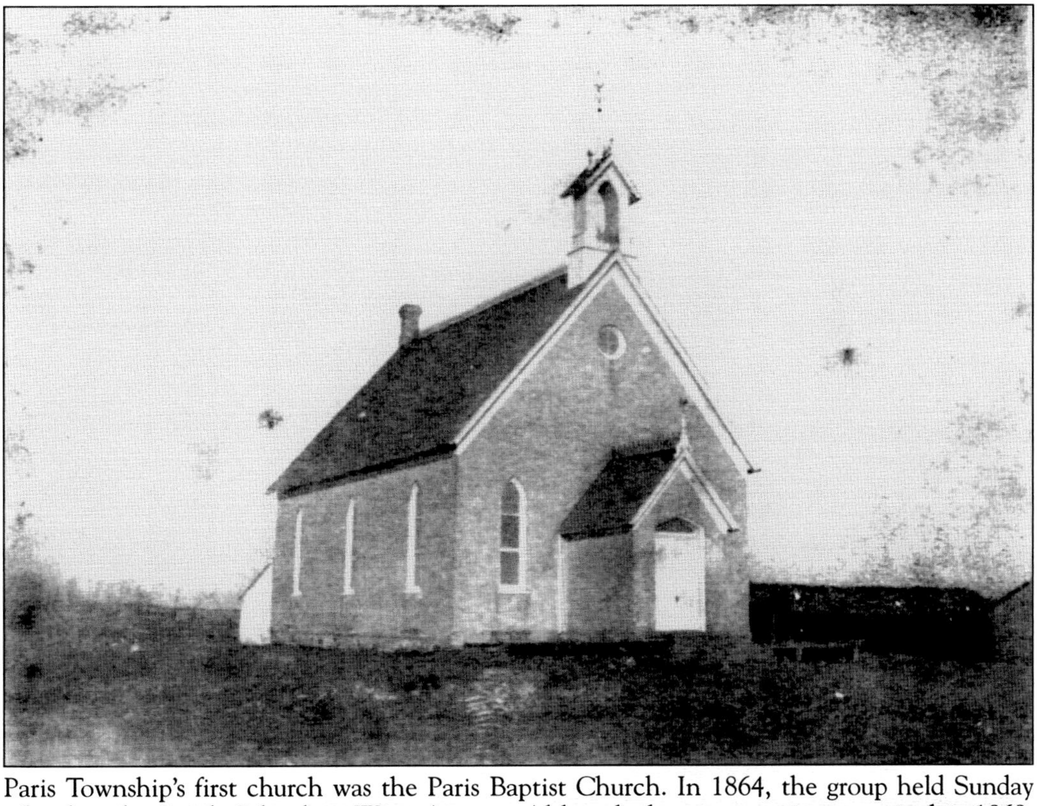

Paris Township's first church was the Paris Baptist Church. In 1864, the group held Sunday school in the Smith School on Wing Avenue. Although the congregation organized in 1869, members met in area schools and homes until 1882, when the first church was built on the corner of Fifty-second Street and Breton Avenue. A new church was built in 1958. In 1967, after Paris Township became Kentwood, the church became Kentwood Baptist Church.

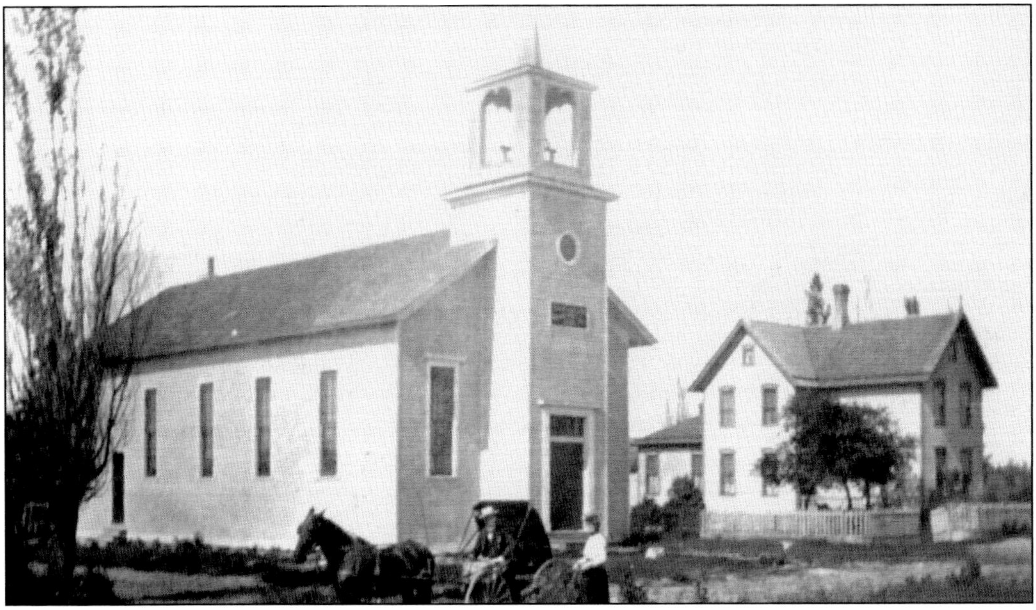

In 1875, Dutch farmers in Paris Township formed the True Holland Reformed Church. At first, the congregation met in the Blaak house and then later in the Troost home. In 1875, the church and parsonage were built on Fifty-second Street between Eastern and Division Avenues. Six years later, the church changed its name to the Kelloggsville Christian Reformed Church and hired Peter Schutt as its first pastor. Services were held in Dutch until 1919.

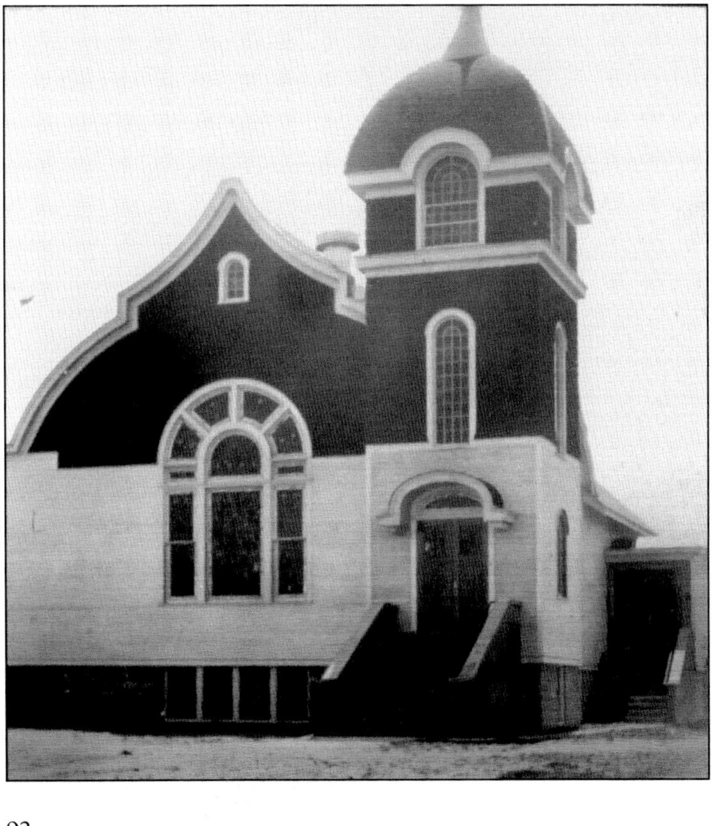

Other than an addition to the building in 1914, little had changed at the Kelloggsville Christian Reformed Church. Then, in 1919, fire swept through the building. Although members of the Heyboer family, along with Joe Postma, tried to stop the fire, their efforts were in vain, and the church was lost. Rather than disband, a new church was built and dedicated in 1920.

The Kelloggsville Christian Reformed Church tore down the church built in the 1920s and built a new facility in 1954 under the guidance of Pastor W. H. Rutgers. An addition to the church was built in 1970. The Kelloggsville Christian Reformed Church continues to serve the faithful in Kentwood in this facility.

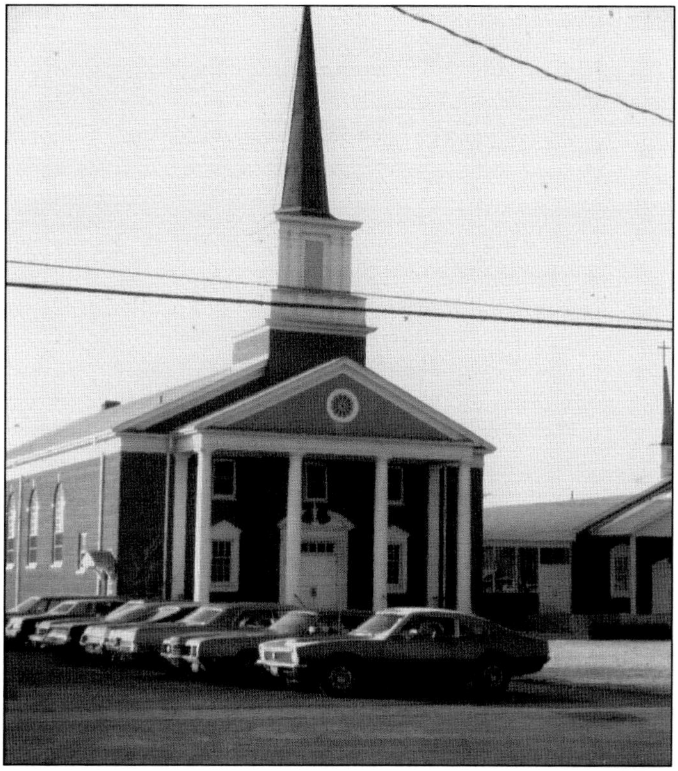

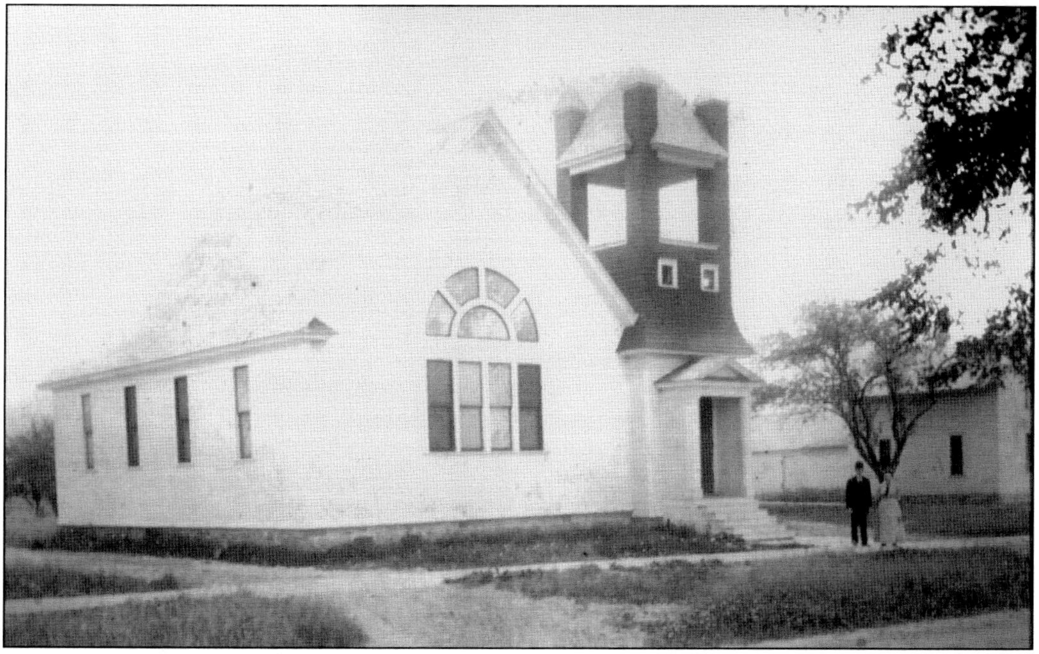

Before the 1900s, Paris Township residents who belonged to the Christian Reformed Church has to travel five to seven miles around the area to attend services. In early 1902, residents met at the home of Jan J. Oosterhuis to organize a congregation. They built the East Paris Christian Reformed Church in 1907.

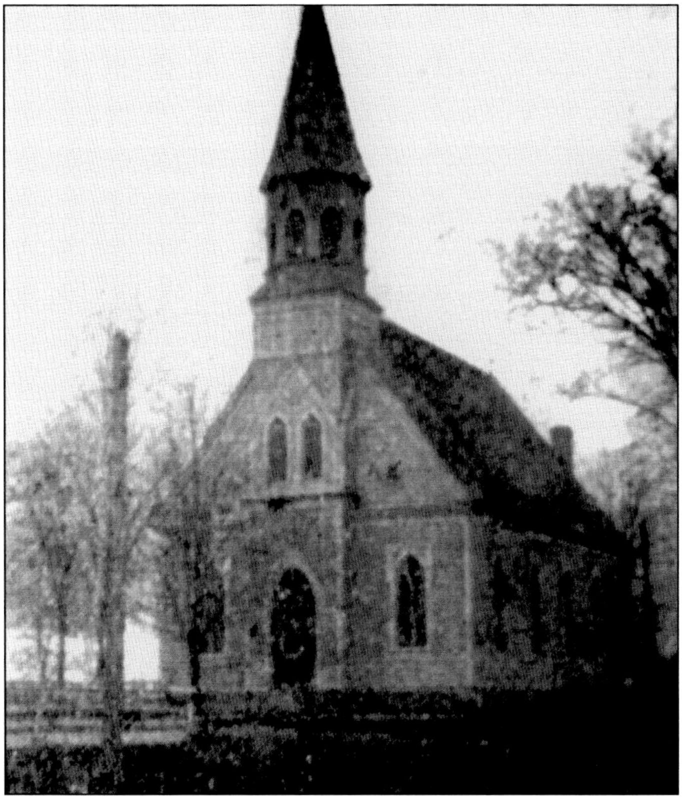

A log cabin near the Paris and Cascade Township border was the first home to St. Mary's Catholic Church in 1861. After the Civil War, a new church was built for the congregation in 1881. The congregation later moved to Caledonia, and for years, Catholic families in Paris Township had to worship in another community.

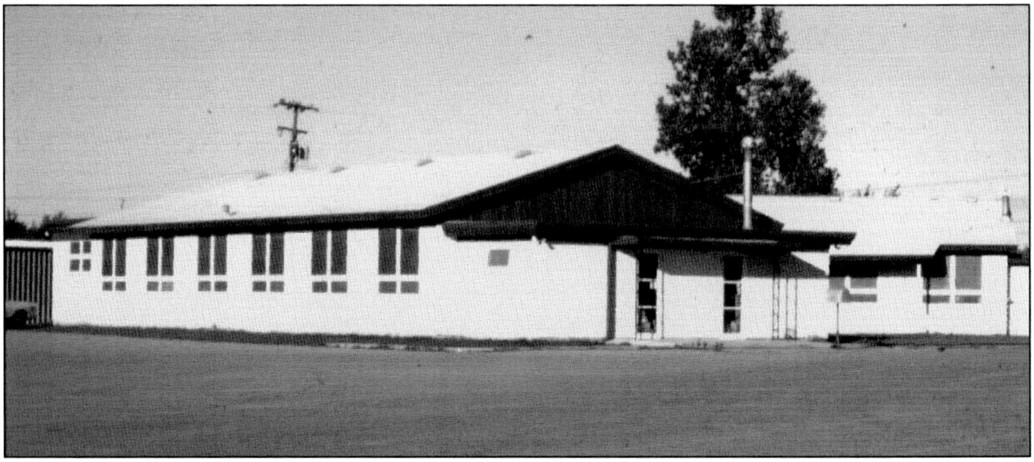

In 1956, a growing number of Catholics in the area generated interest in developing a congregation. Father John Breitenstein held initial services for St. Mary Magdalen in the Bowen Roller Rink. A portable organ and alter were brought in, and carpet samples were given for kneeling during prayer. Within a year, a new church (pictured above) was built on land that was once owned by the Mesnard family.

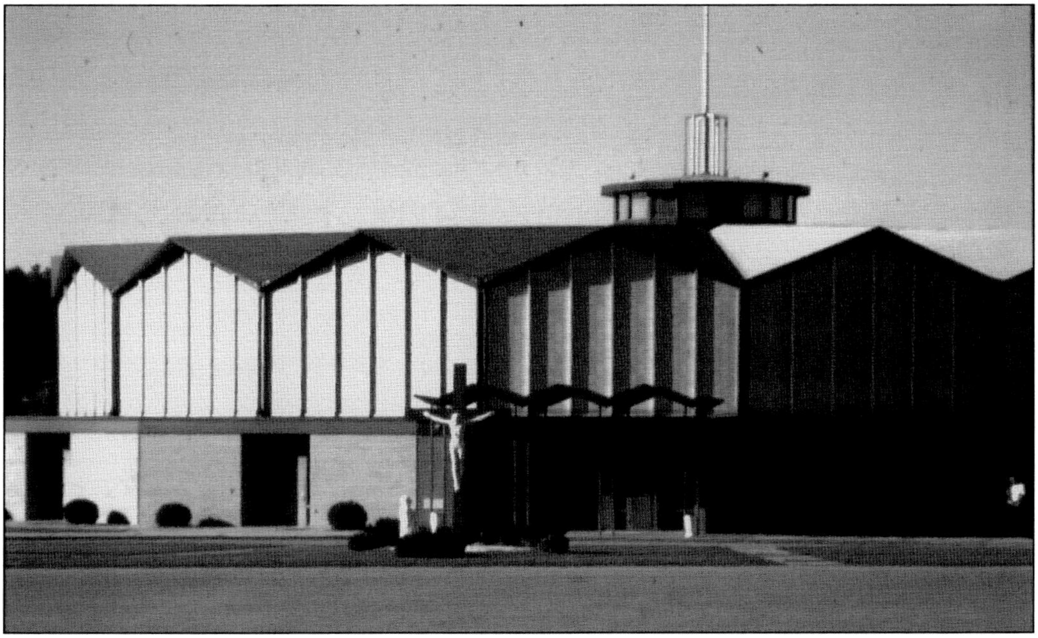

Even though they had a church, Father Breitenstein wanted a more significant structure. The new church had nine doors, each named and dedicated to a religious figure and all leading to the Alter of Forgiveness. Gordon Cornwall, a Traverse city architect, helped oversee the design, along with DeYoung and Bagin Construction. The new church was dedicated on Christmas 1964.

The Princeton Christian Reformed Church was established by Paris Township residents in 1962. The congregation built their church on Kalamazoo Avenue the same year. In 1965, Henry Vanden Heuvel became the church's first pastor, but at the time that this picture was taken, John Medendorp was pastor. Preaching from 1972 to 1991, Medendorp became the church's longest serving pastor.

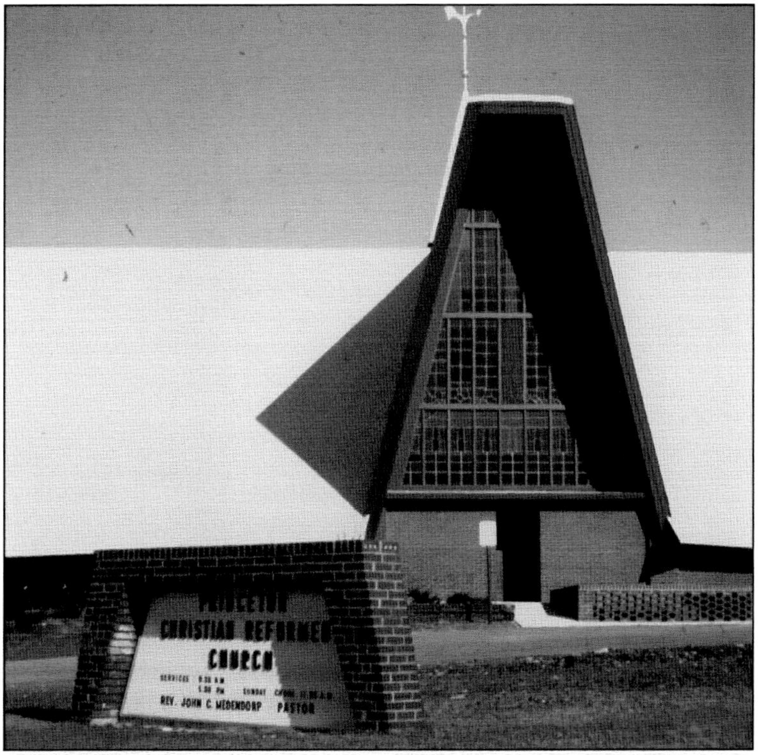

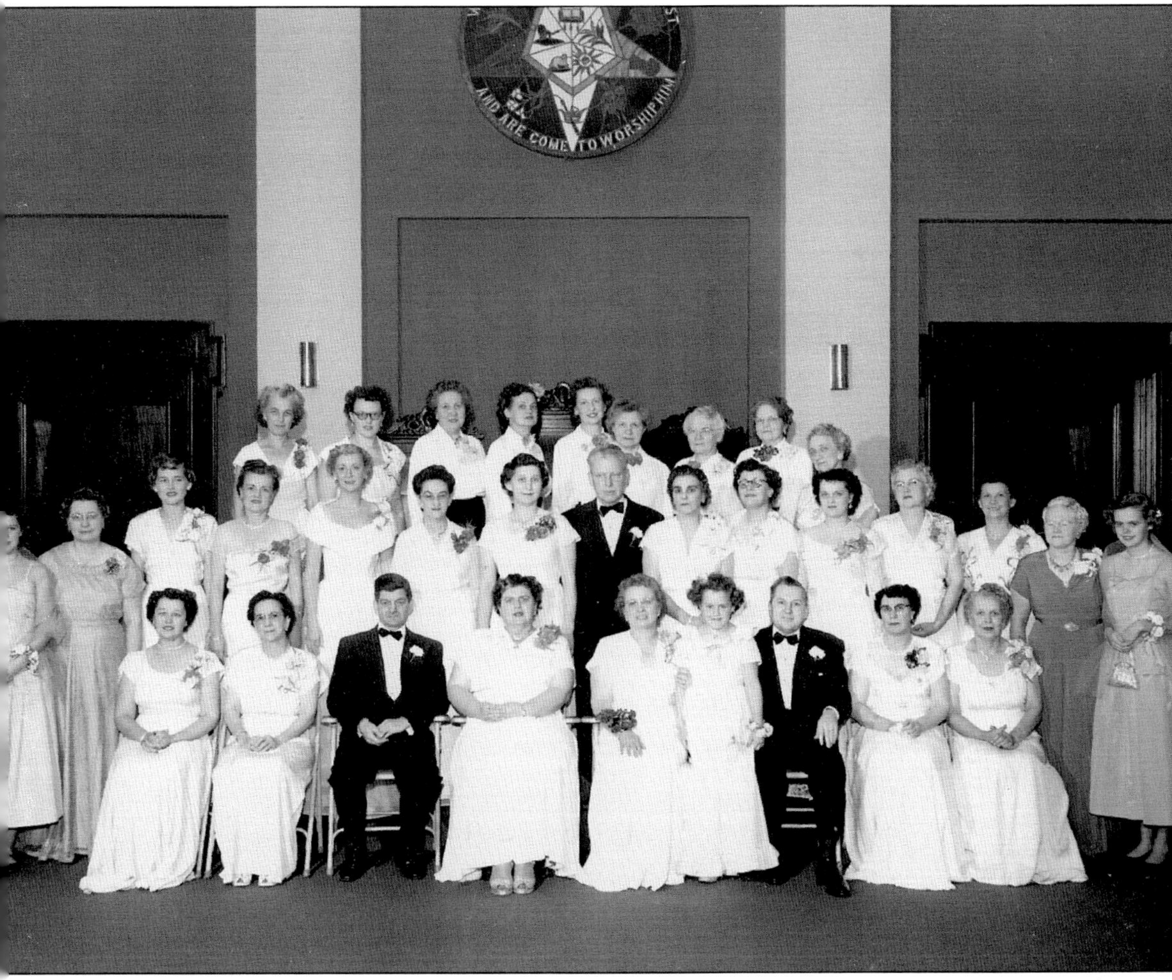

Many churches were dependent on their Ladies Aid Societies. Women in a particular congregation were invited to meet weekly for fellowship, stewardship, education, and charitable activities. The Paris Baptist Church had a very active Ladies Aid Society, which performed a variety of tasks. The East Paris Christian Reformed Church performed charitable work, including raising funds for their fledgling school.

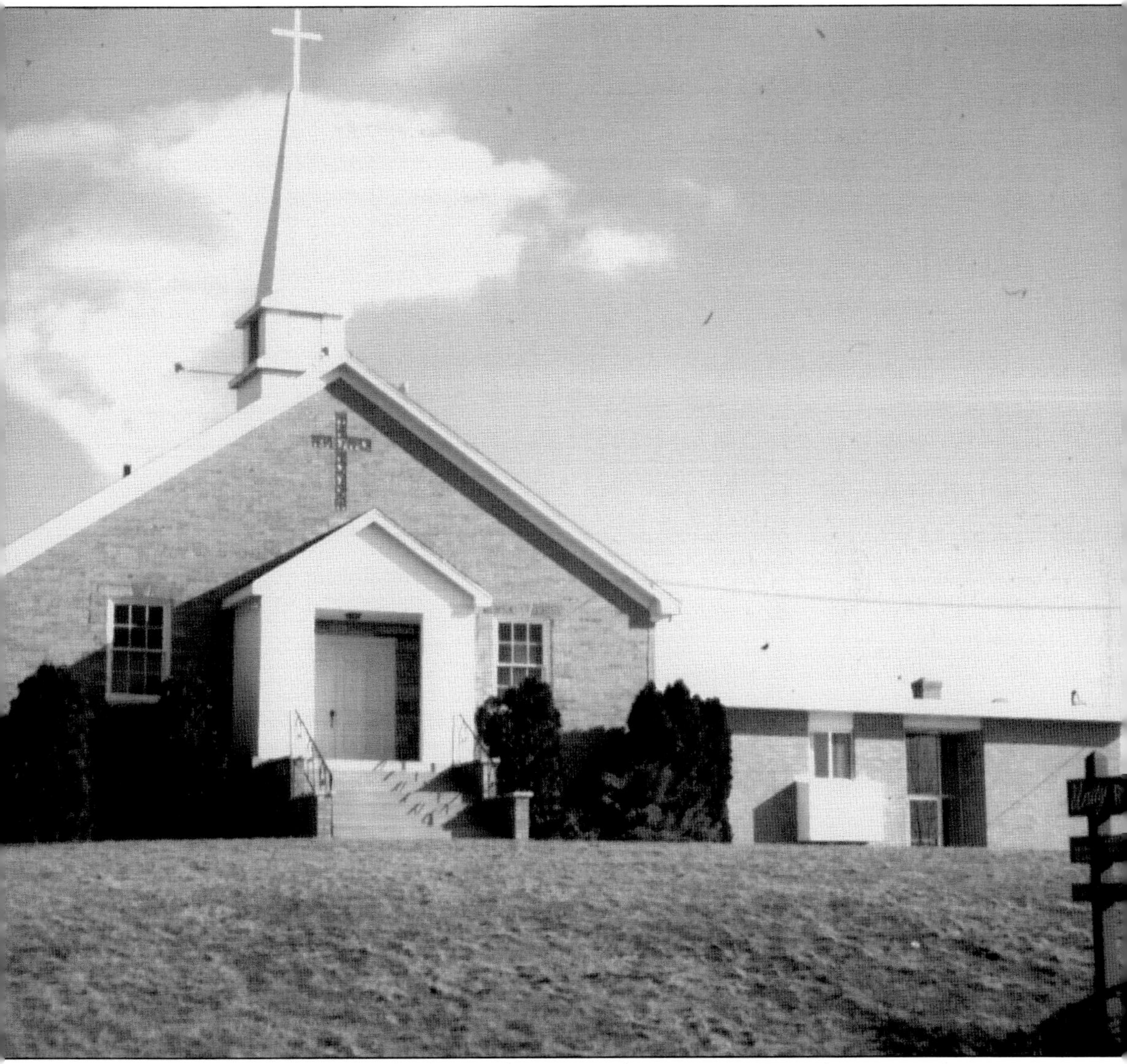

As more residents from diverse backgrounds came to live in Paris Township, a greater variety of churches were established to accommodate the community. The Unity Reformed Church of Paris Township was established in 1956. Its congregation met at the Bowen School until 1957, when the new church was completed. Richard A. Evers was Unity Reformed Church's first pastor. After this picture was taken, the church was renovated in 1965.

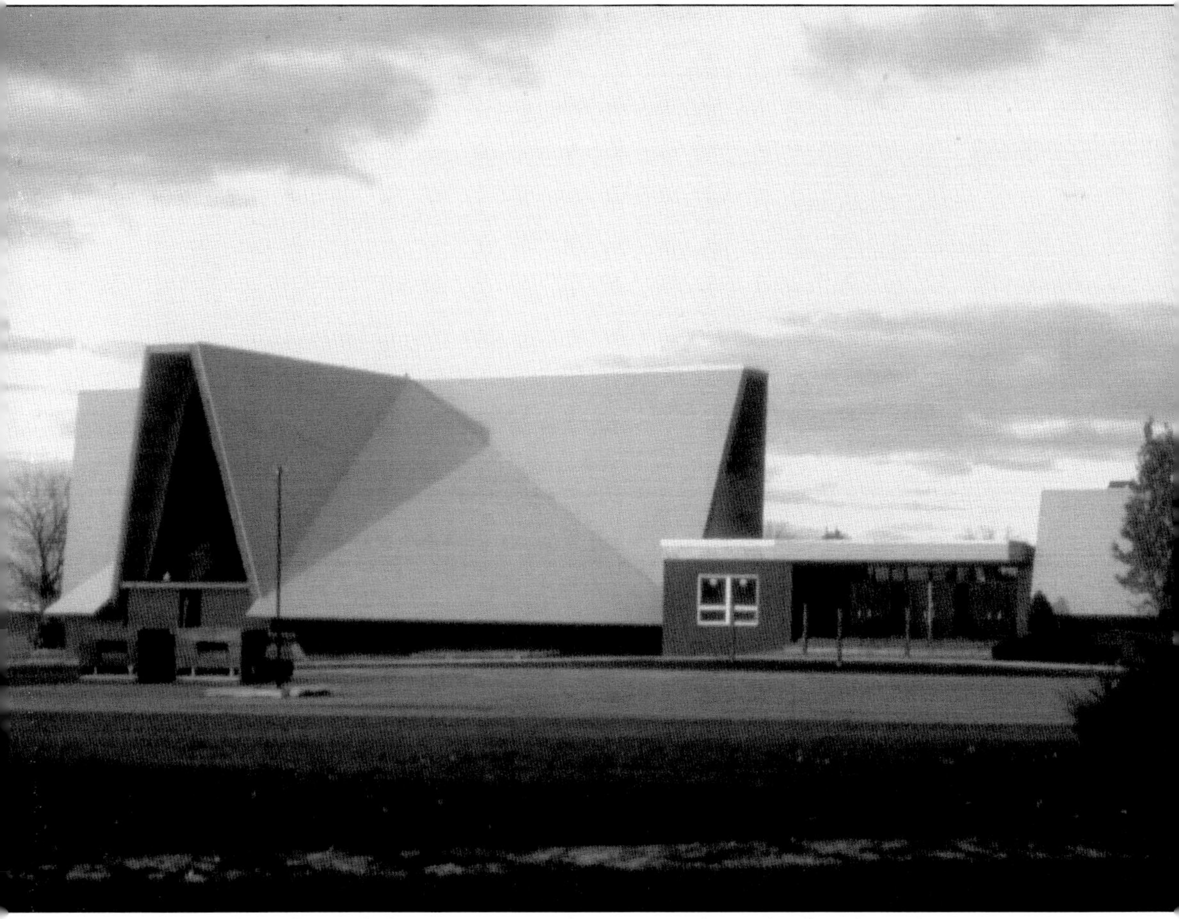

This is another shot of the Princeton Christian Reformed Church. After Princeton was built, other Reformed churches, such as the Vietnamese Reformed Christian Church and the Discovery Christian Reformed Church, were organized in the 1980s and 1990s. No matter the denomination, all of the churches in Kentwood provided area residents with the spiritual support that has defined the area.

Seven

AN EVER-CHANGING AREA

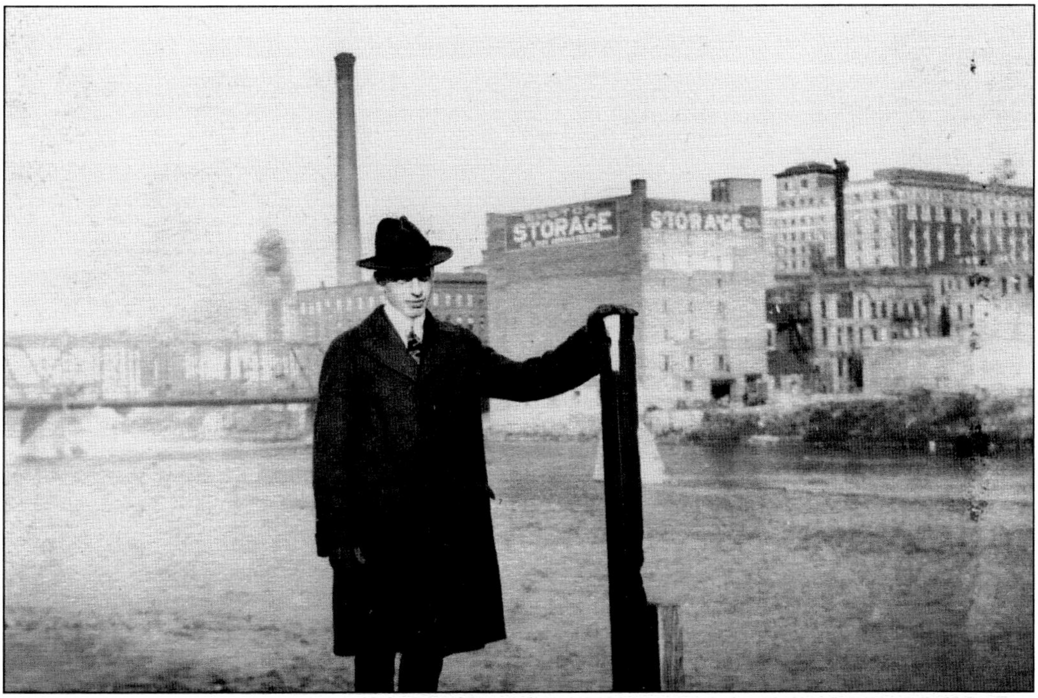

Paris resident and young businessman Morgan Williams stands on the banks of the Grand River with a view of the early 20th century Grand Rapids skyline behind him. As the city became the fine furniture capital of the world, Paris Township was also changing dramatically. Many of the changes would be physical, as farms gave way to more businesses and neighborhoods, while others transformed the way people in Paris Township lived.

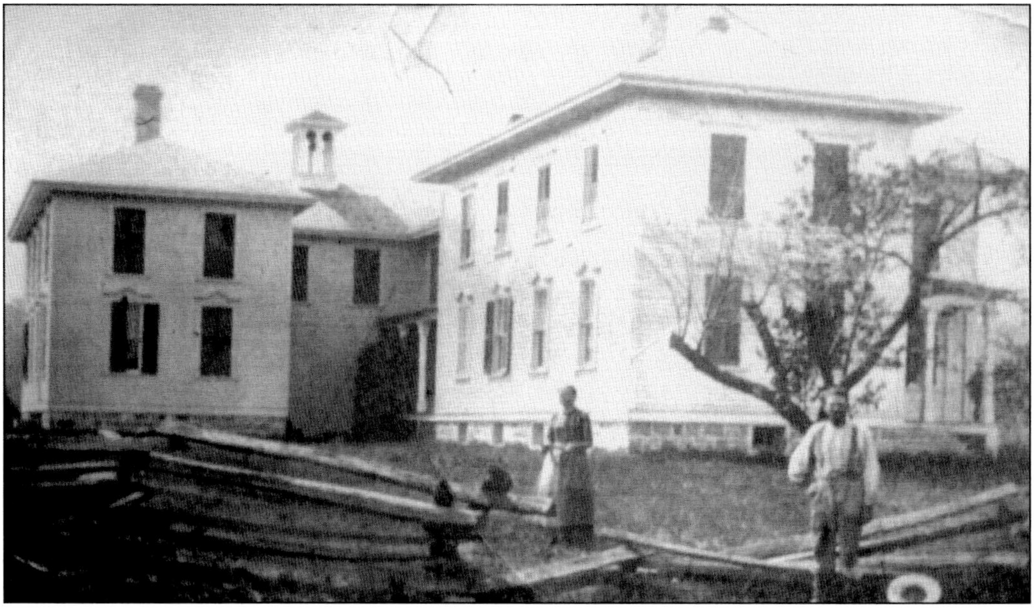

In the late 1800s, farmhouses like these were a sign of the prosperity of the farms in Paris Township. It was also a sign that life in the community was ever changing. The DeBlaay house, which was located at 5626 East Paris, was eventually moved to Fifty-second Street. In the 1950s, part of the house was destroyed by fire.

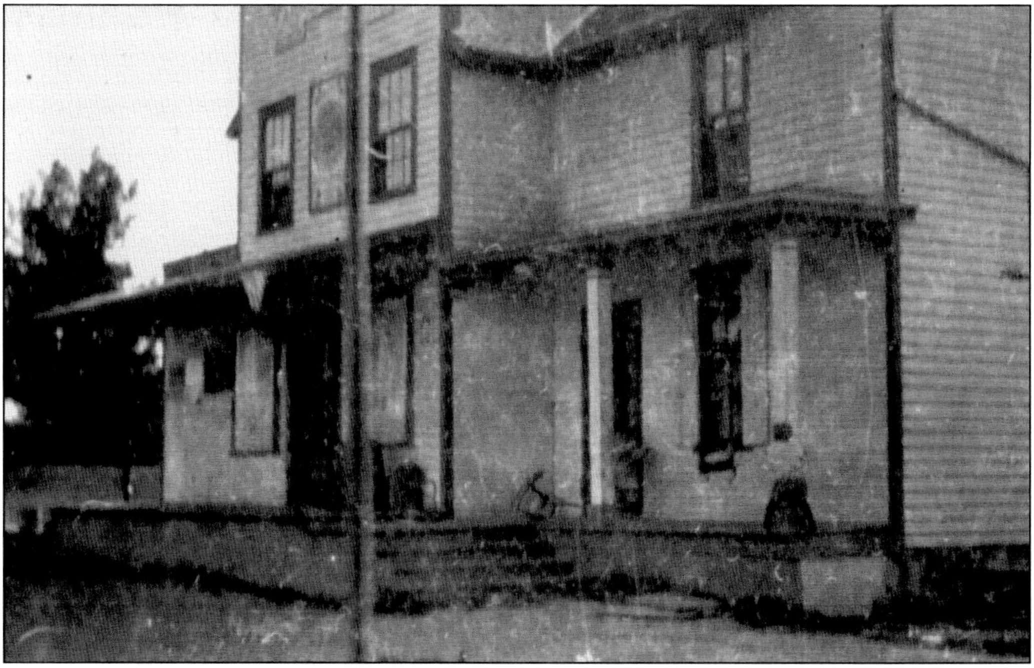

Barkley's General Store was located near the intersection at Forty-fourth Street and Kalamazoo Avenue. Over time, this intersection had a variety of names. When Tanners Mill was there, the area was called Tannerville. After the mill was abandoned, the intersection became Bowen's Corners since it was near the Bowen farm. In 1870, locals called it Bowen's Station since the Grand River Valley Railway Company built a train depot there on land sold by Philonzo Bowen.

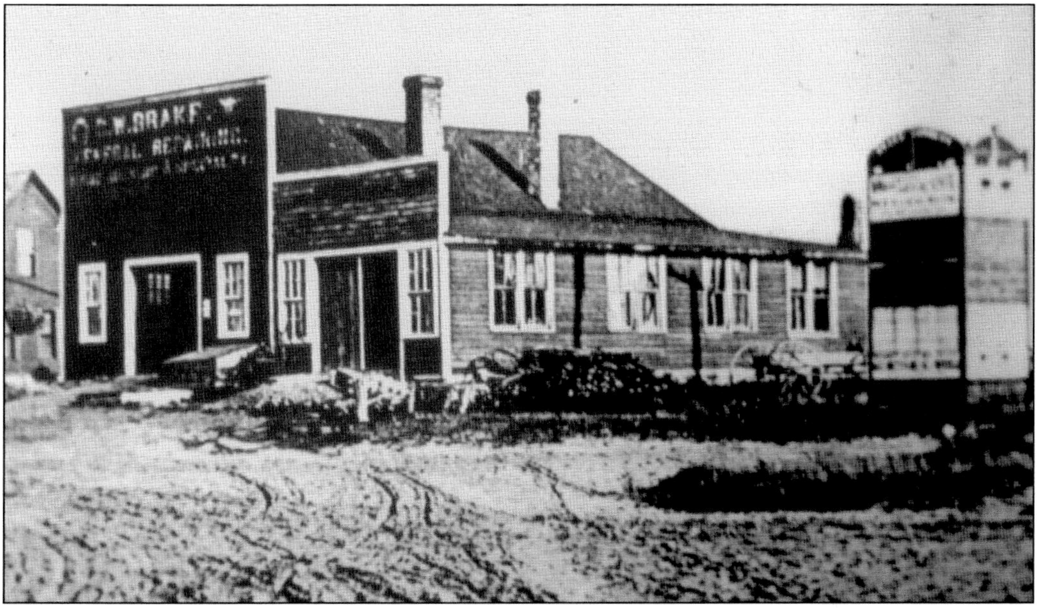

Wesley Brake owned a blacksmith shop at the intersection at Bowen's Corners. Many Paris Township residents became well acquainted with the shop after the Bowen School No. 2 burned down. Brake volunteered a section of his shop for classes, and many children remember watching the smith work. The shop was known as Bowen School No. 3 until 1905, when the new school was completed.

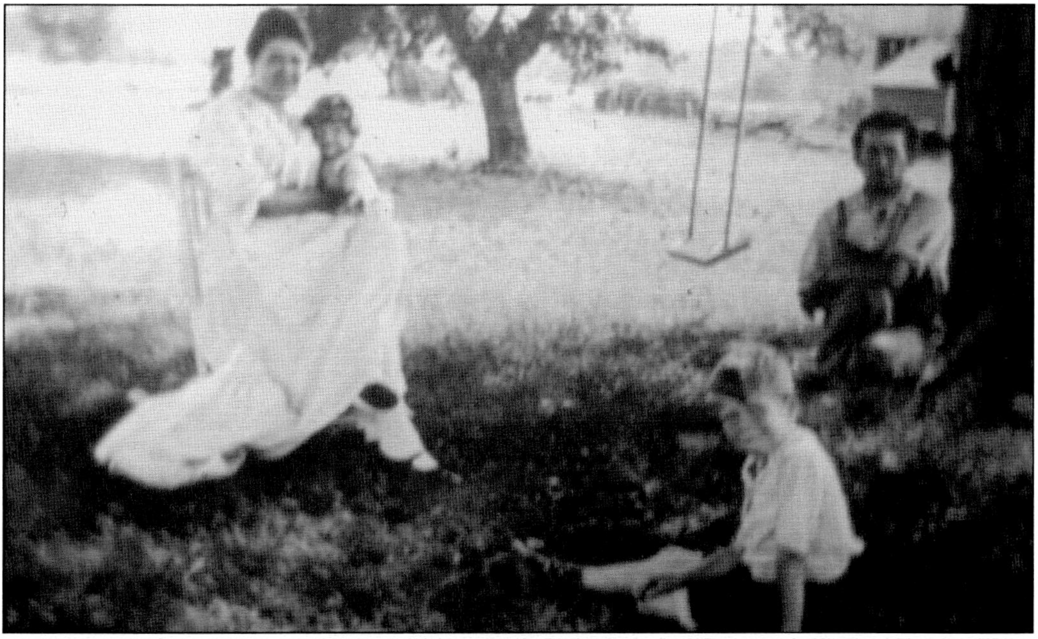

Mable Denison holds one of her children while her husband, Leon, and their son sit in the shade. The Denisons owned a store, which also served as a post office, on the southwest corner of East Paris Road and Thirty-second Street in Baileyville, a small business district near Sluman Bailey's Octagon House. Surrounding businesses near the Denison store included the Bailey Cider and Feed Grinding Mill, Jim Henry's blacksmith shop, and shoemaker Ben June.

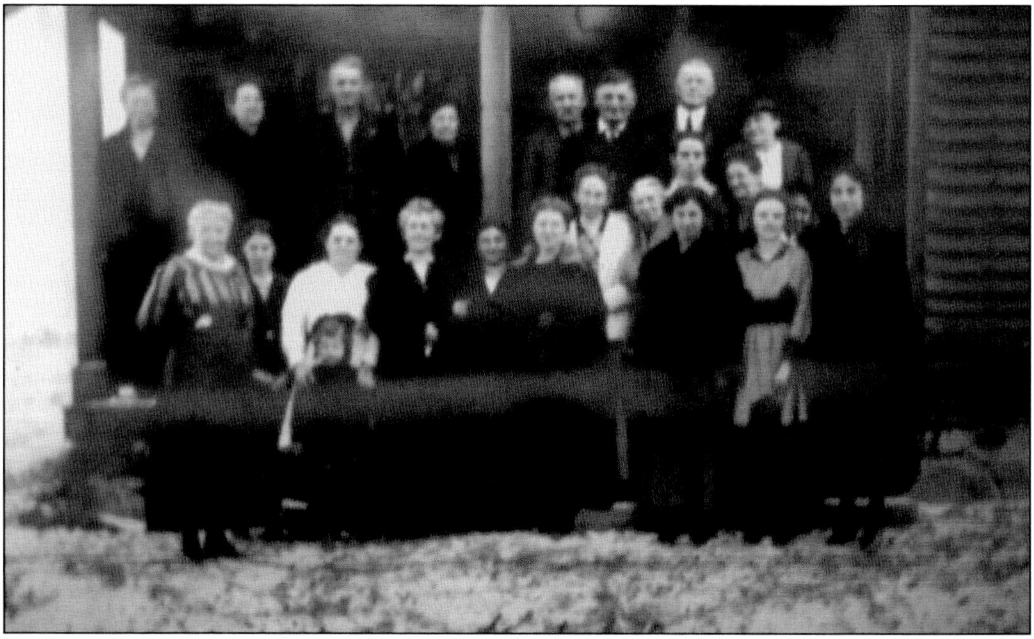

The Ladies Aid Society meets at the VanderBilt house. The VanderBilt brothers opened the first blacksmith shop beside their East Paris store. Unlike Wesley Brake's and Jim Henry's blacksmith shops, the VanderBilts never shod horses. They repaired farm tools and later tractors and cars. Naturally, they filled a niche, which enabled them to help others in Paris Township.

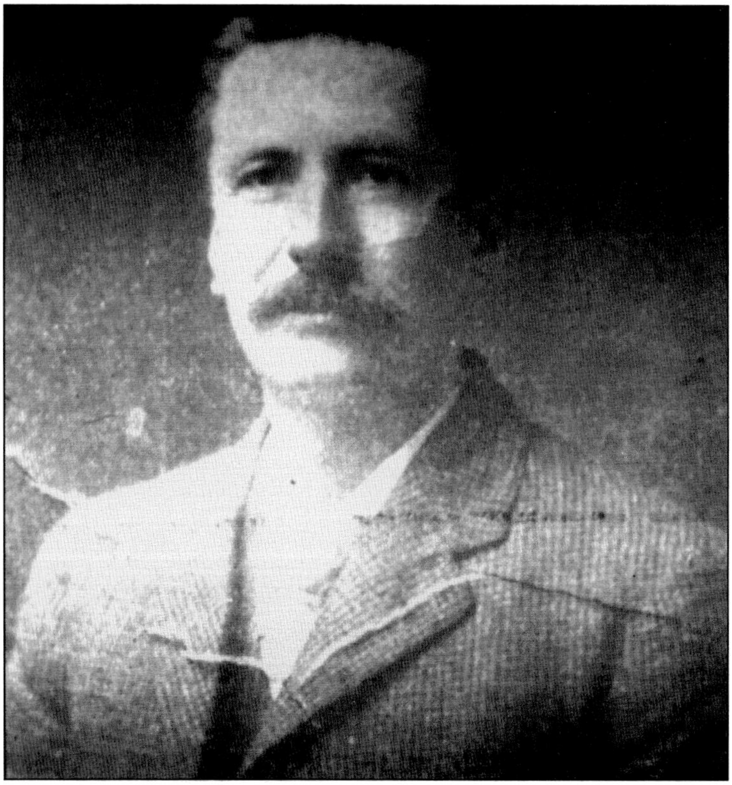

A. G. Burwell, M.D., sits for a portrait in 1907. He was one of many physicians who had an office in Paris Township and served the medical needs of the community. Physicians like Burnwell would have treated patients for common ailments like pneumonia, consumption, or rheumatism. He would have set broken limbs and treated injuries caused on the farm or in local mills.

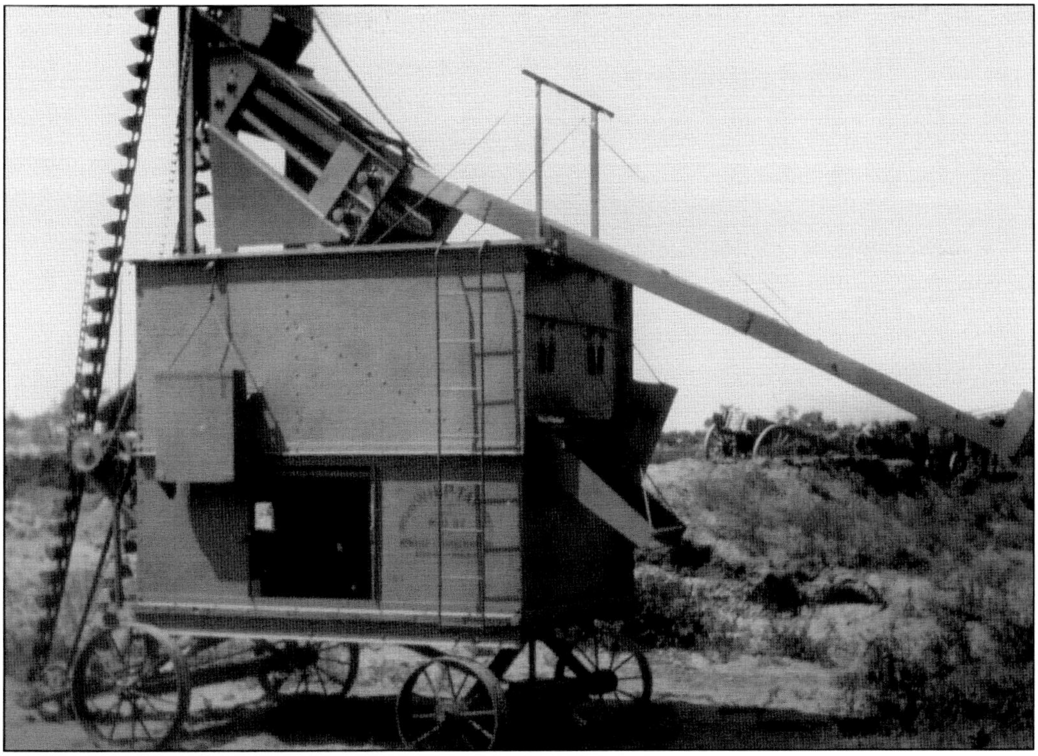

Paris Township produced a little bit of everything. At the corner of Thirty-second Street and Kalamazoo Avenue, gravel was excavated and sold to construction teams for building bridges and other structures, as well as to city governments for road maintenance. Behind this piece of excavation equipment, a gravel wagon and horses pull a grader. Paris Township also produced gypsum, a product used in cement, plaster, and other building materials.

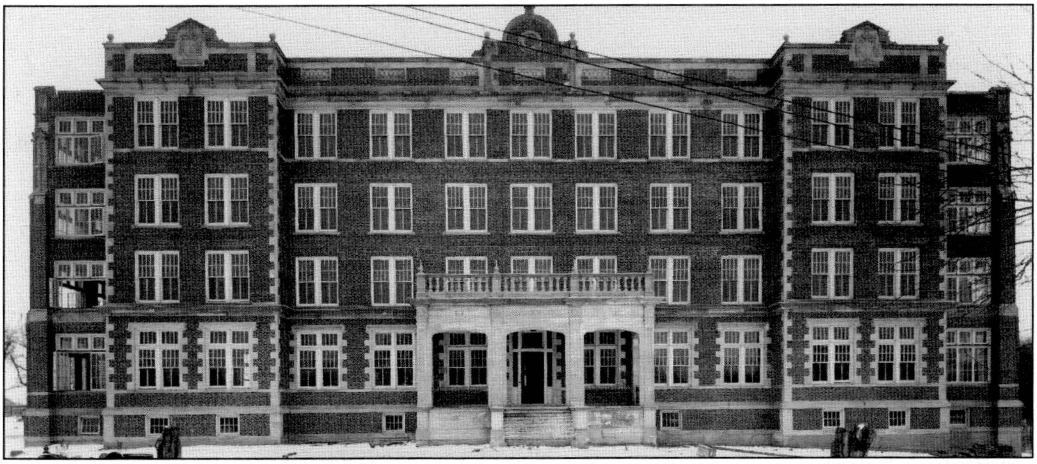

Paris Township was the location of the Kent County's poor farm. Opened in 1855 and supervised by Sluman Bailey, the 104-acre facility housed the elderly, the destitute, and the handicapped. Over time, attitudes about the elderly, ill, and handicapped changed. In the 1950s, the institute became Maple Grove Medical Facility and treated individuals with chronic illnesses. In 1968, the institute moved to the recently annexed Fuller Avenue and became the Kent Community Hospital (pictured above).

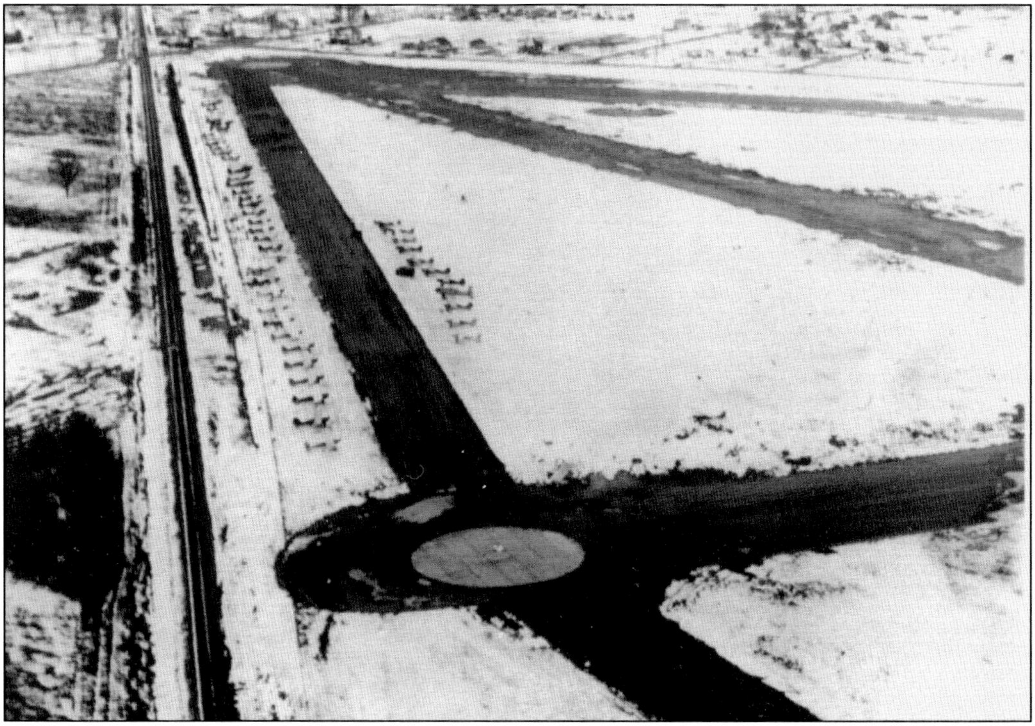

Paris Township was the site of the Kent County Agricultural Society in 1855. By 1900, however, the fairground was abandoned. Over the next decade, it was used as a horse racetrack and a work farm for criminals. In 1919, the land was chosen by the Grand Rapids Aero Club to be Kent County's first airport. This aerial photograph shows a view of the Kent County Airport runway.

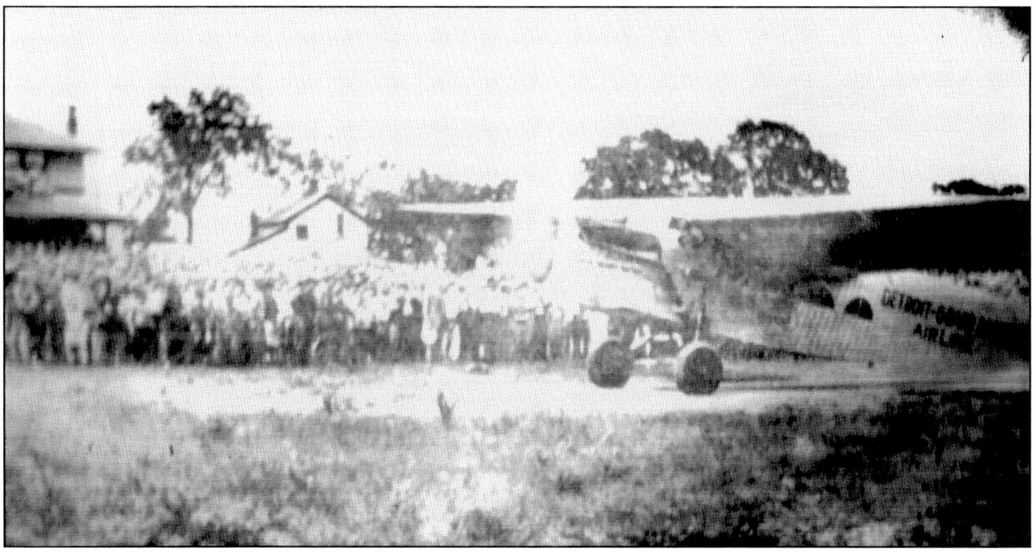

On July 31, 1926, the Kent County Airport became the first airport in the United States to offer regular passenger flights. While leading the country, Paris Township remained a rural area. In the background of this photograph, the VanDyke farm can be seen. The family had moved to the farm the year before the land was selected for the future airport. Over the years, they continued to maintain their farm, which bordered the runways.

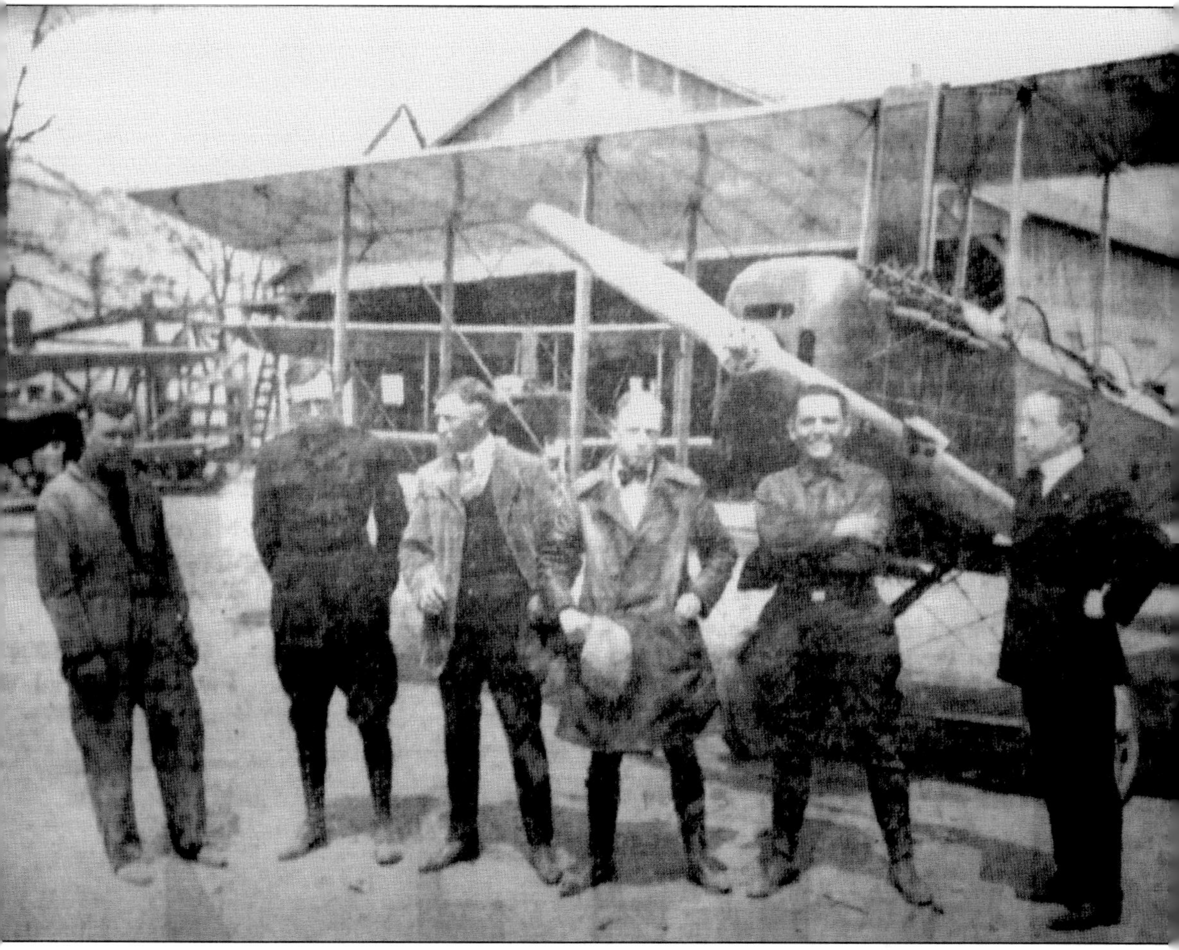

Many local Paris Township residents were bitten with the flying bug and worked in the airport. Pilots pictured here from left to right are Bert Harsell, Mr. Bishop, Bert Kenyon, Jewell Clark, Nathan "Frenchy" Michaelson, and Art Rosenthall. Even VanDyke's oldest son, Joe Jr., worked out of the airport as a barnstormer for area farms.

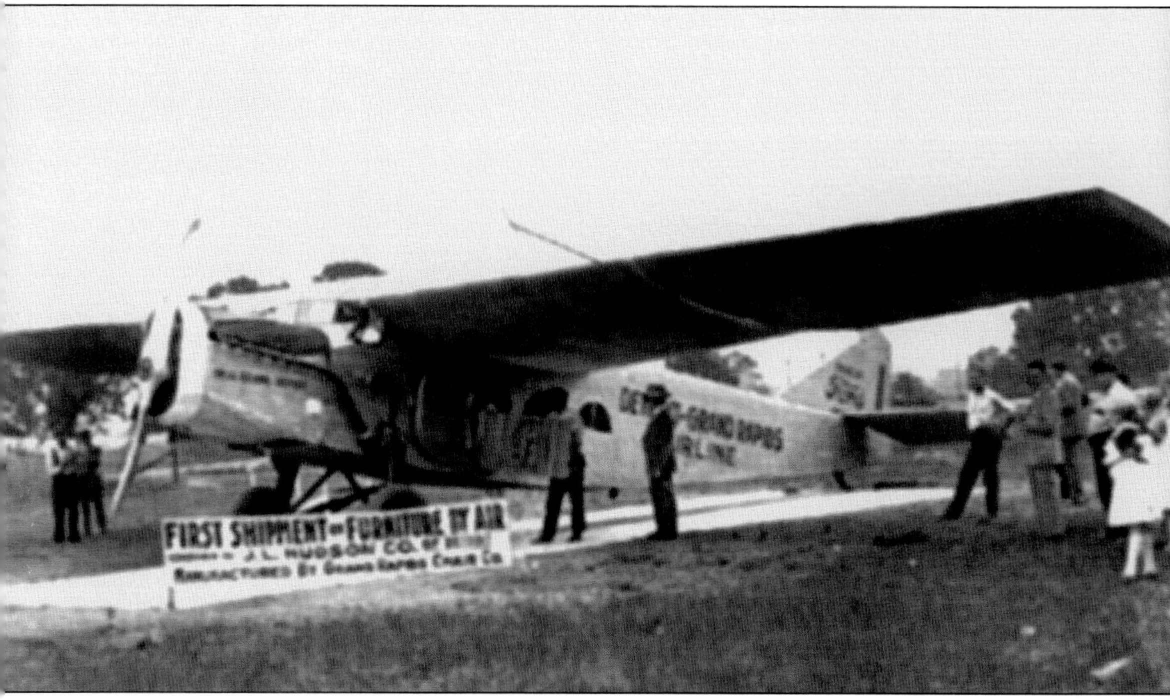

While regular passenger flights between the Kent County Airport and Detroit took off in 1926, Grand Rapids officials knew they were only scratching the surface of the airports capabilities. Two years later, the city promoted its new airport and its status as a furniture center by shipping furniture, including chairs created by the Grand Rapids Chair Company, by air. Miss Grand Rapids went along for the ride.

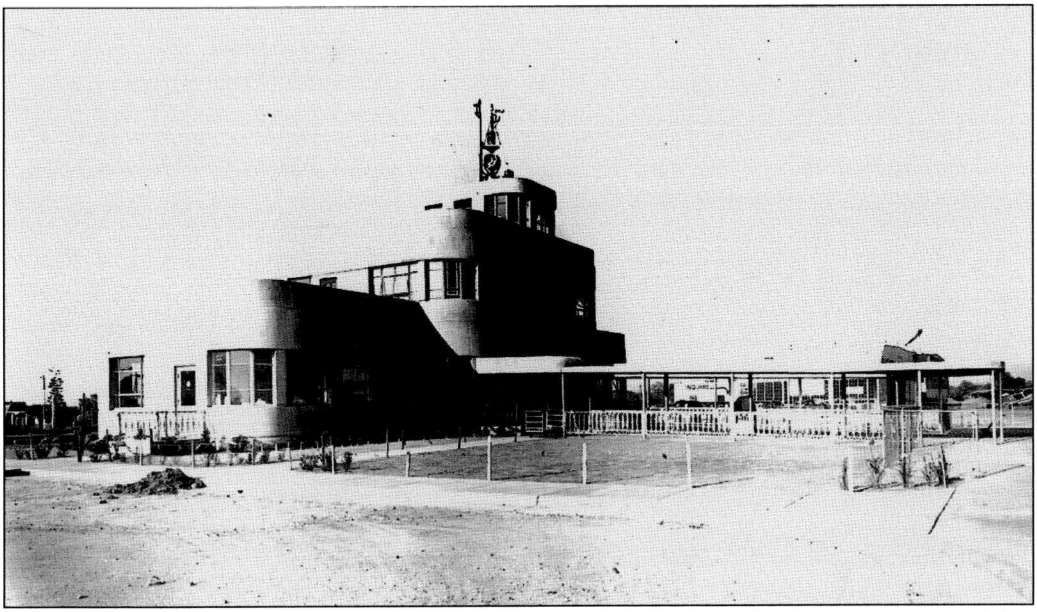

When the airport opened, many of the buildings and hangars were rudimentary structures. After new structures were built, the airfield's manager, Tom Walsh, wanted to bring attention to the airport. During the Depression, the airport received WPA funds. With these funds, they built an art deco–style administration building and terminal in 1939. The airport remained in use until 1963, when a new facility was built in Cascade Township.

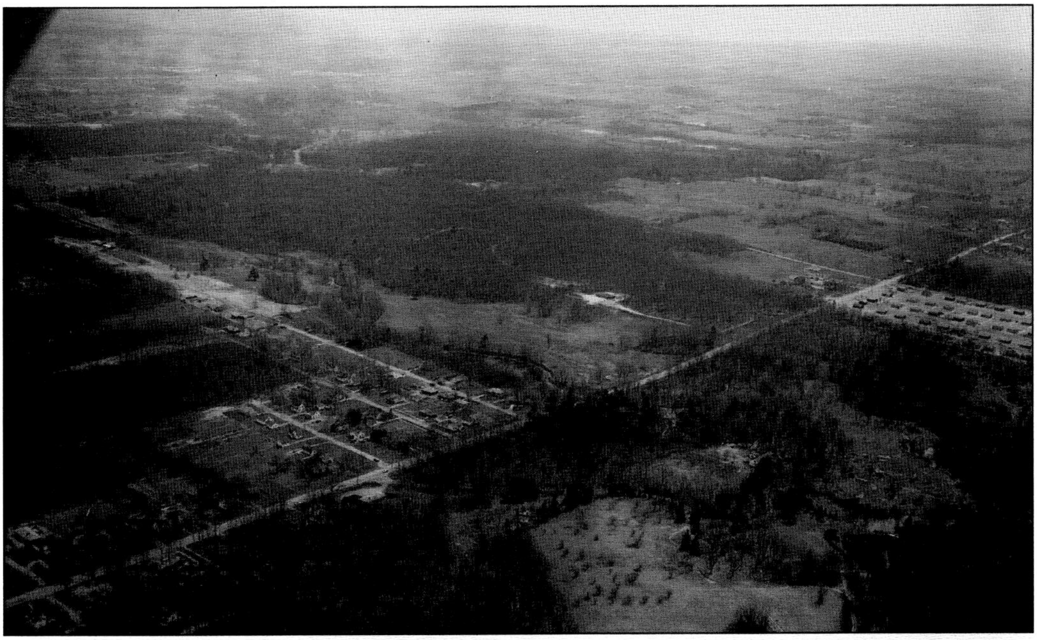

Home Acres was a suburb just south of Godwin Heights. In 1923, realtors Thomas and Cheesman purchased 80 acres of farmland and developed the neighborhood. Situated on both sides of South Division, Home Acres (seen from the air in the 1950s) attracted many local businesses. It also offered Paris Township farmers a place to shop. Other suburban neighborhoods in Paris Township included Kelloggsville (now Kellogsville) and Cutlerville.

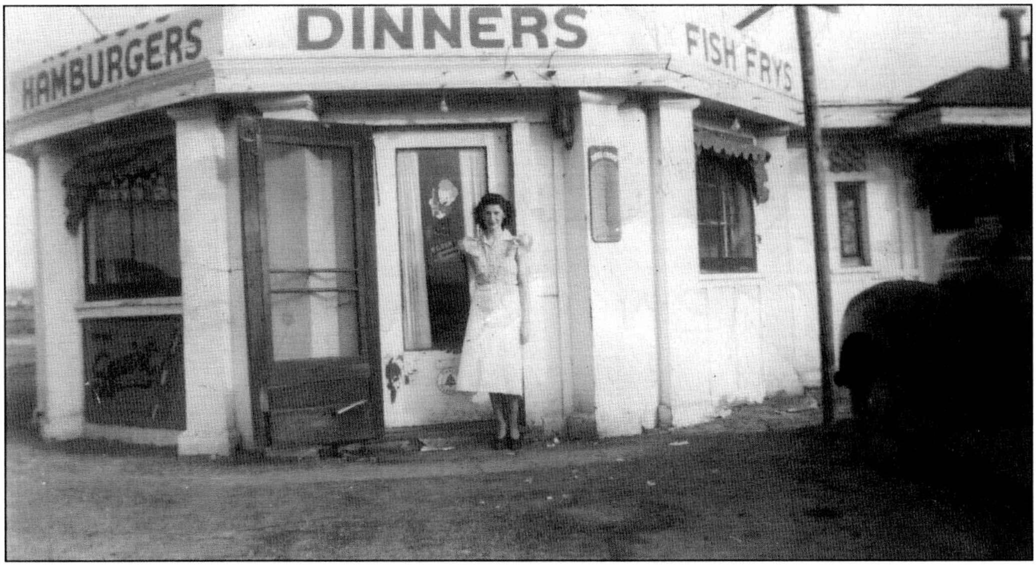

Gwen Haven stands outside her diner in Home Acres in 1948. Her restaurant, with its "Little Squirt" promotional sign and public telephone logo on the door, was typical for a 1940s-era diner. Many Paris Township residents fondly recalled grabbing a bite to eat and shopping at other businesses in this neighborhood. Near the diner were Neil Shippy's pharmacy and an automobile garage.

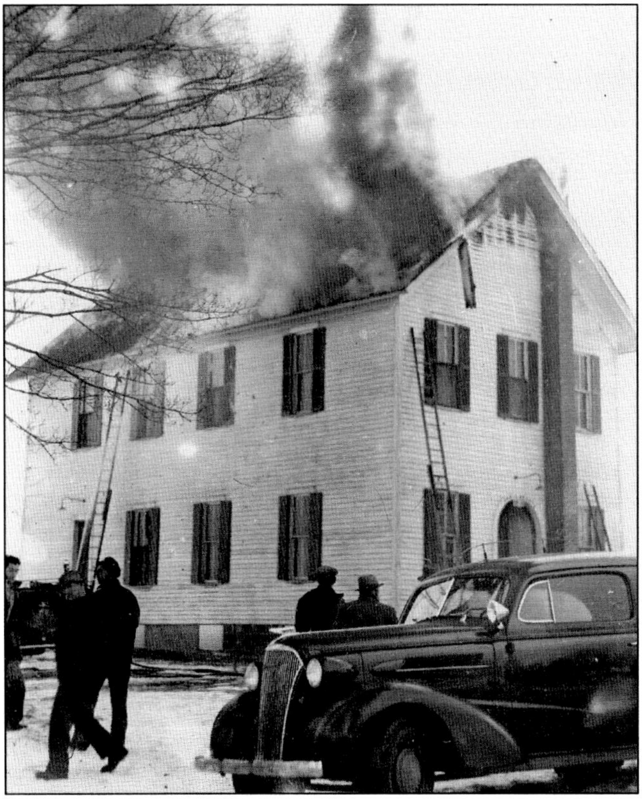

Volunteer firefighters try in vain to stop a roof fire at the Paris Grange Hall on January 7, 1938. Situated on Thirty-second Street and Kalamazoo Avenue, the hall was built in 1873 for farm families to hold meetings and social events. While several granges existed in the area, by 1881, they had all merged with the Paris Grange Hall. Many residents met friends and even future spouses there. Naturally, the fire was a tragedy to the area.

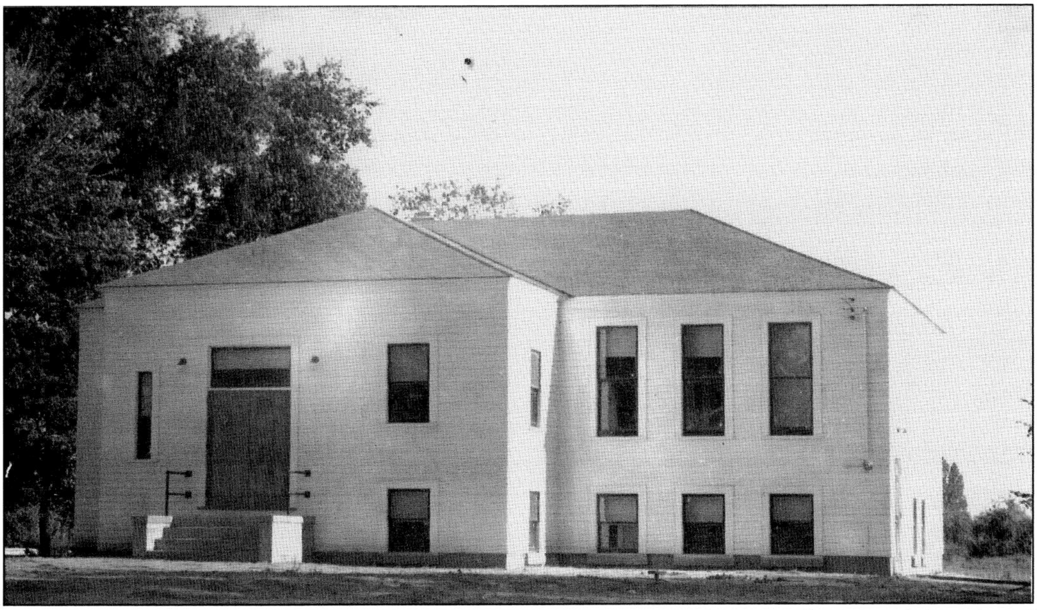

The loss of the Grange hall caused many people in Paris Township to rally around the idea of a new one. Even though the Depression hit many farms hard, residents pooled resources and worked to have a new Grange constructed. The new hall, pictured above, was located on the southwest corner of Twenty-eighth Street and Breton Avenue. The new Grange was dedicated on September 2, 1938.

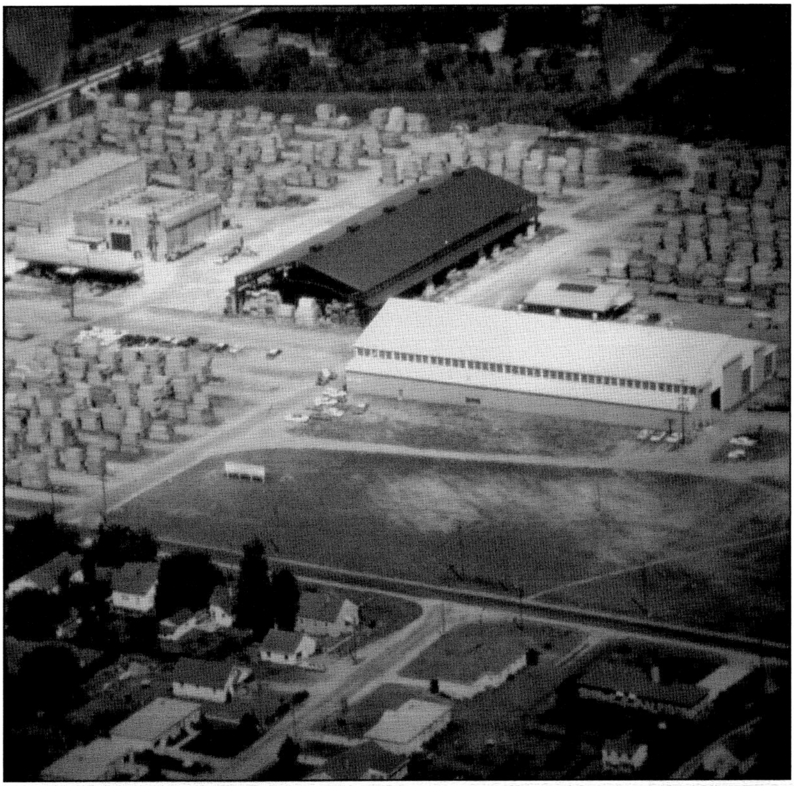

The former Grand Rapids Union Depot building was moved and used as a lumberyard on Fifty-fourth Street. This aerial photograph, taken in the 1960s, shows stacks of lumber ready to be sold and shipped. In a few years, all the growth in Paris Township and later Kentwood would rely on these building materials.

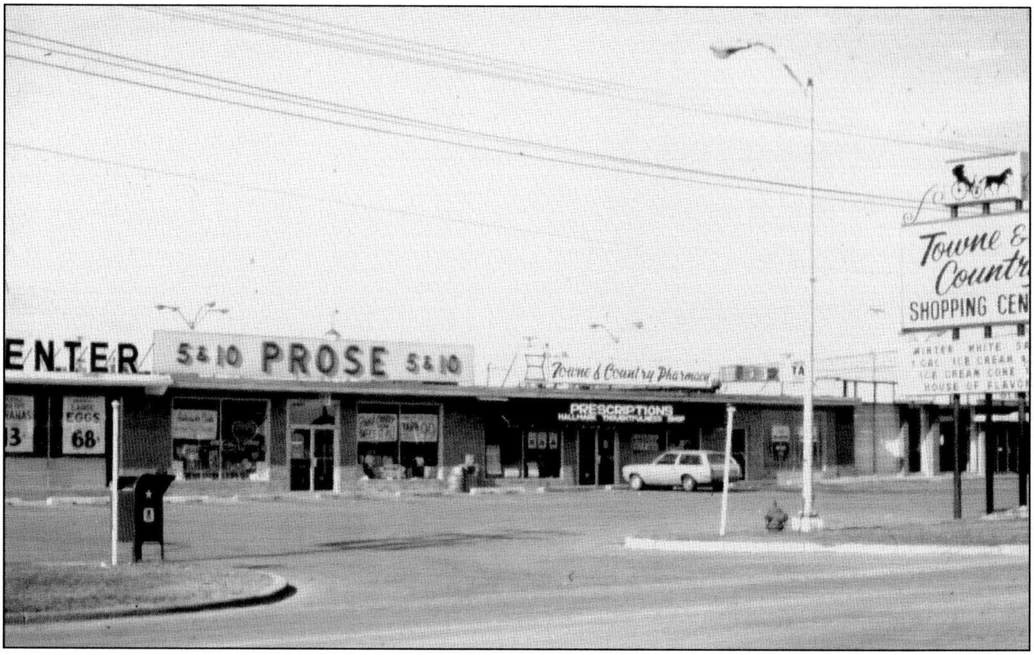

In the past, many residents considered Bowen Station more country than town. In 1956, Chuck Wiersma wanted to open a lumber business at the intersection, so he built the Town and Country Shopping Center. The center included a pharmacy, hardware store, barbershop, grocer, and other businesses, but never a lumberyard. Wiersma was too busy leasing space in his center.

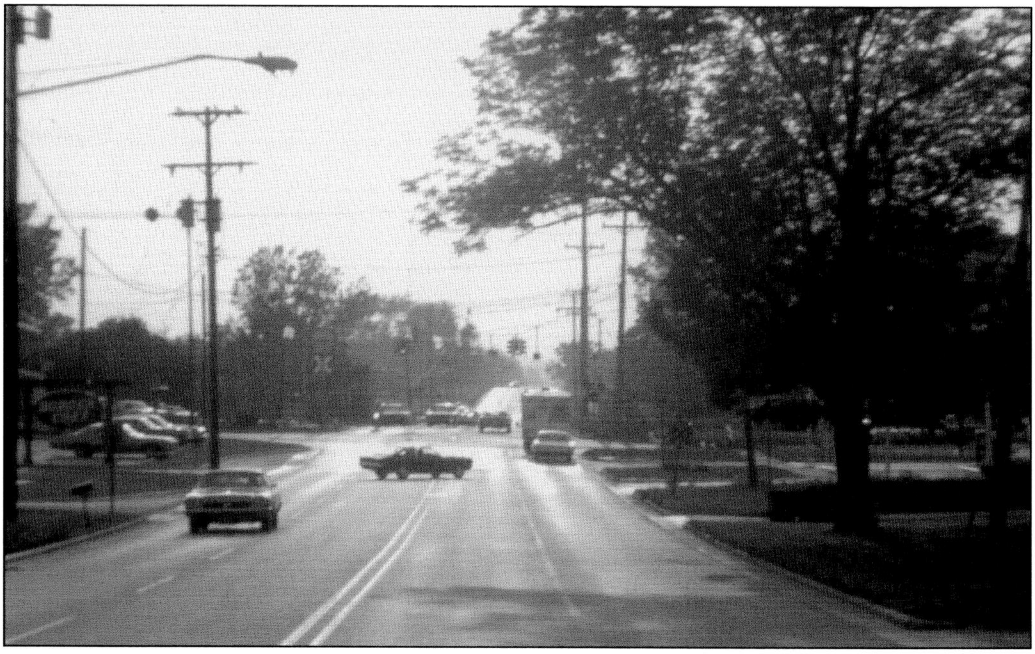

The Town and Country Shopping Center was the largest shopping building in Paris Township before Woodland Mall was built. The success of the center changed the area, as can be seen in this picture. The Burger Chef on the left was once the location of Wesley Brake's blacksmith shop. The road was also widened to four lanes.

Eight

Becoming Kentwood

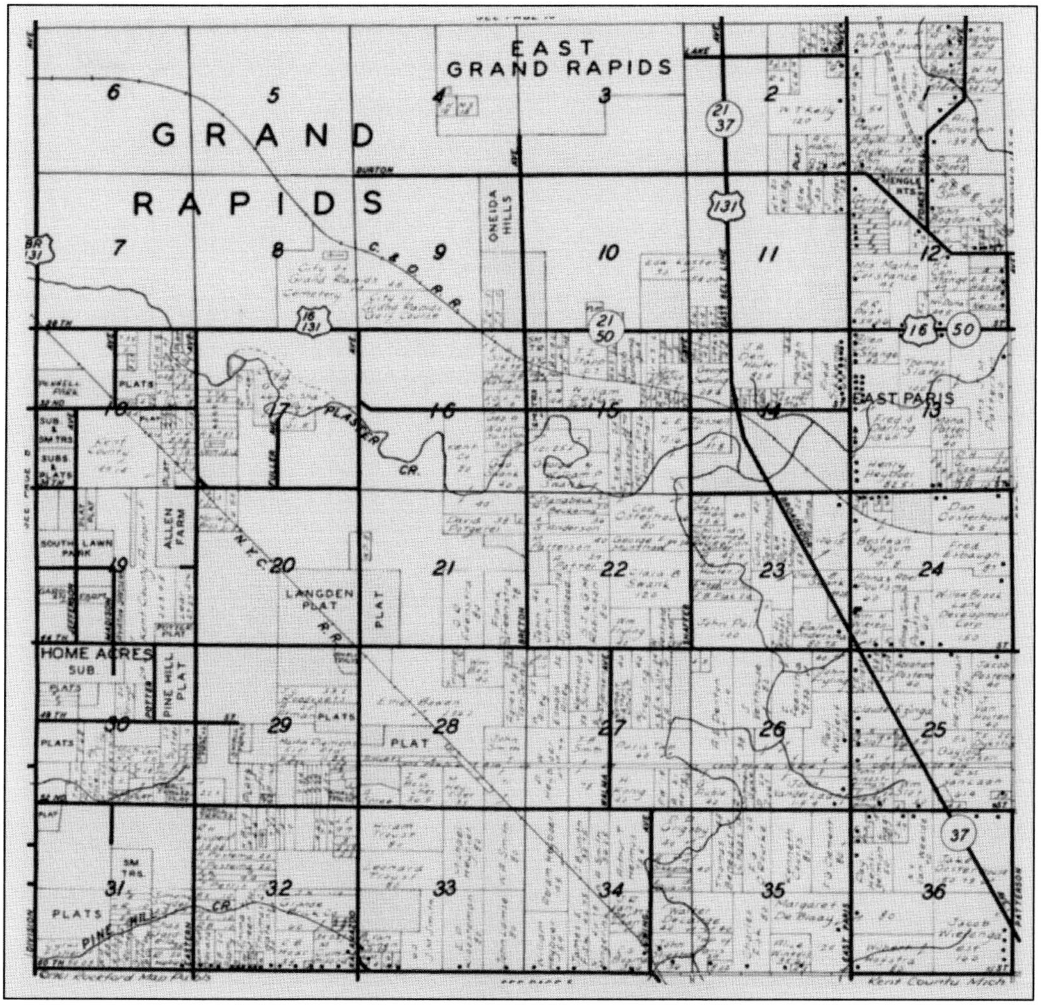

A 1961 plat map shows the original boundaries of Paris Township and the boundaries of Grand Rapids. Over the years, Grand Rapids annexed sections of many of its surrounding townships. By the 1960s, however, continual annexations hurt Paris Township, costing the community population and tax revenue. At election time, the annexation voting always favored the bigger city. By the end of the decade, however, Paris Township residents were ready for a change.

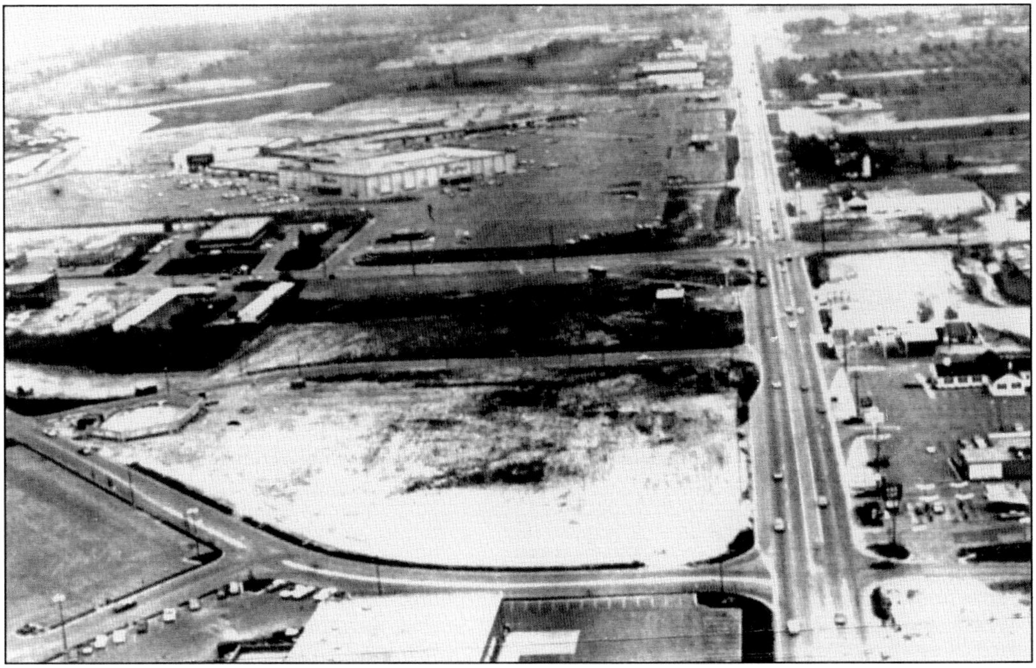

Paris Township tried to become a city three times and failed. In 1965, the Taubman Business Group wanted to build a shopping center on Paris Township farmland. Officials agreed and sold land on the border of Paris Township (pictured above) that once belonged to the Slater and Darling families. Knowing that the mall would be an annexation target, township trustee Peter Lamberts and other area officials rallied the community to become a city.

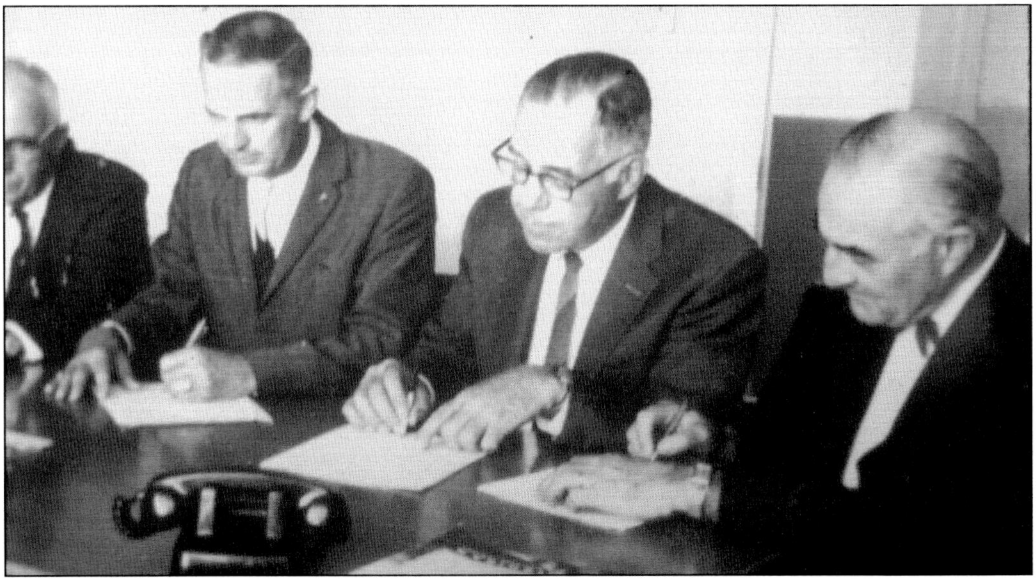

Angry about the mall, Grand Rapids officials refused to extend water and sewer service to the Woodland Mall construction site. After also losing land in annexations, Wyoming city officials agreed to help. In this picture, taken in 1965, they sign a water and sewer agreement with Paris Township Supervisor Peter Lamberts. Grand Rapids's response was one more indication that Paris Township needed to become a city.

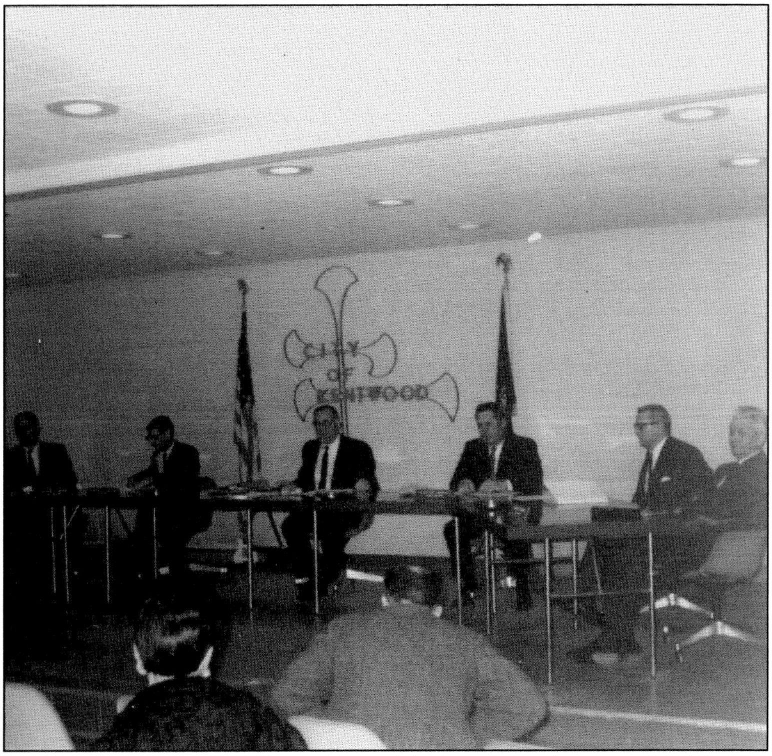

Paris Township used the fleur-de-lis as its symbol for 130 years. In a special election, the community overwhelmingly voted to become a city and prevent further annexation. On February 27, 1967, the fleur-de-lis became the new symbol of the city of Kentwood. Mayor-elect Lamberts called a meeting of the city commission at 8:00 a.m. Lamberts and others were sworn in later that day in a special ceremony at the Bowen School.

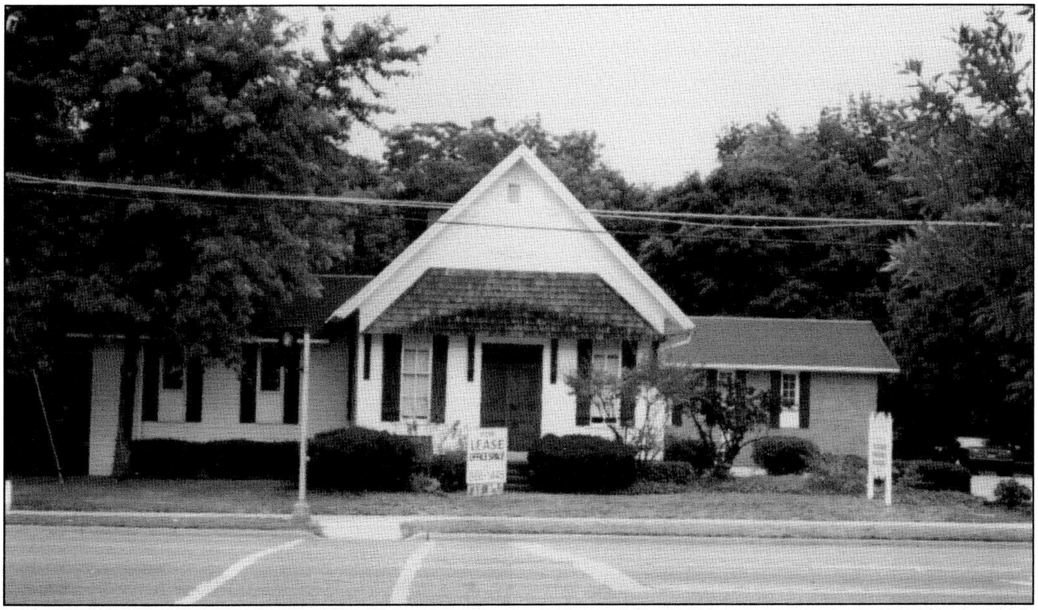

The first Paris Township City Hall was built in the late 1800s. Although updated several times, most township officials did not use the building pictured above. Elections were even held at other locations. One of the first actions of Mayor-elect Lamberts in 1967 was to propose the construction of a new city hall.

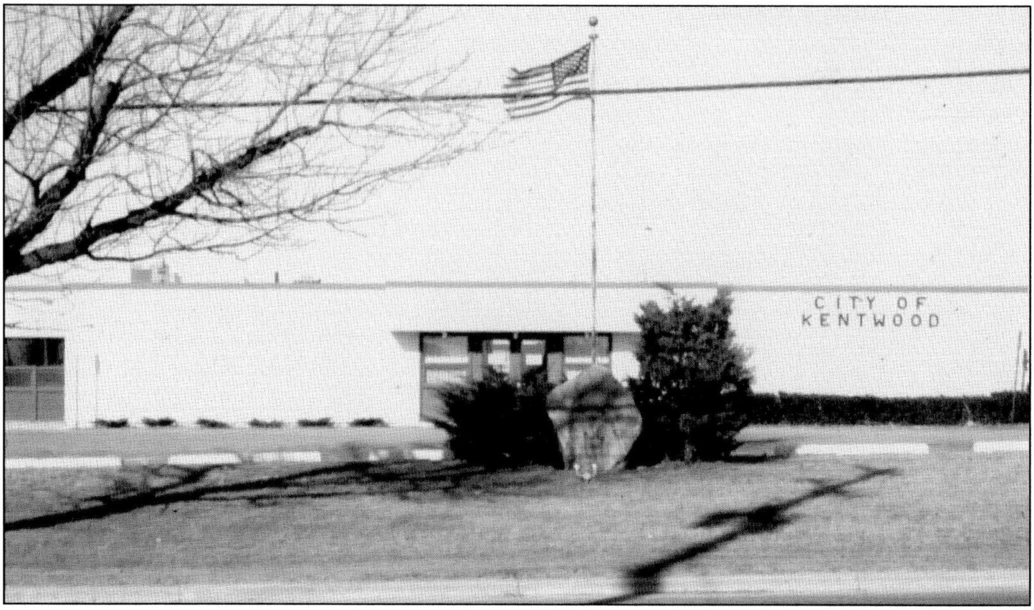

The new Kentwood City Hall on Forty-fourth Street was completed in 1975. Ironically, the land the building was on had been annexed earlier into Grand Rapids. In order to get the new city hall within Kentwood's borders, Mayor Lamberts negotiated with Michigan Attorney General Milt Firestone to have Grand Rapids return the land and several other sections of Paris Township.

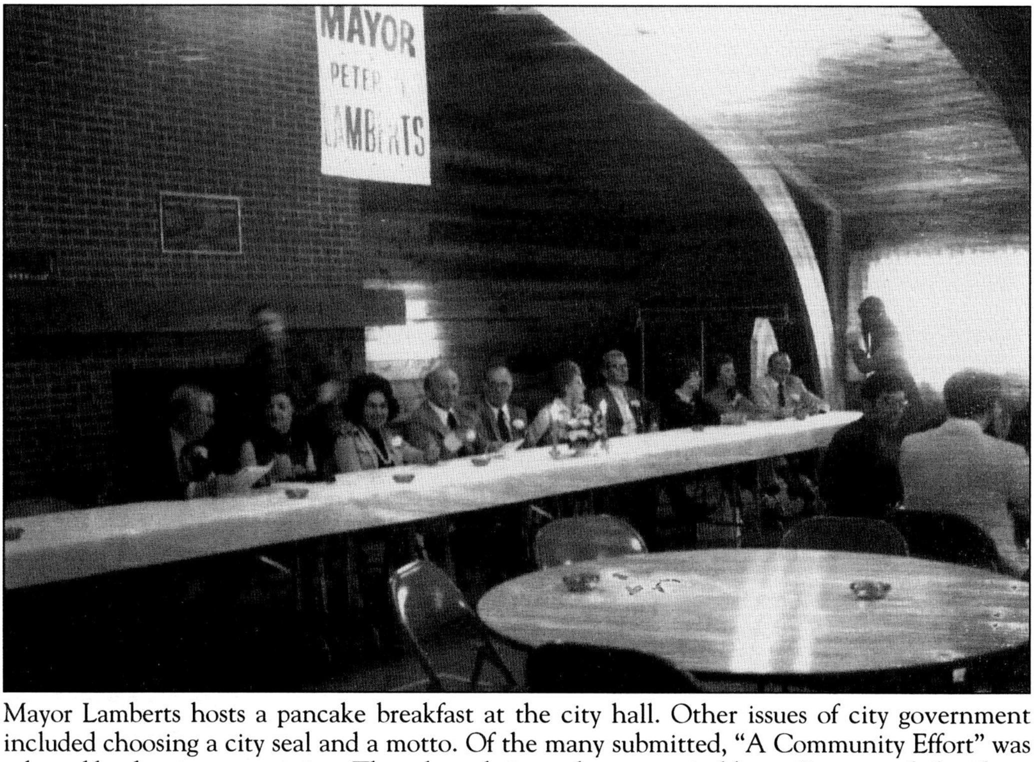

Mayor Lamberts hosts a pancake breakfast at the city hall. Other issues of city government included choosing a city seal and a motto. Of the many submitted, "A Community Effort" was selected by the city commission. The selected city seal was a capital letter K surrounded with an olive wreath. The seal was used up until the 1990s, when it was updated.

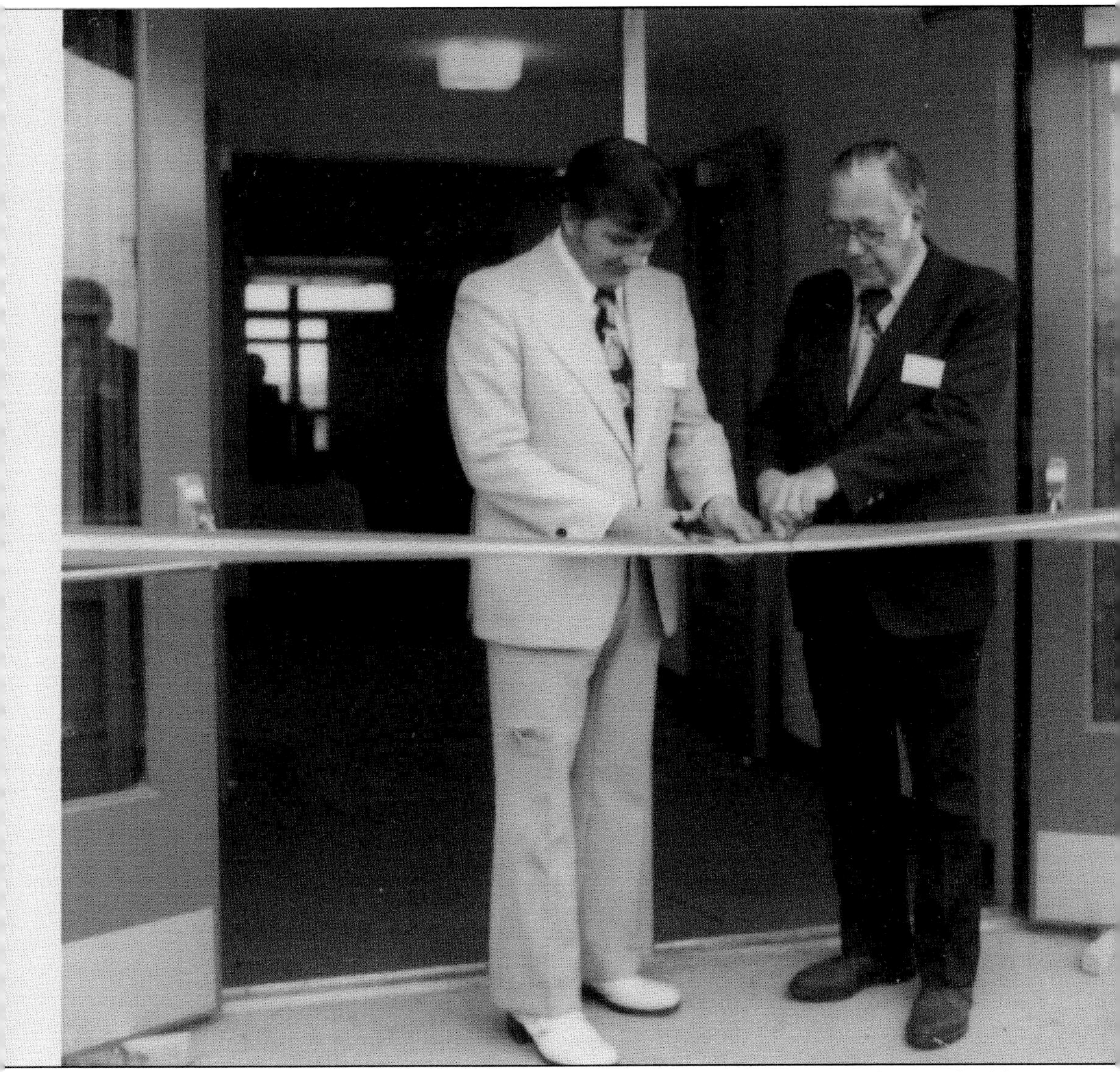

Mayor Lamberts, on the right, helps cut the ribbon on the new city hall. While the new building met Kentwood's needs, Lamberts and others felt that the city needed to be represented by a more stately building. A few years after the city hall was built, construction began on a new city center.

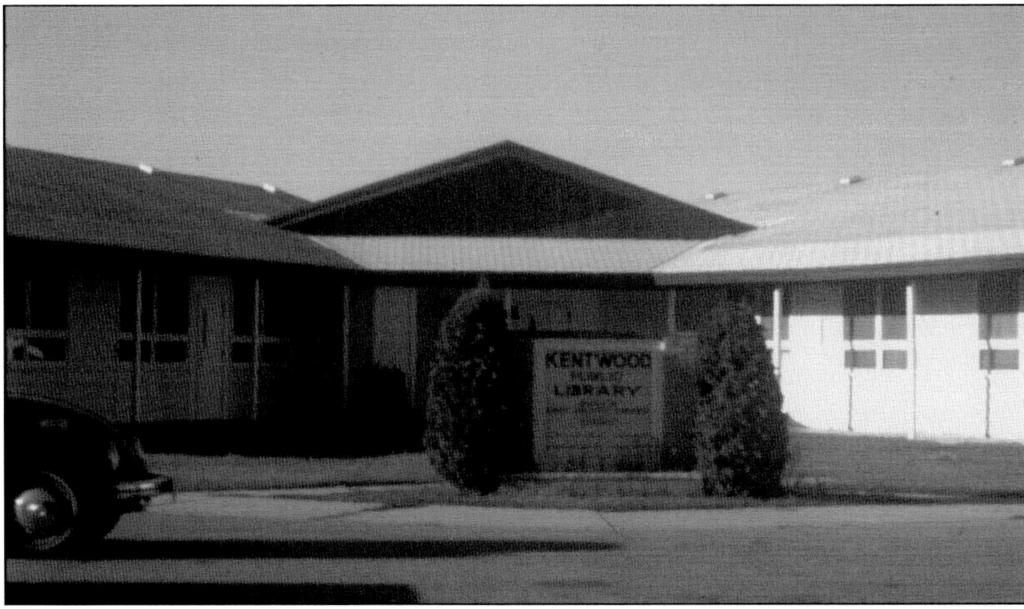

Another issue of the new city was its library. The Paris Township library used to be at 200 Forty-fourth Street. When Kentwood became a city, the area police department was in the basement of the library. City officials knew this was no longer a good arrangement. To accommodate fire, police, and other areas of government, Kentwood moved the library into the building that was once St. Mary Magdalen Church.

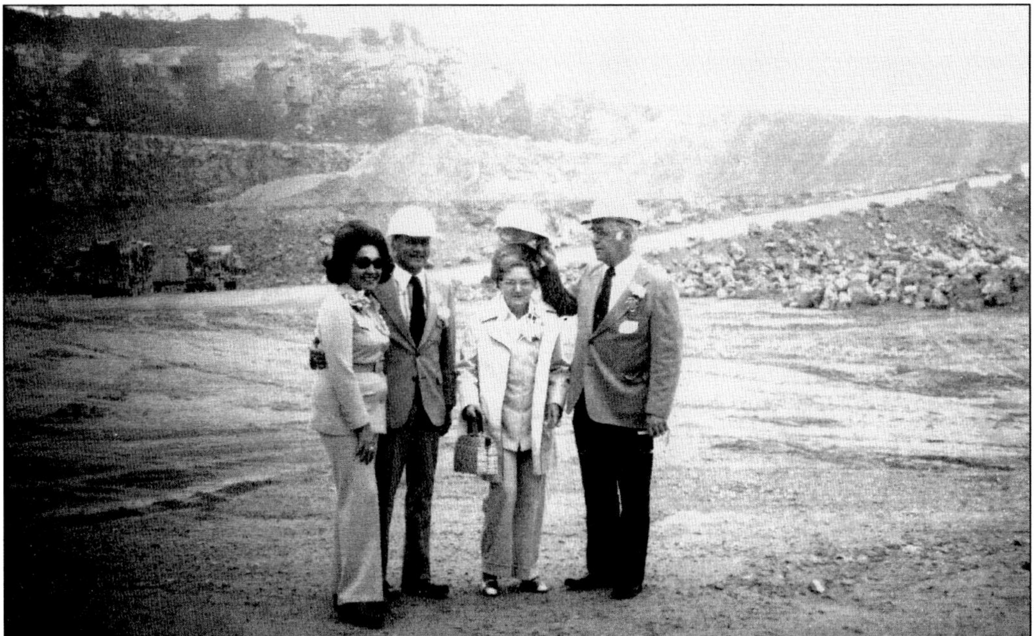

Ground was broken on the new city center in 1977. In this photograph, Mayor Lamberts places a construction hat on Cora Bowen Stauffer's head at the site of the future city center. The complex was intended to sit atop the highest spot in the city. The site chosen was more than 800 feet above sea level.

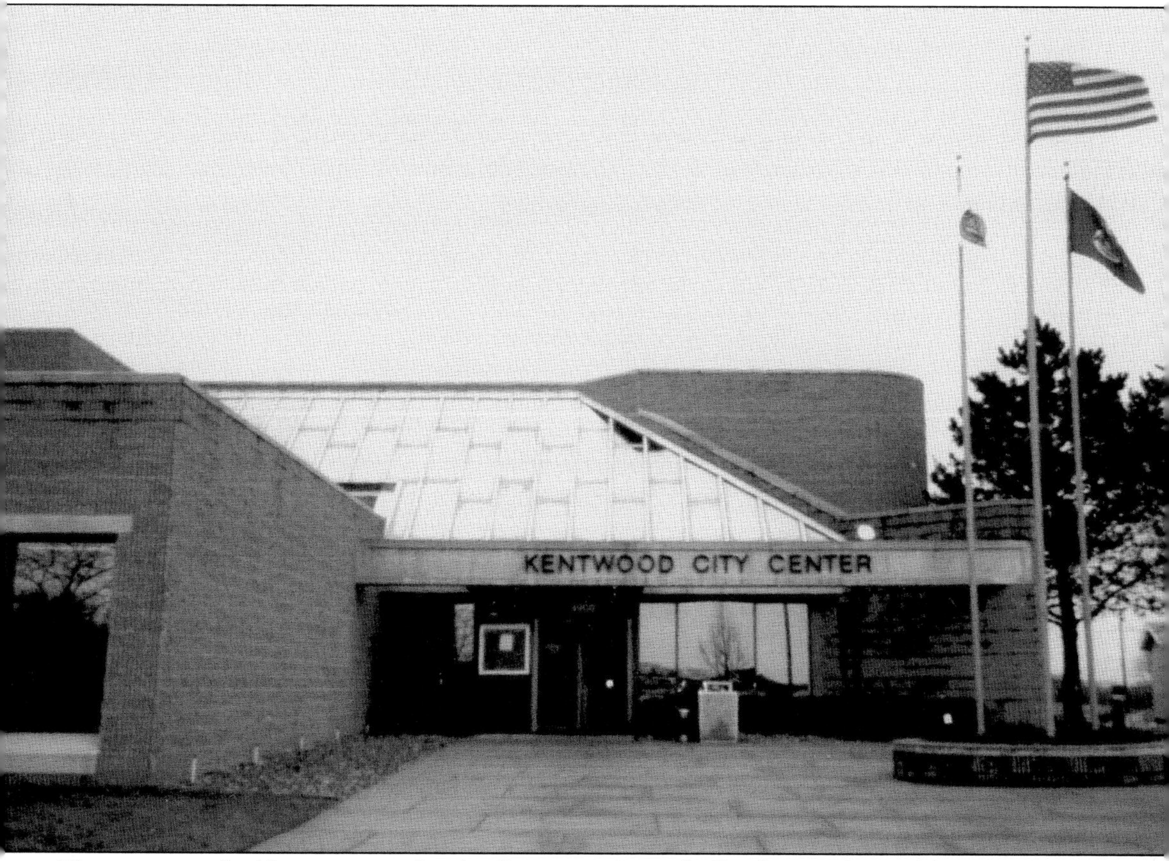

The city center building was completed in January 1979, and officials moved out of the Forty-fourth Street building and into the new facility. On St. Patrick's Day of that same year, a ribbon-cutting ceremony officially opened the city center to the public. Since then, the Kentwood City Center has remained the seat of the local government.

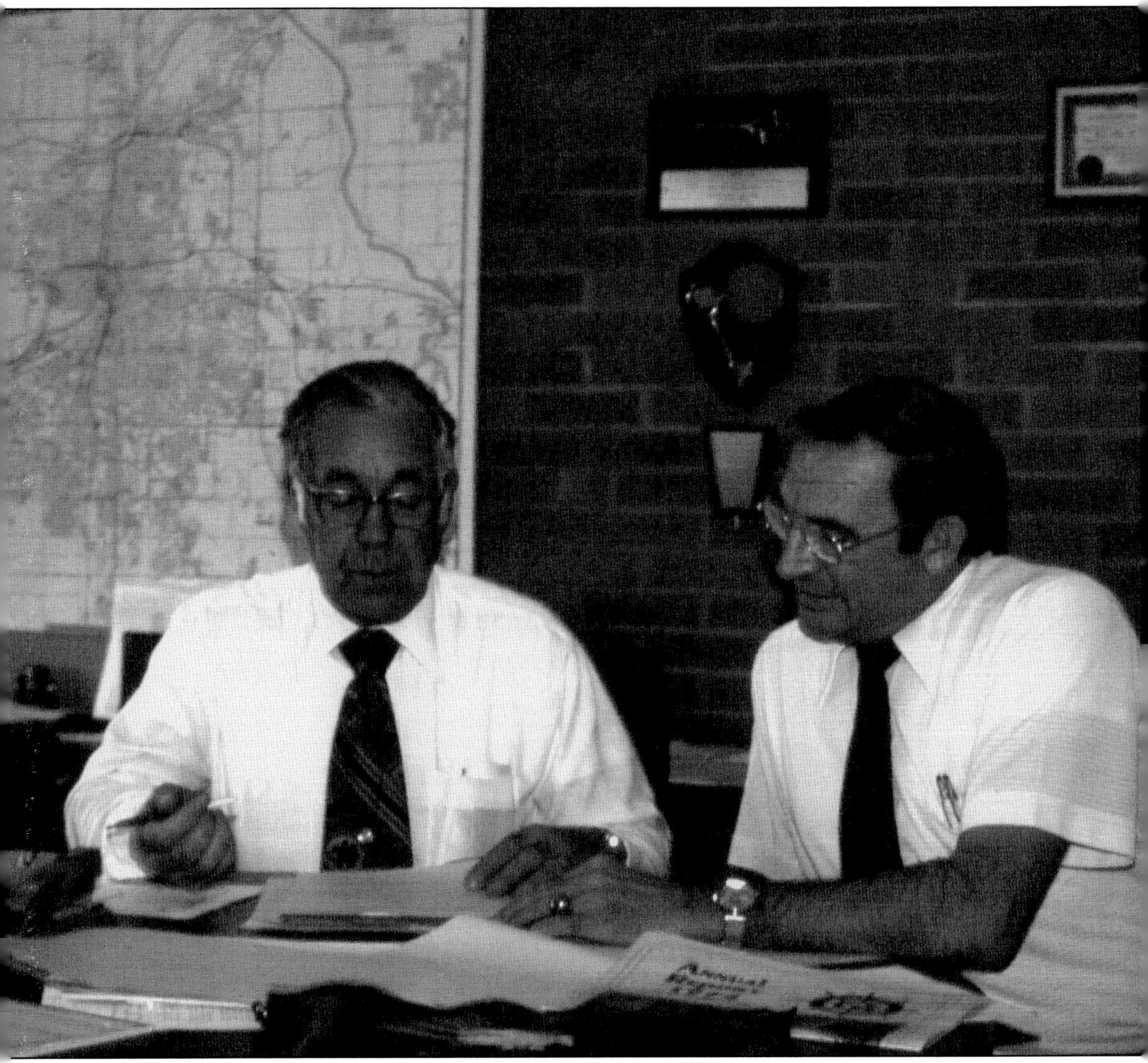

Mayor Lamberts reviews city regulations with an official at city hall. He served 12 years and six consecutive terms as mayor before announcing he would not seek re-election. City officials who worked with him remembered Lamberts as a friendly, funny man who wrote poetry while in office. Kentwood's next mayor was Marvin Hoeflinger.

Nine

New Beginnings

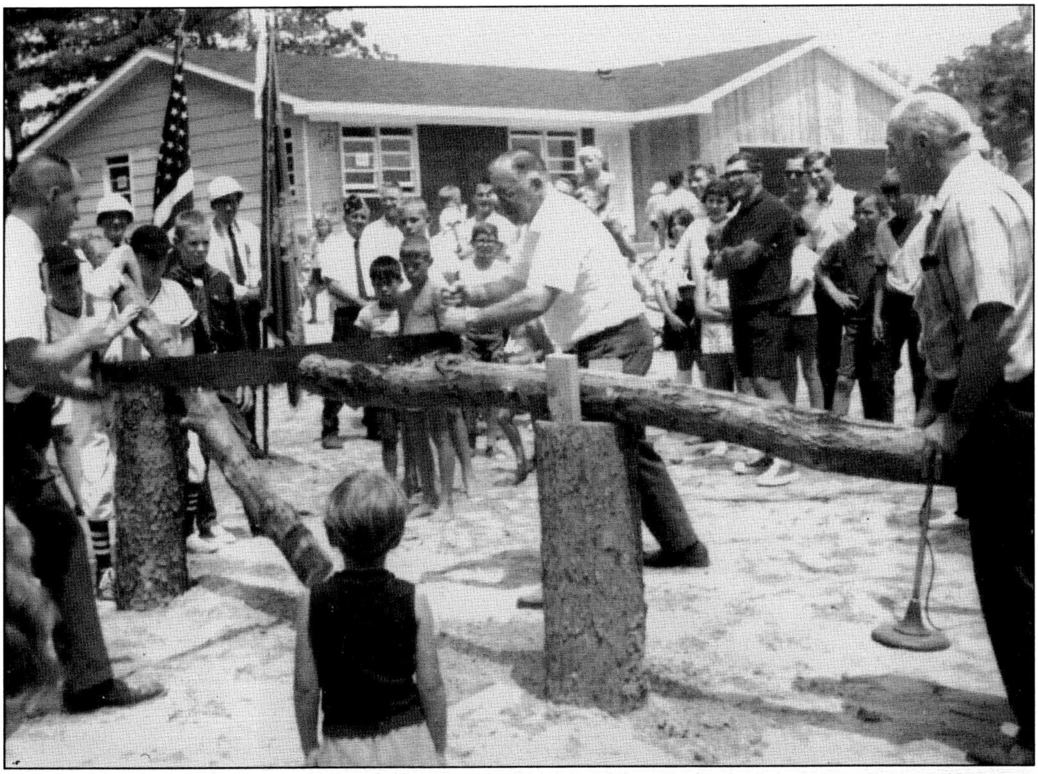

Mayor Lamberts and his son saw through a log the way the original Paris Township settlers did. Although settlers needed to cut and haul their own wood to make a house, new residents to Kentwood could move into one of its recently constructed homes, seen in the background, in many of the city's neighborhoods.

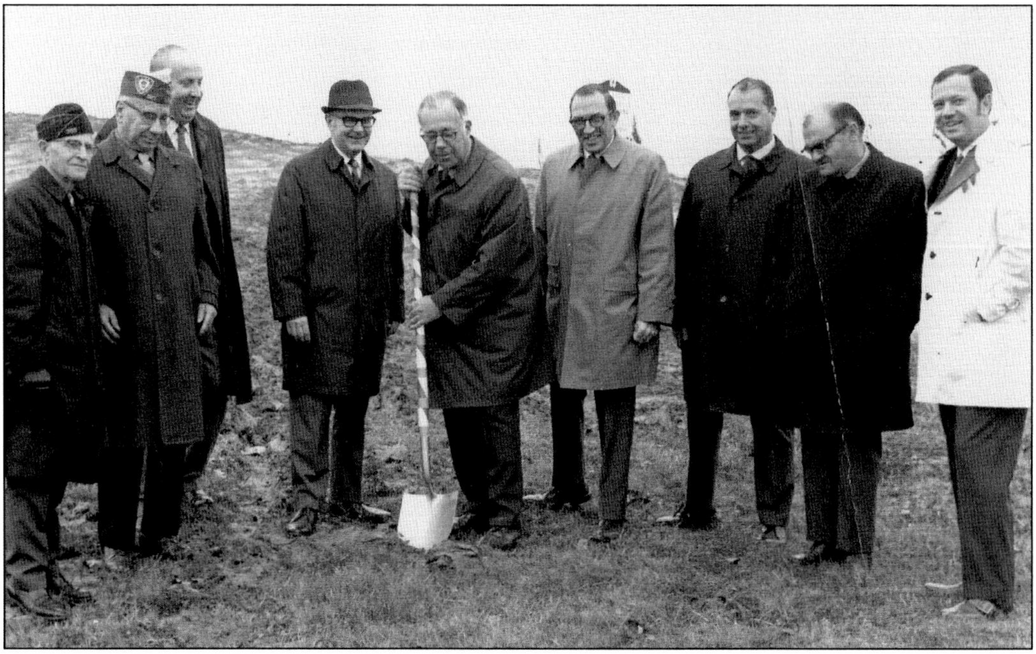

Mayor Lamberts prepares to take the first ceremonial shovel at a local groundbreaking. The population of Kentwood increased by more than 50 percent over the 1970s. By 1980, Kentwood was the seventh largest city in the region. This was the first of many groundbreakings for Lamberts and future city officials.

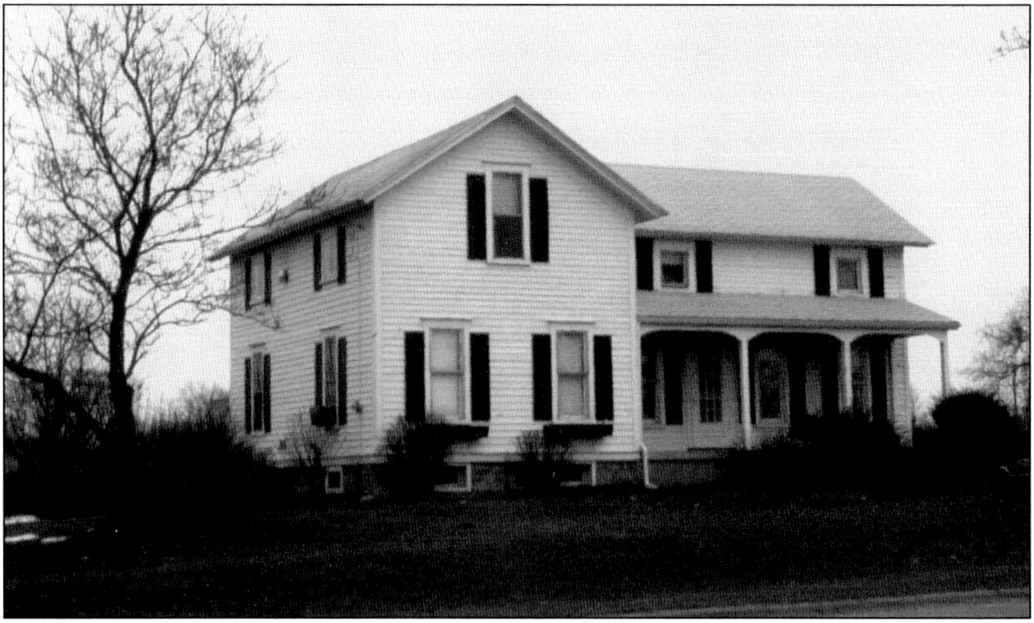

Mayor Lamberts and subsequent mayors carefully cultivated businesses and industries to establish themselves in Kentwood to serve the community. The city was dramatically changing, and residents sometimes struggled with merging remnants of an old township with the new city. Residents considered preserving several houses, including the Whitford house, photographed in 1974.

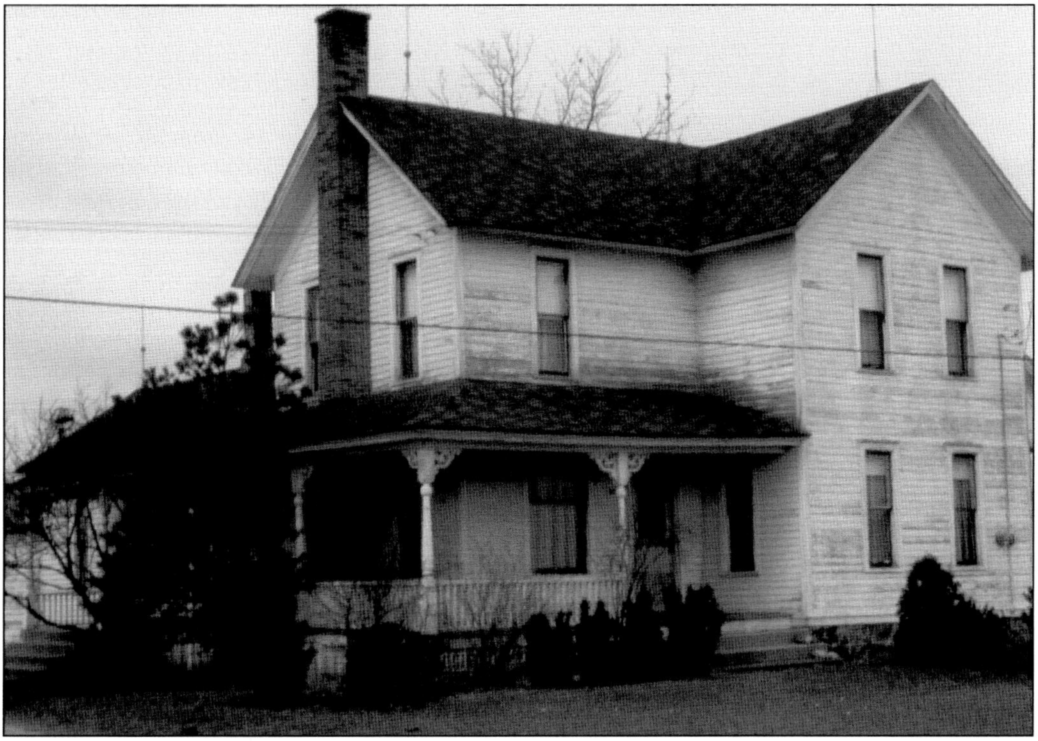

Rachel Patterson was a widow who moved to Paris Township with her 10 children in the 1830s. Despite incredible odds at the time, the Pattersons built a successful farm. Their farmhouse was home to several generations of Patterson descendants, even into the 21st century.

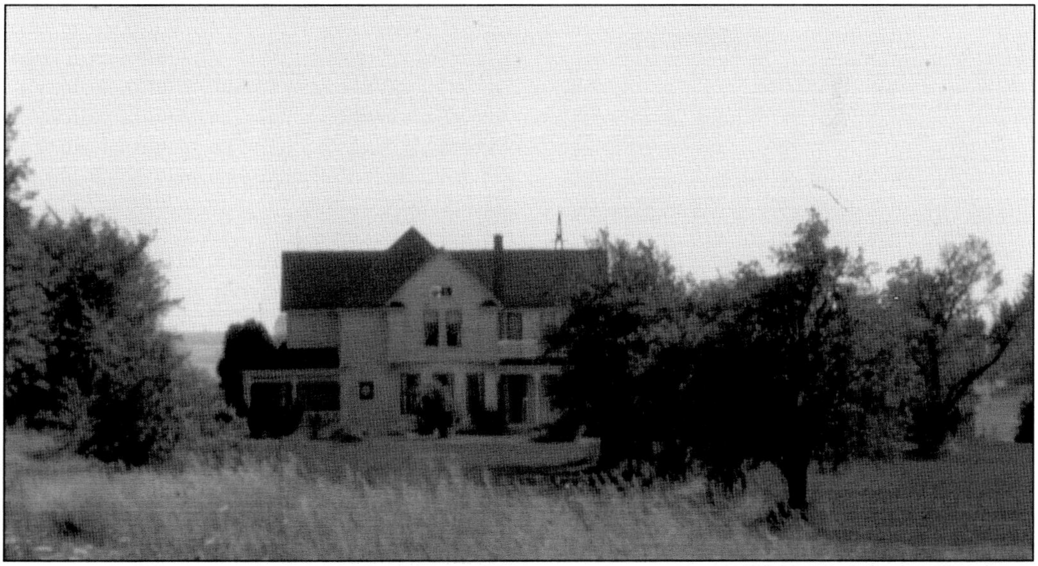

The Rawlings were another early settler family to Paris Township. Their house, located on Kalamazoo Avenue, was built in 1896 and purchased by Ed Rawlings in 1905. The last descendant to live in the house was Gretchen Rawlings, a former Paris Township schoolteacher. The house had three bedrooms and a bathroom upstairs and a bedroom, parlor, living room, dining room, and kitchen on the main level.

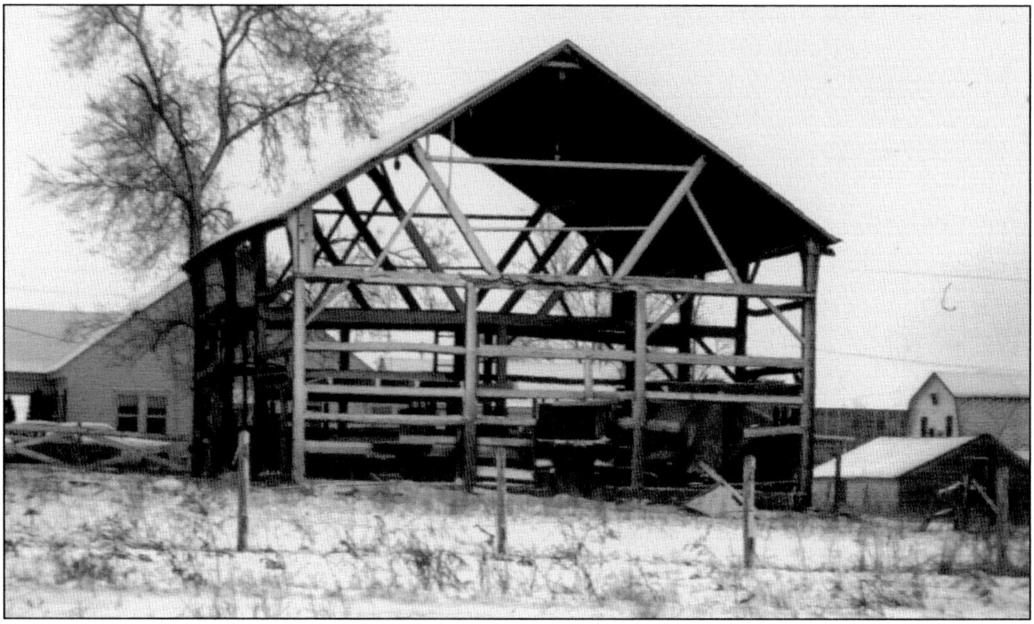

Many Paris Township children fondly remember climbing into a hayloft or swinging on ropes in a family or neighbor's barn. With more businesses and fewer farms, new barns were not being built in Kentwood. Existing barns were either being sold and razed for new businesses or being neglected from disuse and collapsing. Very few families, such as this one, tried to repair them.

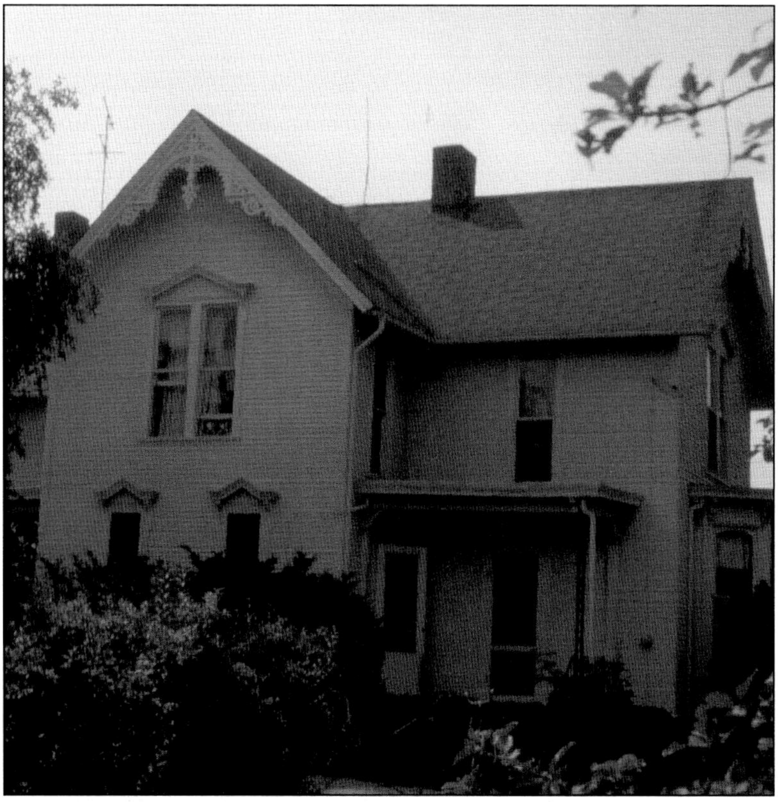

Several generations of Munshaws lived as farmers in Paris Township since emigrating from Canada in the mid-1800s. Their house, located on the corner of Forty-fourth Street and Kalamazoo Avenue, was evaluated for its historic value by the Kentwood Historic District Study Committee, created in 1976 by the city commission and chaired by longtime Kentwood resident Dale Heyboer.

The Karel family moved from the Netherlands to a farm on Fifty-second Street in Paris Township in 1862. Over the years, they lived in several Paris Township neighborhoods, including Home Acres. In 1952, the Karel family built this house, which is still standing on Fifty-second Street today.

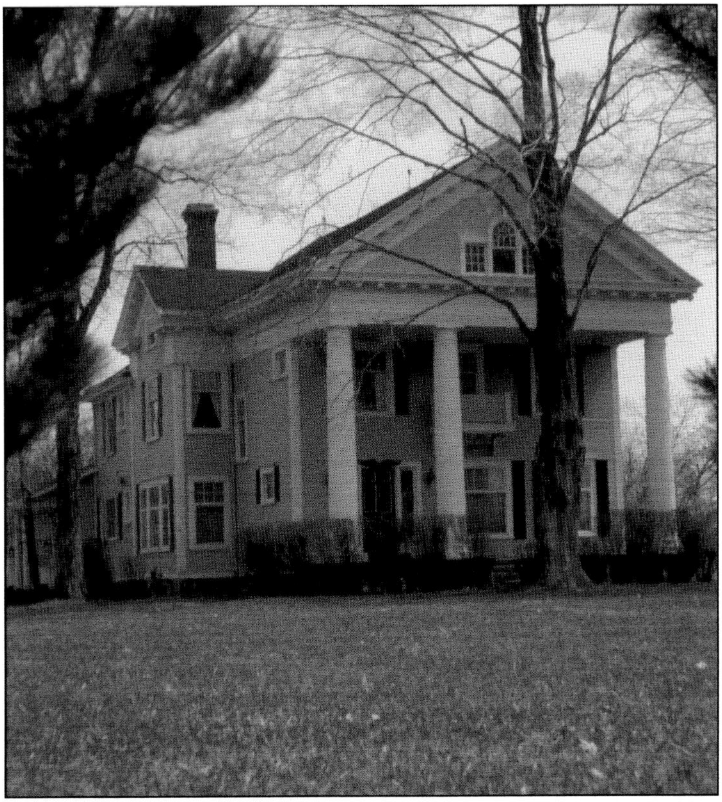

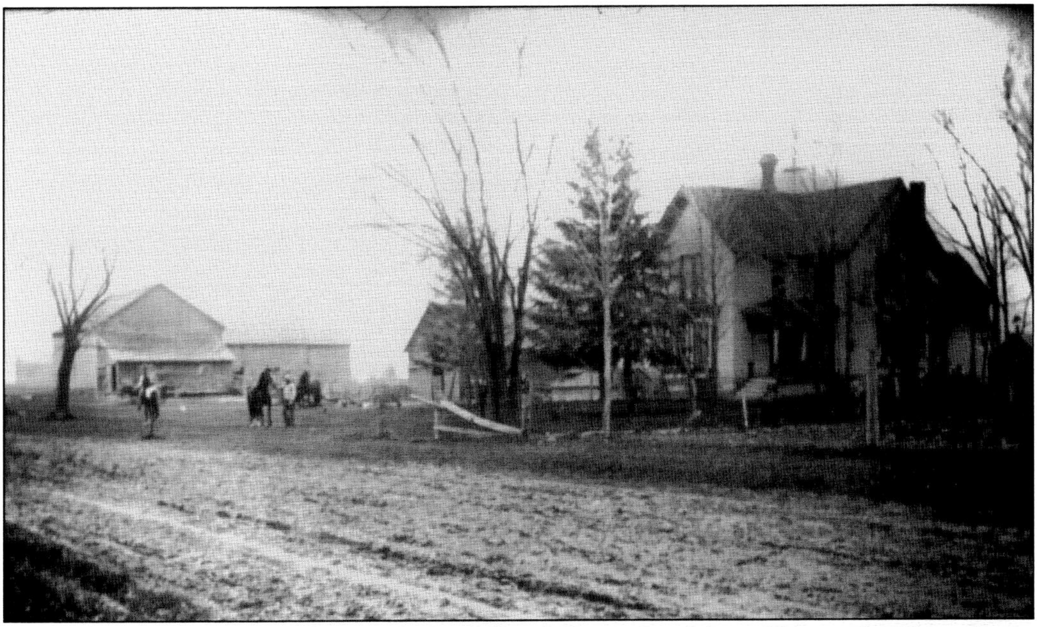

Orson Bowen lived in this house on Forty-fourth Street until he sold it to the Oosterhouse family. When Breton Avenue was extended in 1972, the house was demolished. The Oosterhouse family's other home was bought by the Heyboer family. Currently, it is one of the last working farms in the township.

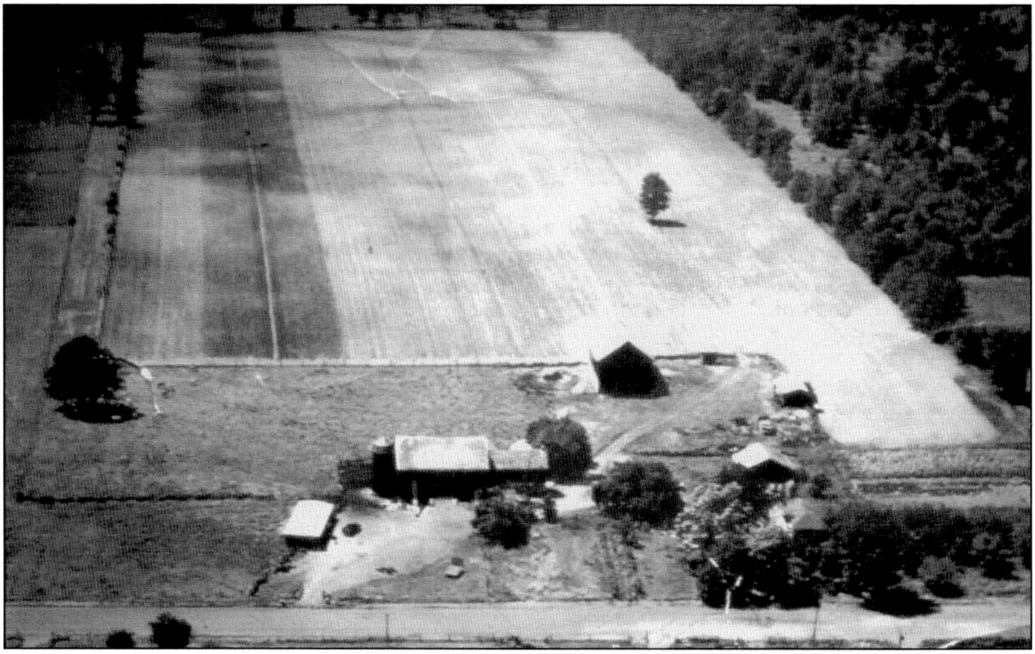

John DeBlaay was one of the many settlers in the area who moved from Holland to Paris Township. He and his wife, Mary, had several children who later helped shape the community. This aerial photograph shows the DeBlaay property located along East Paris Avenue in the southwest part of the township.

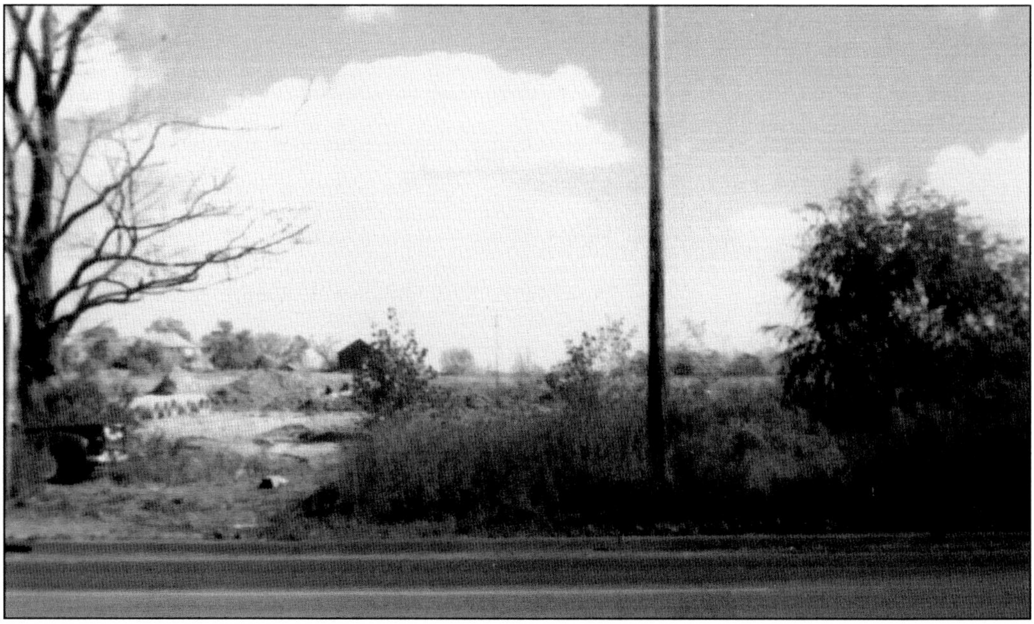

The Bowens had farmed their land for 100 years. Burr Bowen, the only son of Bostwick Bowen, died in 1922. Ethel Bowen had never married, and Cora Bowen Stauffer did not have any children to run the farm. As the sisters grew older, sections of the land were sold or, as in the case of the Kentwood Public Library, donated. This photograph shows a view of the Bowen property under development from Kalamazoo Avenue.

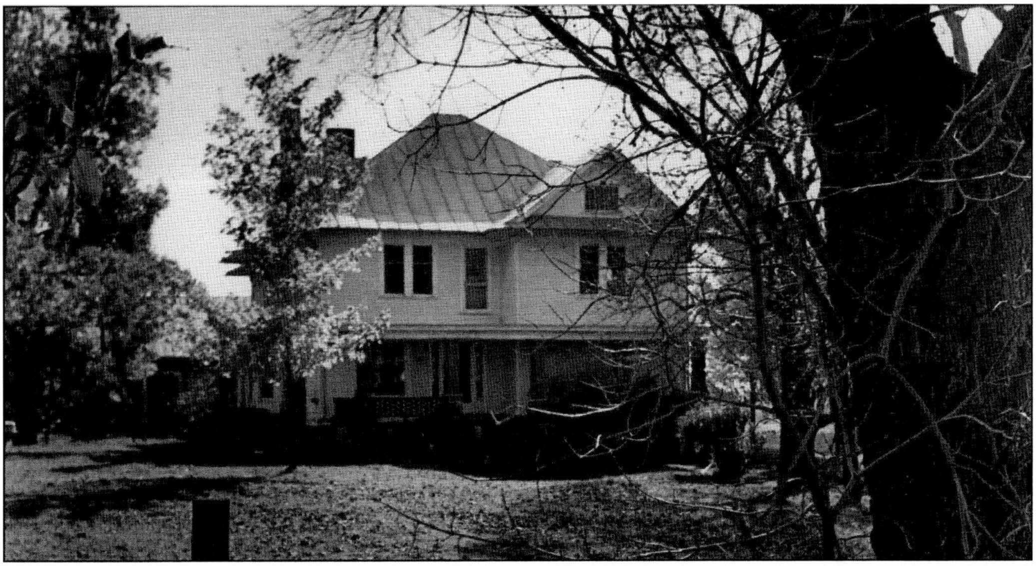

The Bowen farm and barn stands as the land around it is developed. Ethel and Cora lived together for many years until 1973, when Ethel died. Cora sold the house to an architectural firm and moved into Luther Village, a retirement home built on the same land as the original Kent County poor farm. Kentwood officials recognized the home's historical significance, and various plans for the house were suggested as businesses and residential neighborhoods crept around it.

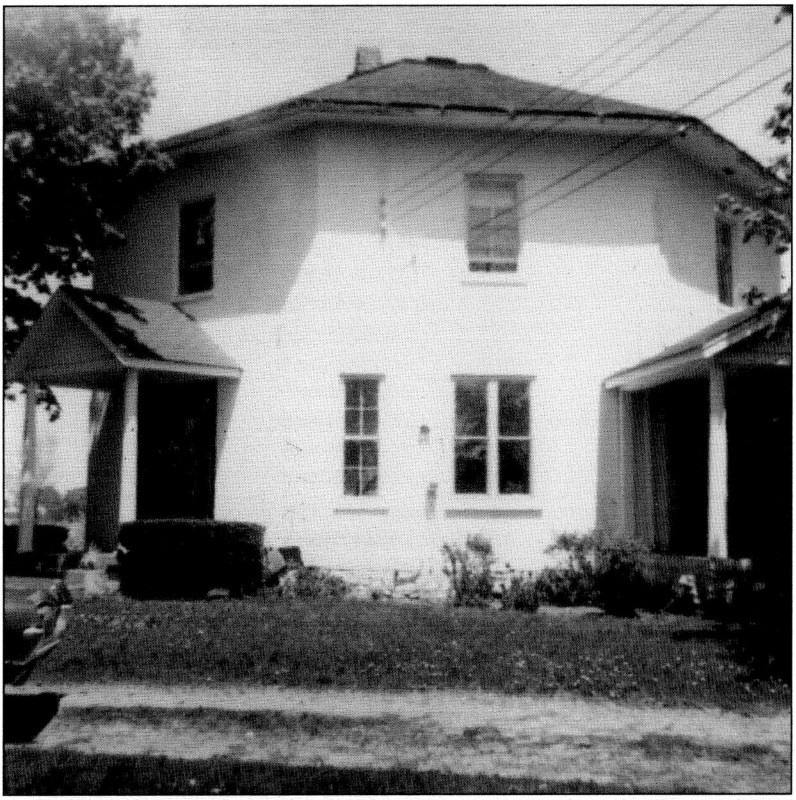

Nearly 300 acres of land around the Bailey Octagon House was sold to Eastbrook Companies. They created Bailey's Grove, a residential community of 725 homes and condominiums and 375 apartments. A school, park, and nature preserve are also located on the site. The Bailey House was restored and declared a Kentwood historic site in 2001.

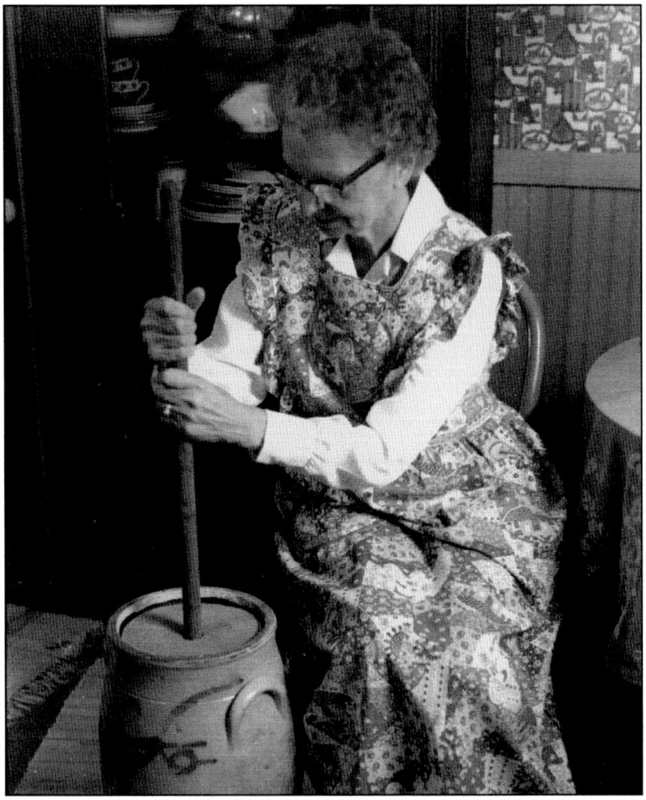

By 1975, many residents of Kentwood realized that the community was drastically changing. Connie Udell and Shari Boisvenue, of the then Kentwood Historical Society, visited elementary classes in Kentwood dressed in 1920s garments. They showed organizations how women may have prepared food during that time. In this photograph, a volunteer shows how cream was churned.

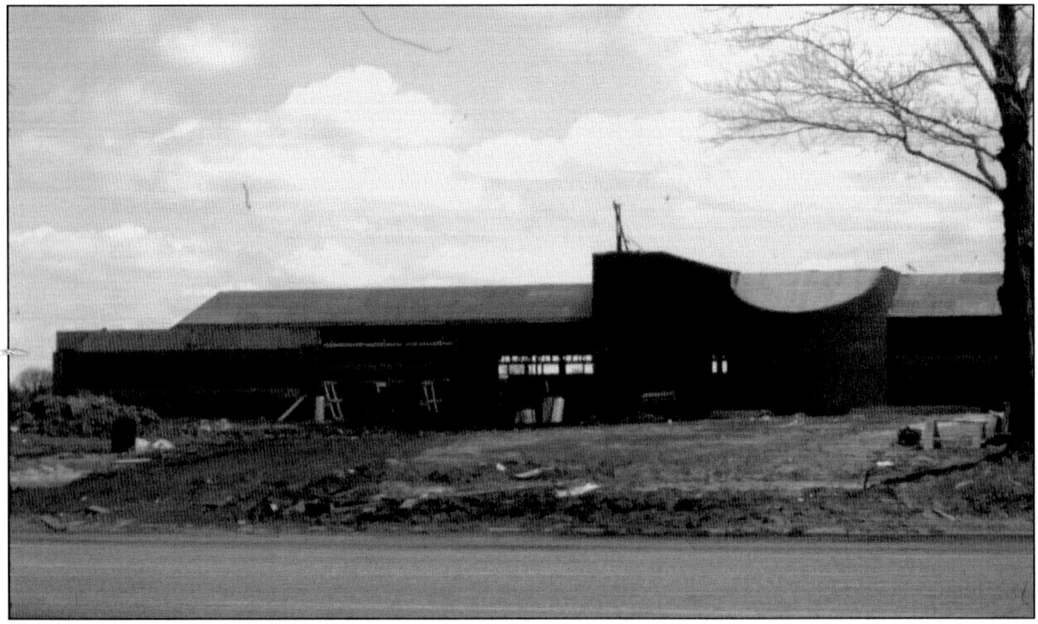

With other concerns on the mind of city officials, funding for a new Kentwood District Library was delayed. Local individuals and groups helped get the library on its feet. In 1973, Cora Bowen Stauffer donated four acres of land. The Paris Grange donated $15,000, and city funds eventually enabled the city to begin construction on the $725,000 facility.

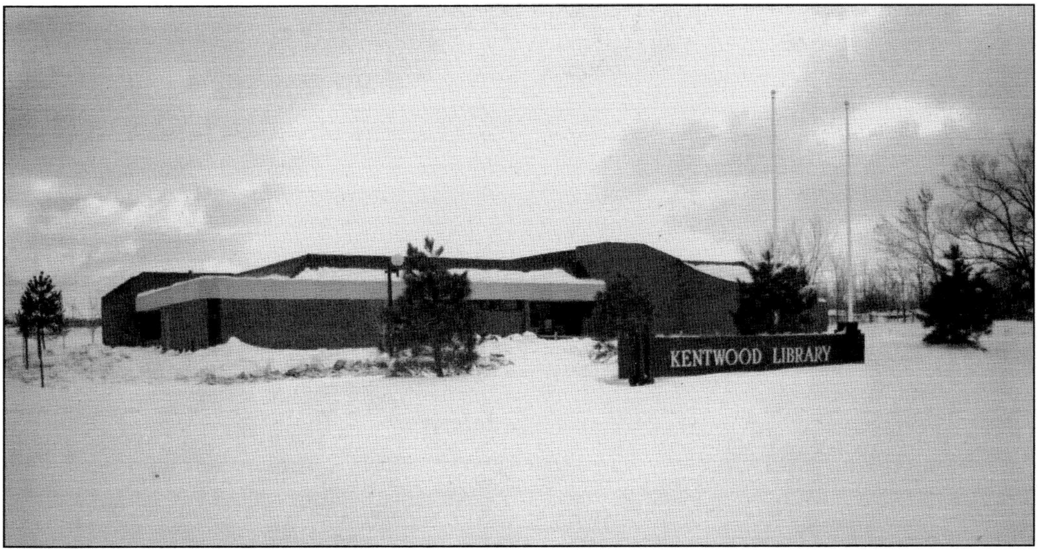

The Kentwood Library was finally completed in 1975. As part of the Kent District Library System, it houses over 96,000 books, videos, and other lending materials. The library is also home to the Kentwood Historical Room, a collection of photographs, oral histories, records, and other memorabilia from the history of Paris Township and early Kentwood.

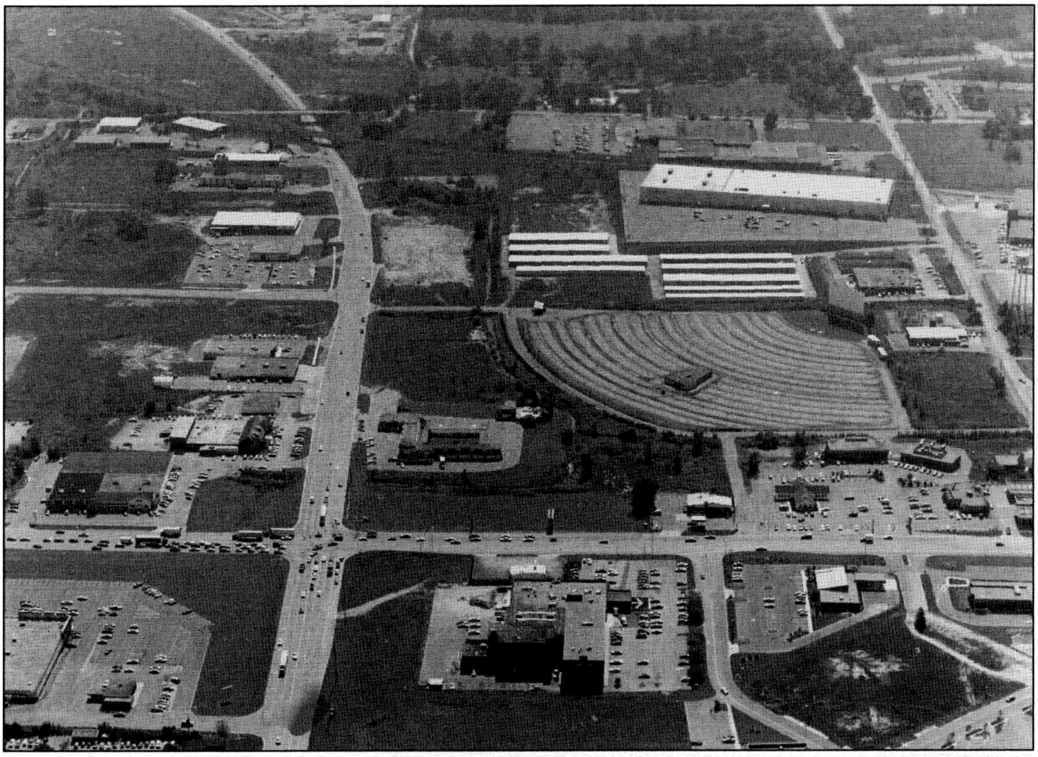

As the area rapidly grew, Kentwood area officials had a number of different aerial photographs taken. This one shows Twenty-eighth Street at M-37, before Twenty-ninth Street was extended from Broadmoor Street over to Shaffer Avenue. The triangle-shaped section in the middle of the picture is the drive-in theater.

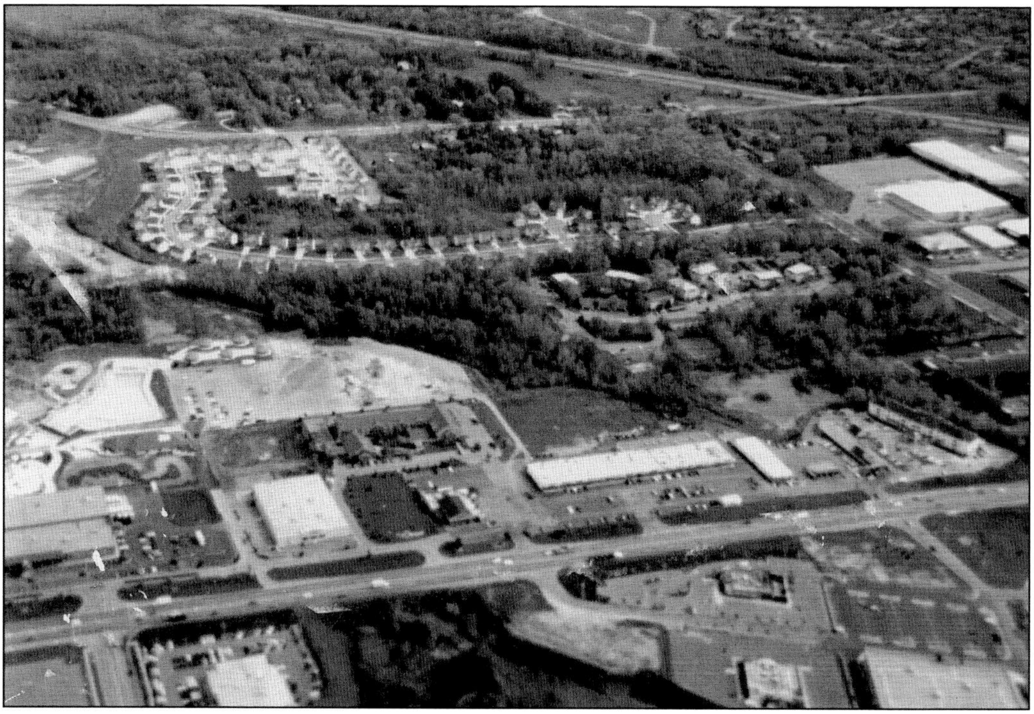

This aerial photograph captures the eastern section of Twenty-eighth Street in Paris Township. The left-hand side of the photograph shows A. J.'s Water Park, a popular destination for Kentwood and Grand Rapids young people throughout the 1990s. Around the park, local businesses, organizations, and new residential neighborhoods have developed.

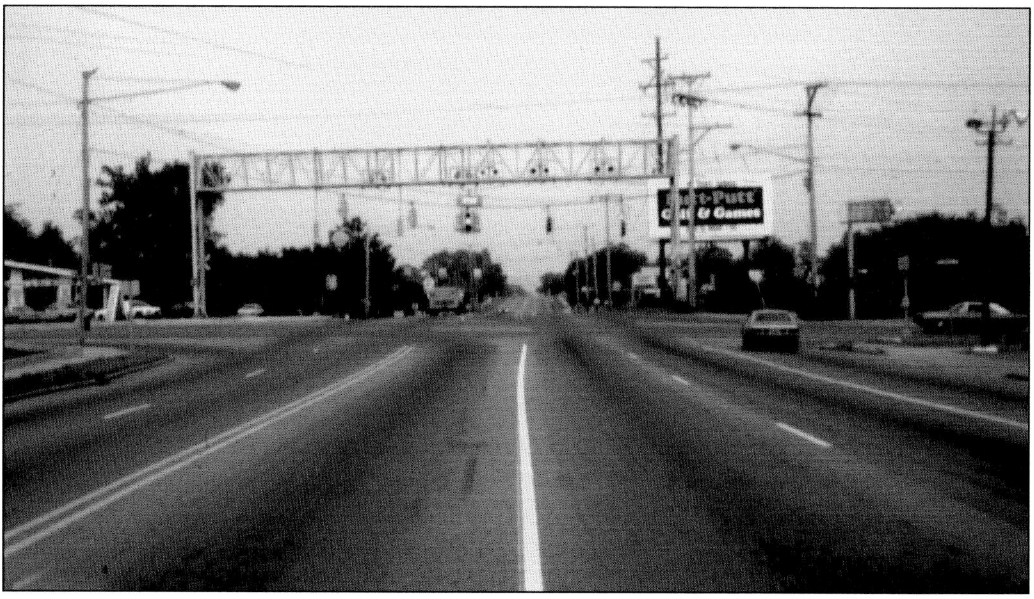

This is another shot of Forty-fourth Street looking west toward the intersection at Kalamazoo Avenue several years later. The street had been widened from two lanes to four to accommodate for the high volume of traffic going through the area. How this road will look in the future is anyone's guess as Kentwood journeys into the future.